HARBINGERS
OF
HOPE

HARBINGERS OF HOPE
CLAIMING GOD'S PROMISES
IN TODAY'S WORLD

William E. Hull

Inaugural Publication of the Hull Legacy Series
Sermons Preached in the
Mountain Brook Baptist Church
Birmingham, Alabama
1991–2006

Samford University Press
Birmingham, Alabama
U.S.A.

William E. Hull is Research Professor, Samford University, and Theologian in Residence, Mountain Brook Baptist Church, both in Birmingham, Alabama

Samford University Press
Samford University
800 Lakeshore Drive
Birmingham, Alabama 35229, U.S.A.
www.samford.edu
©2007 by Samford University Press

Printed and bound in the United States of America

Samford University Press books are distributed by The University of Alabama Press. For editorial matters, contact Samford University Press at the address above; for book trade information, contact The University of Alabama Press Sales Department at 205.348.5180 or www.uapress.ua.edu <http://www.uapress.ua.edu/>; to order books please call 800.621.2736 for U.S. accounts; international orders, 773.702.7212; fax orders only 800.621.8476.

Inaugural Publication of the Hull Legacy Series
ISBN-13 978-1-931985-16-1
ISBN-10 1-931985-16-2

Cataloging-in-Publication Data available from the Library of Congress.

Production Coordinator: Jack E. Brymer, Sr.
Editorial Supervisor: Sandra L. O'Brien
Cover Design by: Scott E. Camp

Typeface: New Baskerville, NatVignetteTwo, Trajan

For
the Ministers in our Family
Past, Present, and Future

—➤•◄—

David William Hull, son

Susan Hull Walker, daughter

Jane Shannon Hull, daughter-in-law

Emily Katherine Hull, granddaughter

*The very least you can do in your life is
to figure out what you hope for.
And the most you can do is live inside
that hope.
Not admire it from a distance but live
right in it, under its roof.*

—Barbara Kingsolver, *Animal Dreams*

CONTENTS

PREFACE

—➤•◄—

When most people explore the future, they seldom venture far from the present. In our personal lives, some think of their future in terms of the next few weeks or months, while others live almost entirely on a day-to-day basis. Even large organizations that once projected ten-year strategic plans have cut back to a five- or three-year framework, while many now limit their planning to an annual projection. One reason for this shortsightedness is that the rate of change is accelerating so rapidly that we cannot predict, or even imagine, what may happen next.

At the same time that we are pulling our sense of a human future closer to the present, however, we are pushing our sense of God's future farther from the present. For many, heaven defines the future with God, and its enjoyment is assumed to begin only at the end of our earthly life or, even more fully, at the end of human history. Our culture is saturated with sensationalistic views of the last days that locate the fulfillment of God's promises in the aftermath of a series of catastrophic events of global proportions rather than in the lives of individual believers here and now. The divine future becomes more distant from daily life, while the human future almost merges into the present, opening a great gap that separates our spiritual pilgrimage here on earth from the promises that await us "in the sweet by and by."

Jesus offered his followers a way to overcome this chasm between a foreshortened human future and a far-away heavenly future. The heart of his message was that "the kingdom of heaven"—that is, the eternal realm where God reigns—is not remote but *"near"* (Mt. 4:17 NRSV), so near that it was already in their midst (Lk. 17:21) and could enter the lives of those who were open to its presence and power (Mt. 12:28). That is why his disciples were to pray that the realities of heaven become actualized here and now on earth as well (Mt. 6:10). By faith they could embrace an entirely new future, one determined not by the circumstances in first-century Palestine but by what God was doing in and through their master's ministry (Mk. 9:1). Because the heavenly kingdom was "at hand" (Mt. 4:17 RSV), they could reach out and claim God's long-awaited promises in their lives without delay.

When we appropriate this new future offered by Jesus and make it our own, we are given a lively hope for a better tomorrow. Such hope is not based on secular optimism in human progress but is grounded in the unshakable confidence of Jesus that God is at work fulfilling his promises (Mk. 1:15). As such, it is a "tough hope" that remains sure and steadfast regardless of the adversities we may face (Rms. 15:4; Col. 1:23; Heb. 6:19). Because Jesus knew the kind of future that God had planned for his creation, he was able to anticipate that future in his earthly ministry long before many were ready to accept it. Likewise, those of us who share his hope are to live out that vision, in advance of its widespread arrival, as a way of challenging others to claim these promises for themselves.

The Apostle Paul stated the obvious when he said, "Now hope that is seen is not hope. For who hopes for what is seen?" (Rms. 8:24 NRSV). This absence of outward confirmation means that hope is a fragile assurance at best, which is why it needs a home in which it can be nurtured and protected. Jesus established the church as a fellowship of reinforcement that gathers so that "we who have taken refuge might be strongly encouraged to seize the hope set before us" (Heb. 6:18 NRSV). In that gathering, a prime task of preaching is to point the congregation toward God's horizon of promise in such compelling terms that hope is both awakened and sustained. The sermon, like the Scripture on which it is based, seeks to put that future into words so that those who hear it will determine to put it into deeds.

In selecting the sermons to be included in the volume, I was keenly aware of addressing a very diverse readership, which explains why these messages differ greatly in both style and content. Although grouped in five clusters that explore our search for God, for salvation, for growth, for renewal, and for service, each sermon stands alone as a self-contained treatment of its topic, thus you may skip about in choosing what to read in light of current interests and needs. If a particular selection lacks relevance for your life at the moment, look elsewhere with the realization that it may have someone else's name on it or that it will speak to you later when facing other circumstances. Despite their differences, all of these chapters are united by a common purpose to kindle a sturdy hope that will abound as it takes root in your heart and is nurtured in that habitat provided by the people of God (Rms. 15:13).

Sermons flourish best as an integral part of the act of worship when we gather to sing, pray, confess, listen, and wait upon the Lord. I cannot reproduce here that undergirding sense of support that reinforced every word uttered from the pulpit. Nor can I reconstruct the immediate context that called forth and gave cutting edge to what was said. But I can devoutly hope that these messages in printed form will convey some of the energy and excitement that we experienced in the original preaching event. Read these chapters as a road map to God's tomorrow, a new future bursting with unclaimed potential for the living of these days.

INTRODUCTION

SEEKING TREASURE IN EARTHEN VESSELS

But we have this treasure in clay jars, so that it may be made clear that this extraordinary power belongs to God and does not come from us.

2 Corinthians 4:7 NRSV

What does it mean to become an engaged participant in the preaching event, whether as a listener in worship or as a reader of these pages? How does the significance of such an experience differ, for example, from hearing an academic lecture or a political oration? In other words, what is unique about the very nature of a sermon?

The Apostle Paul provided an insightful clue when he sharpened the paradox of preaching by likening it to a precious treasure in a fragile clay pot (2 Cor. 4:7). That is, the glorious gospel with its transcendent power to change lives is proclaimed by ministers whose weaknesses make them vulnerable to the whole gamut of human trials (2 Cor. 4:8–12). Unlike the learned and the influential whose words gain credibility from the brilliance and status of the speaker, preachers depend entirely on God to validate the message given them to declare (1 Cor. 1:18–25).

To prepare you for what follows, I have chosen two sermons designed to help you ponder this paradox of preaching. The first takes the Baptist practice of giving one's testimony and puts it in a kind of pulpit memoir that seeks to show the shape of the modest "clay pot" that has been my life as a minister. The second heightens the contrast between messenger and message by describing the exalted work that preaching

1

intends to perform. Once you accept the paradox of preaching in my life, you may be ready to accept it in yours as well. Consider: if God would use me as a receptacle of his riches, then he is willing to fill the clay pot of your life with spiritual treasures as well!

1

"THIS IS MY STORY"

". . . we cannot help speaking about what we have seen and heard."
Acts 4:20 NIV

While serving as a pastor in Shreveport, Louisiana, during the 1970s, I sat one afternoon with a young couple discussing ways in which our worship services might become more meaningful to them, particularly at the point of my pulpit ministry. One request that surprised me was for more autobiographical preaching. In effect they said, "You preach the Bible so much that we can't tell what you personally believe!"

Rather than flattering myself by concluding that what was offered as a criticism was actually a compliment, I sought instead to probe their desire more deeply. Merely to have responded that, when I preach the Bible, I am declaring exactly what I believe would not have met their need. They wanted more of my sermons to include the traditional Baptist practice of giving one's "personal testimony," not in competition with the Bible, but as a witness to how Scripture is being applied in my own life.

Even though the apostle Paul insisted that "we preach . . . not ourselves, but Jesus Christ as Lord" (2 Cor. 4:5 RSV), he was ready to share the story of his spiritual pilgrimage at every opportunity (Acts 22:1–21; 26:1–23). Nor did his witness compromise a Christ-centered gospel, because Paul was not recounting what he had done for Christ, but what Christ had done for him. The sacred story we tell includes not only what Christ did for his earliest disciples

3

but what he continues to do for us today.

Therefore, I want to tell you my story because it discloses some of the ways in which I have experienced the reality of Christ. Though mine is no Damascus Road drama such as Paul's, its very ordinariness may carry the suggestion that your story is worth telling as well.

The Grace That Waits to be Discovered

When Paul started to tell his story, he went back before he was born (Gal. 1:15), and so must I. My parents came from the red clay of central Alabama where their parents eked out a meager existence in the cruel aftermath of the Civil War. As a child, I frequently visited the "home place," my grandparents' little farm a few miles down a nameless road from a post office crossroads in Coosa County, called Titus, Alabama. There was no central heating for warmth, only a fireplace in each bedroom and a wood stove in the kitchen; no plumbing for baths, only a washbasin filled by buckets of water brought from a nearby spring; no electricity for light, only kerosene lamps that cast eerie shadows in the twilight.

In that Spartan setting where life was lived close to its elemental forces, religion was serious business. Brother Hughes came over from Clanton every fourth Sunday to preach in the one-room Providence Baptist Church. The men sat on one side, where coffee cans were judiciously placed to receive well-aimed streams of "chawin' tobacco" juice; and the women on the other side, covered from head to toe in dresses made from flour sacks with only a cardboard fan furnished by the friendly funeral director to combat the stifling summer heat.

I can still remember when they would call on "Uncle Emmett" to pray. Rising to grasp the slat-back pew in front of him, that toothless old man would

4

begin, softly and slowly, to celebrate the Lord's doings in his life until, overcome by the wonder of it all, he would simply throw back his head and cackle, sometimes with the snap of giant yellow galluses that held up his baggy beltless britches. Something about that laugh always made me peep, even in the middle of his prayer, allowing me to see how the light of the Lord shown on his face as he waited for emotions to subside so that he might find his next words.

Shortly after World War I, my parents transplanted this rural heritage of unwavering faith to the young city of Birmingham. No sooner was I born than the Great Depression that dominated the 1930s devastated my father's real estate business, requiring our family to flee for shelter to a chicken farm run by a bachelor friend who offered us a roof over our heads in exchange for my mother's cooking and housekeeping. Those were financially desperate days when we literally lacked for enough to eat despite my father's efforts to tend a garden after chugging home in his Model A Ford from a fruitless day at work. Nevertheless, when time came for me to enter first grade, we moved back to town so that I would not have to attend a one-room country school. The best we could manage was living for years in a basement apartment, then moving to a home where my mother cooked for yet another bachelor to pay the rent!

Despite these deprivations, there was never any question that we would be in church every time the doors opened. My earliest memory of worship at the Hunter Street Baptist Church is that of lying with my head in my mother's lap and my feet in the lap of the lady next to her, while both of them fanned to keep me from becoming restless. Even some of the larger congregations in Birmingham had not yet discovered either nurseries or air conditioning. As I began to grow, there were no "Sunday clothes" to wear, but this familiar excuse meant nothing to my folks. I can still see my mother cutting up one of my father's threadbare suits trying to find enough good cloth to make me at least one decent outfit to wear to church. I was too young then to understand anything about the Christian faith, except that it was the most important thing in my parents' lives—more important than the bankruptcies and failures and despair that caused once-powerful businessmen to jump to their death out of tall buildings in downtown Birmingham.

When I was nine years old, we moved and began to attend the Central Park Baptist Church in Birmingham. The pastor's wife was our Sunday School departmental superintendent who, in response to many a childish prank, never failed to let me know that she was praying for my urgently needed salvation! During my tenth or eleventh year, the annual revival meeting began to claim some of my schoolmates. I remember sitting one afternoon on the back steps of our home resting from play with a little girl from across the street. Without a trace of self-consciousness she described how she had recently "gone forward" to profess her faith, then asked with disarming candor, "When are you going to join the church?" I quickly mumbled something about attending to that matter shortly, then changed the subject so that she could not tell just how wildly my heart was beating. It had taken only her simple question to let me know beyond any shadow of doubt that I had been *claimed*, that it was only a matter of time before I would seek the waters of baptism as she had done.

The decision was made, as I remember, on a Tuesday or Wednesday evening of the next year's revival series.

Like so many, I cannot now recollect who was preaching or anything about the sermon. But I do know that it was my own decision, freely made, with a remarkable awareness of its ultimacy granted my tender years. Looking back, more than a half-century later, I would have to say that, even though the commitment was entirely uncoerced, it was shaped to a large extent by a faith that had first dwelt in my parents and grandparents (2 Tim. 1:5). From the dawning of my consciousness, they had made church as essential an ingredient of our family life as school or work or play. The Lord's Day was just that: it belonged to Someone else regardless of what conflicts might arise. "Saying the blessing" was so predictable a part of every meal that I could not think of eating food without first acknowledging its Giver.

But, most important of all, in and through and beyond this patterning of my existence until faith became as instinctive as breathing or sleeping, I was given to understand that *Christ mattered ultimately*, that his lordship was the difference between life and death, that there was simply no way to face the heartbreak of life without his help. Those convictions did not come to me, as they did to Paul, with the force of blinding light, but by gradually absorbing them, almost by osmosis, from the spiritual atmosphere in which I lived. If the New Birth from above, like the first birth from below, has its period of gestation, then my home was like a womb and my parents' devotion was like a placenta through which I was nourished by their faith until I was old enough to partake of the Bread of Life on my own. To be sure, I was saved by God's grace, not by my parents' or grandparents', but it was a grace that was *already there*, living in those closest to me even before I was old enough to ask for it, waiting to be appropriated

7

and acknowledged as soon as I was ready.

The Growth That Responds to a Latent Potential

Shortly after becoming a Christian, I entered adolescence, that awkward transitional stage when one tries to put away childish things in order to become an adult (1 Cor. 13:11). My churchgoing habits were too deeply entrenched to be dislodged, even by the ceaseless experimentation of this impulsive period in life. But I did shift from the front pews to the back, and began to sit by girls instead of boys, to whom I passed cute little notes written on the back of offering envelopes during the pastor's sermons. After Sunday School, before the worship service began, some of my peers would slip down to the corner drug store, but I found this furtive escape entirely too daring to risk the displeasure of my parents, even though they never tried to keep me on a tight leash.

As I reflect back on those early teen years, it at first seems strange that I made so little of my newly found Christian commitment. Even though I had been thoroughly saturated in the environment of faith for a dozen years, the climactic exhilaration of baptism seemed to lead nowhere. The next half-dozen years I merely marked time, responding to what was provided and expected. Oh, I made the required meetings, glanced at the Sunday School quarterly, and put a little money in my offering envelope, but, in truth, I was letting the church carry me while I merely capitulated, half-willingly and half-reluctantly, to its routines. To be honest, I was getting, not giving; I was holding on, not helping out; most importantly, the great gift of new life in Christ was lying dormant rather than developing into maturity.

I have often wondered about this pause in my

spiritual pilgrimage. Why did I "tread water" during the half-dozen years between ages twelve and eighteen? Was it that I was so busy growing physically, mentally, socially, and emotionally that I was distracted from growing spiritually? Was it that we were all preoccupied with World War II and its uneasy aftermath? Was it that my pastor was growing elderly, and my parents with him, thereby losing the vitality to challenge a brash teenager? Whatever the causes, I must confess to a fallowing time at the very outset of my discipleship when the problem was not that I was burned out from spiritual exhaustion, but that I had never even caught fire! Just as a baby must lie in a crib for months or even years before it is able to walk unaided, so it was a long time after my spiritual birth before I was ready to stand on my two feet and go to work for God.

Someone has said that grace grows best in winter. If so, this parenthesis in my pilgrimage was a time for the seed to grow secretly, waiting for the warmth of springtime to burst into bud and then into bloom. The springtime of my faith began about 1948. Spellbinding speakers such as Chester Swor and C. Roy Angell were in their prime at the Ridgecrest Baptist Assembly in North Carolina which we attended for several summers. A great youth revival movement, ignited at Baylor University in Texas, spread across the Southland, led by dynamic young preachers such as Charles Wellborn, Jack Robinson, and Howard Butt. At that time I left for college at the University of Alabama and became involved in a very different Christian culture through the Baptist Student Union. Frank Leavell, its Southern Baptist leader, was calling my generation to maximum discipleship. It made sense to an increasing number of my contemporaries, even to the Baptist girls I was dating, and soon it began to make sense to me as well.

My first realization was that the human dimensions of my life had far outgrown the transcendent dimensions. I was now six-feet-four in my stocking feet but pygmy-sized in my soul. I was making grades good enough for Phi Beta Kappa in pre-med but had a kindergarten knowledge of Bible and theology. Socially, I was a "Big Man on Campus" in student organizations—there were so many keys on my chain that it hung almost to my knees!—but I did not understand the first thing about true community based on service rather than on merit. Suddenly I came to a crossroads where these discrepancies became unbearable! This time my decision was called "rededication," in accordance with the idiom of that era, but what it really meant was a commitment, not only to know a grace that saves, but also to grow in a grace that matures.

Once I had shifted from a holding pattern to a growing pattern, I became actively involved in the ministries of the church. One childhood elective had been serious training in music, first the violin and then choral groups, hence it was easy to turn these talents toward leading "singspirations" or directing the BSU choir. With broadening experience came a clearer assessment of my gifts. Even though I had been doing well in pre-med and was virtually assured of a slot in medical school, it would not be true to say that this vocational option was fulfilling my highest dreams. In October 1949, when a junior in college, I attended the statewide Baptist Student Union convention at Shocco Springs—half-impulsively I must confess—primarily in hopes of seeing some of my "old flames" from high school days now studying on other campuses. But what I really saw during that weekend were college youth like myself giving their lives to Christian service in ways that I had never dared consider. By the time of the final service on Sunday morning, my decision was made to enter a church-related vocation, a commitment that had been growing within me even while I was refusing to recognize it.

Entering the ministry was for me a leap in the dark. No one in my family had been a preacher. I had not talked with anyone about this possibility, nor did I have any idea what it would entail in terms of training or skills. When I wrote my parents of the decision, it took them completely by surprise. And yet it was the most certain thing I have ever done, a resolve from which I have never wavered. If my conversion was by God's grace mediated through family, my vocational calling was by that same grace given, as Paul put it, apart from conferring with flesh and blood (Gal. 1:15–16). When I was a child, God worked through the earthly continuities with which I was familiar, but, when I became a man, he must have felt that I was ready for a crisis that would turn my life in an entirely new direction determined by his initiative.

The Gratitude That Elicits an Undying Devotion
Once the call was heard, I responded much like Abraham who "went out, not knowing where he was to go" (Heb. 11:8 RSV). Immediately I changed schools and majors, from pre-med at the University of Alabama to religion at Howard College (now Samford University). Here, I was initiated into the larger Baptist fraternity and, even more important, found my future wife, who was studying for a church-related vocation in religious education. I also served my first student pastorate, a country church near Wetumpka, Alabama, where patient folk loved me dearly despite my amateurish efforts that bordered on ministerial malpractice.

11

Upon graduating, I was off to Southern Seminary in Louisville, Kentucky, to complete my theological training at both the professional and graduate levels. During those years I served two more student pastorates, was married, and both of our children were born. Seminary opened to me a vast world of theological thought which has been endlessly fascinating ever since, particularly in my chosen specialty of New Testament Interpretation which I stayed to teach at Southern for twenty years. I was also provided opportunities for administrative leadership at every level from departmental chairman to chief academic officer as provost.

During those decades of service in our denomination's oldest seminary, I was constantly speaking in a wide variety of Baptist churches and denominational conferences, which led to the frequent question of whether my first preference was preaching, teaching, or administration. The truth is that I have always found great fulfillment in all three avenues of service. My vocation has made me an incurable workaholic, not because extra effort would lead to additional prominence or financial reward, but because every facet of the ministry is so fulfilling! If I were independently wealthy, I would gladly pay someone to let me do exactly what I have done during all of my adult life.

This consuming love for every aspect of ministry was doubtless a factor prompting me to consider the possibility of a call to the First Baptist Church in Shreveport, Louisiana, for the pastoral role is the most comprehensive position in the Christian ministry. There I found endless opportunities to preach and teach and administer, as well as to work with many individuals, families, and civic groups. Over the period of a dozen years (1975–1987), I formed the most intimate relationships imaginable with those who turned to me to help them find the deepest meaning of the great ventures of life: birth, marriage, family, divorce, work, disease, death. My congregation was filled with influential members, and, through them, I was privileged to become significantly involved in the life of the city and its surrounding region.

Then why did I consider returning to my home-town of Birmingham and to my alma mater of Samford University after an absence of thirty-six years? Partly because of the compelling vision of its energetic new president. Partly because the university stood poised on the threshold of a new level of usefulness in its long and colorful history. Partly because work as provost would permit me to gather up all of my efforts as theologian, seminarian, and pastor and seek to integrate them in the cause of Christian higher education. In a phrase, I returned to help build a community in which faith and learning enrich each other. In the face of skepticism in the academy and anti-intellectualism in the church, I wanted to demonstrate afresh that, at their best, education is good for religion, and religion is good for education.

To be sure, my duties in every position have been very demanding, often to the point of exhaustion, and the problems with which I have dealt often proved intract-able to the point of frustration. But that agenda, however challenging, has always fascinated me because it lies at the very heart of human life. The issues with which I have chosen to wrestle are often viewed as controversial, but that is only because they really matter. Their resolutions have given me deep fulfillment, despite whatever struggles may have been involved, simply because these are the issues that shape our eternal destiny.

My chosen path has not been easy. I have experienced a full measure of setbacks and defeats. But even in failure, I know that I am slowly but surely being saved: from depending upon my own strength to depending upon God's strength, from self-centered isolation to community-centered fellowship, from conformity to the world to conformity to Christ. Such is my story: of a grace that was already waiting as soon as I was ready to receive it, of a growth that shattered my inertia and lethargy of spirit and set me on a pilgrimage toward maturity, of a gratitude that I can spend my days helping you to live out a story worth telling to others!

2

"WE PREACH NOT OURSELVES"

—→►•◄—

We preach . . . not ourselves, but Jesus Christ as Lord . . .
                                        2 Corinthians 4:5 RSV

When Paul stood to speak on Mars Hill, some of the
Athenian philosophers voiced the question which
congregations may well ask when a preacher begins a
sermon: "What would this babbler say?" (Acts 17:18 RSV).
There is no better way to answer that query than with
an affirmation of the great Apostle, "we preach . . . not
ourselves, but Jesus Christ as Lord . . ." (2 Cor. 4:5 RSV).
Let us explore the implications of this text for an
understanding of Christian preaching.

"We Preach"

Why did Paul say, "we *preach* . . ."? His training as a rabbi
was in synagogue argumentation rather than in gospel
proclamation (Acts 22:3). The itinerant philosophers of
Greece and Rome were not preachers, nor were the
apocalyptic sectarians of Palestine. Indeed, there was a
dearth of preaching in the religion of Paul's day. Most
people either looked back to the golden age of
prophecy that had ended centuries earlier with the
collection of its sacred writings, or they looked forward
to its revival in a final age at the end of history.

No, Paul did not define his role from the religious
fashions of his time but from the nature of the
Christian movement into which he had been thrust by
the call of his Lord. Its founder, Jesus, like his
forerunner, John, had come preaching (Mt. 3:1; 4:17),

thereby breaking the silence of the centuries. So well did the Master train his first followers that the launching of the church at Pentecost was essentially an explosion of preaching, the gift of a new tongue to address all mankind with the gospel as the Spirit gave utterance (Acts 2:4).[1] Long before Christianity had any institutions, organizations, or even the New Testament writings, it lived and grew by its preaching! It may well be that the seeds of conversion were planted in Paul's life through the fearless sermon of Stephen which precipitated his martyrdom (Acts 7:58; 9:4).

The letters of Paul reflect his keen awareness that, at best, preaching is a precarious, even scandalous, business. For this kind of declaration depends neither on the wisdom of its substance (as with philosophy), nor on the cleverness of its structure (as with debate), nor on the elegance of its style (as with oratory). This is why, in a profound discussion of his preaching in 1 Corinthians 1:18–2:5, Paul frankly admitted that for most of his hearers, whether they be Jew or Greek, preaching was "foolishness" (1 Cor. 1:18 NRSV).

The scandalous nature of preaching is still with us today. A good case can again be made that its golden age lies in the past. Even in the nineteenth century, the great British preacher F. W. Robertson lamented the decline of the pulpit with these words: "By the change of times the pulpit has lost its place. It does only part of that whole which used to be done by it alone. Once it was newspaper, schoolmaster, theological treatise, a stimulant to good works, historical lecture, metaphysics, etc., all in one."[2] Now, there are multitudes of competing authorities: scientists, journalists, psychiatrists, the ubiquitous radio and television commentators, plus a host of religious bloggers on the Internet.

Let us candidly confront this chilling claim that the pulpit is no longer the prow of the church, much less of civilization, as Herman Melville visualized it in *Moby Dick*. Ask any pulpit committee after months of intensive investigation and travel: How many pastors have you found who give preaching a central place in their ministry? Instead, reputations are often made through promotional techniques, advertising skills, political adroitness, and ideological conformity. Subtle but excruciating pressures are brought to bear on ministers to spend all of the week engineering some spectacular scheme designed to draw attention to their church, then on Saturday night to dust off somebody else's clever sermon outline for use the next morning.

Against that swift-running tide, I have sought to base my ministry on the primacy of preaching. After a lifetime observing every kind of church imaginable, it is my conviction that preaching, more than any other ministerial activity, sets the tone of congregational life. To be sure, a Sunday morning soliloquy is no substitute for pastoral counseling or committee meetings or mission endeavors, but I would observe that trivial preaching quickly trivializes these essential weekday endeavors. The theologian Paul Tillich was right in his contention that religion is nothing if it is not "ultimate concern,"[3] and urgent preaching is the wellspring of a seriousness that should pervade everything a church does. Turn the sermon into nothing more than a jingle of artificially alliterated phrases augmented by pious moralisms and soon the curse of blandness will settle like a choking cloud over the entire enterprise.

But some view preaching as a "sitting-down exercise" that easily becomes a substitute for action. The point is well taken—but consider that one must first make the point by preaching a sermon on it before anything is *done* about it! More, note that to say the needed word of rebuke to our apathy may in itself be the most courageous act possible. How many centuries did we wait for somebody to speak up and say that sweatshops, slavery, and segregation were wrong? How many more centuries must pass before we learn to say with equal clarity that war, poverty, and oppression are also wrong? In each case, fearless action will be required, but the word is an essential prerequisite to the deed. Only when we break the conspiracy of silence are we able, with a web of words, to weave together our isolated interests into a community of shared concerns that clamor for needed change.

There is more than editorial modesty in the pronoun used here by Paul. The plural *"we* preach" points to the solidarity of the people of God in one shared proclamation. Preaching is no isolated "one-on-one" encounter; rather, it is the crucible in which authentic fellowship is formed. Speech itself is the most social act of which we are capable. When that speech fails to voice the one true gospel, then "how are they to believe in one of whom they have never *heard?"* (Rom. 10:14 NRSV). But those who do hear receive a gift in common which reconciles their fragmentation caused by the babel of earthly tongues (Gen. 11:1–9).

In the strength of that bond by which we all cling to one common word there is help for the inner crisis of meaning. We do not really need more deeds to do— our lives are already full of constant activity. Rather, we need to discover a dimension of significance to the harried pace of the daily round. For instance: "My best friend died of leukemia last week at age forty-two— what does it *mean?"* "The courts handed down a controversial ruling on religion last week—what does it *mean?*" Preaching at its best need not scurry about looking for some new agenda to address. Rather, it takes the givenness of life as it was lived yesterday, refracts it through the prism of the gospel so that all of its dark hues and bright colors are transfigured into some mosaic of meaning for today, then offers those healing insights as light by which to venture resolutely into tomorrow.

James Russell Lowell wrote eloquently of this "transfiguring" function of preaching when he described the lectures of Ralph Waldo Emerson. "We used to listen," said he, "to that thrilling voice of his, so charged with subtle meaning and subtle music, as shipwrecked men on a raft to the hail of a ship that came with unhoped-for food and rescue." Why? "The delight and the benefit were that he put us in communication with a larger style of thought, . . . gave us ravishing glimpses of an ideal under the dry husk of our New England; made us conscious of the supreme and everlasting originality of whatever bit of soul might be in any of us; freed us, in short, from the stocks of prose in which we had sat so long that we had grown wellnigh contented in our cramps." Then Lowell asked and answered the key question: "Did our own imaginations transfigure dry remainder-biscuit into ambrosia? At any rate, he brought us *life*, which, on the whole, is no bad thing."[4]

"Not Ourselves"

Strange that Paul should inject this negation into the center of our text. For he, more than anyone, had much to preach about himself (2 Cor. 6:3–10): a dramatic conversion (Acts 9:1–19; 22:3–21; 26:4–23), impressive evangelistic results (Acts 13:4–12; 16:25–34), heroic missionary service (2 Cor. 11:22–28), remarkable heavenly visions (2 Cor. 12:1–4). Indeed, would we not consider ourselves fortunate to be able to sit all day and listen to Paul preach about his amazing exploits!

Moreover, we know that the opponents of the Apostle were certainly preaching about themselves (2 Cor. 11:12–21). One group, the Judaizers, were boasting of the laws they kept, of the circumcision they practiced, of the festivals they observed (Gal. 1:6–9; 4:10; 5:7–12). Another group, the Gnosticizers, were proud of their special knowledge, of their separation from ordinary people, of their resurrection out of the mundane world (1 Cor. 3:18–21; 4:8–13; 5:9–11). Yet a third group, the original followers and relatives of Jesus, were making much of their participation in the earthly ministry of the Lord and hence of their foundational status in the life of the church (Gal. 1:11–2:10).

On every side Paul was sorely tempted to outshine the claims of his adversaries by preaching about himself, but he steadfastly refused. Why? Because Paul realized that the proper subject matter of the gospel could never be himself. Nothing he had done provided any basis for proclamation—after all, he viewed himself as chief of sinners (1 Tim. 1:15 KJV). The Apostle realized that, more often than not, true preaching is in spite of, rather than because of, its spokesmen (Phil. 1:15–18). For the subject matter of the gospel is God. Its plot is the story of Jesus. Its validation is the power of the Holy Spirit. Preaching is not a recital of what we have done for God but of what God has done for us! It is not a discourse on the power of God but is a demonstration of that power at work for human redemption (Rom. 1:16). The proclamation of the gospel is not an informed opinion on spiritual issues; rather, it is a divine occurrence in which the Christ-event actually happens all over again. This does not mean that confessional preaching is invalid. Rather, it means that our personal testimony concerns Christ as the object of the gospel, not ourselves as the subject of the gospel.

How strange that, in the face of this fundamental distinction, the motto of many pulpits today might read, "We preach ourselves . . ." That is not a charge of ministerial egotism or of personal self-centeredness. Rather, many preachers, recoiling from massive criticisms lodged against the ancient message, are openly insisting that they have only themselves to preach. There is no longer thought to be any certainty in the "pre-scientific" views of Scripture, now two thousand and more years old. Even our theology is said to have been formulated in concepts that are obsolete. The terminology of yesterday is dismissed as having lost its potency in speaking to the sophisticated intellectuals of today. The last retreat for the preacher, therefore, is to take a stand behind the bulwark of his own experience.

Many factors have contributed to this self-conscious religious humanism in the pulpit. Philosophically, existentialism has nourished a passionate intro-spection that values the subjectivities of the immediate and the inward more than the objectivities of the ancient and the external. Psychologically, the pastoral care movement has stressed clinical data from autobiographical reflections as the basis for religious awareness. Culturally, the sense of modernity has been so overpoweringly strong that many theologians have subordinated their gospels to the dominant intellectual currents of the day. On every hand we see evidence that Western scientific empiricism is being yoked to Eastern mystical privatism to reinforce the assumption that nothing is real and true unless we have experienced it for ourselves.

It is not surprising, therefore, to observe that the calling described by Paul as a "scandal," which got him labeled as a "fool" (1 Cor. 1:18–25 AT) has in our day become instead a cult of heroes. For once we begin to preach ourselves, then those with the most fascinating selves will have the most to say. They may be All-American athletes, or reformed politicians, or media superstars. Nor is there anything wrong with these achievements as such. In fact, religiously there is nothing either good or bad about such credentials, since they are quite irrelevant to the gospel—which means that ordinary preachers need be neither contemptuous nor jealous nor deferential to these overnight stars who suddenly steal the pulpit limelight. The real problem with the celebrity approach to preaching is that, because of all the ballyhoo created, most people will come to hear such preachers preach *themselves*, even though some may sincerely attempt to do otherwise.

Why is it so crucial to emphasize that what we preach is "*not* ourselves"? In part because that sharp negation sets the scandal of the gospel in proper perspective. There are controversial themes in the Bible that I would just as soon not touch. Left to myself, I might be tempted to choose safety and security by muting or ignoring these dangerous issues. But that is just the point: I do not preach my preferences and priorities. Rather, I preach a word that is fire in my mouth (Jer. 5:14), that is bitter to my stomach (Rev. 10:9–11). It is a word that I may quake to speak as much as my listeners may quake to hear. It is a word that judges me just as severely as it does them. But it is a word that cannot be silenced, not because I want to be cantankerous or troublesome but because I am not in control of my pulpit agenda! As Hugh Thompson Kerr put it, "We are ambassadors not diplomats."[5]

"But Jesus Christ as Lord"

That being so, what, then, are we to preach? Paul had his answer ready: "Jesus Christ as Lord" (2 Cor. 4:5 RSV). The name "Jesus" identified a life and ministry lived out in Palestine for a few short years around A.D. 30. The title "Christ" pointed to the meaning of that life and ministry as fulfilling the highest hopes of Israel anticipated in Holy Scripture. The appellation "Lord" meant that this fulfillment was no isolated achievement limited to one place or time or people. Rather, it asserted the supremacy of Jesus the Messiah over the totality of human existence whenever and wherever it may be found.

It was no easier for Paul to preach "Jesus Christ as Lord" in his day than it is for me to do so in ours. He had not participated in the earthly ministry of "Jesus" and so was at a disadvantage in preaching to the Jews who had. He knew that the messianic claims implied by the title "Christ" were viewed as narrowly nationalistic and so held in contempt by the Greeks to whom he preached. And he knew that Caesar was murderously hostile to any rival who would claim the status of "Lord" among the Romans to whom he preached. Despite every difficulty, however, Paul was determined to preach this message because it declared that his Savior was the climax to human history, the clue to human hopes, and the comfort of human hurts as the cosmic potentate of the universe. To affirm anything less would have compromised the uniqueness and finality of his redemptive work.

By comparison, what midget claims we make for our Master today! How seldom do we hear preaching that sets Jesus at the centerpiece of history, that views his life as the apex of Old Testament revelation, that installs his authority above that of political, economic, and ideological rulers of the present age. In his spiritual autobiography, *A Sort of Life*, Graham Greene quotes Flaubert: "Human language is like a cracked kettle on which we beat out tunes for bears to dance to, when all the time we are longing to move the stars to pity."[6] We sometimes suppose that we have gotten "results" when we see a lot of "action," but often it is nothing more than the bears dancing to our pulpit tunes while the great shaping forces of life, the stars that guide human destiny, remain unmoved by our cliché-ridden rhetoric.

There is a profound sense in which the greatest conflict in modern history, World War II, was a war of words. It all began when a fanatical paperhanger named Adolf Hitler used spellbinding speeches to rally a broken nation with visions of conquest and glory. Soon his frenzied oratory had whipped Germany into a military juggernaut that quickly brought Europe to its knees. Across a narrow channel lay the last holdout, Great Britain, with Winston Churchill at its helm. Reeling under the blows of Nazi aggression, England committed every plane to its skies, every boat to its shores, every able-bodied man to defend its streets, but even that valiant effort was not enough. With disaster staring him in the face, Churchill took up the weapon of his adversary and began to do battle with words. From a concrete bombshelter deep underground, he spoke to the people of Britain not of superiority but of sacrifice, not of conquest but of courage, not of revenge but of renewal. Slowly but surely, Winston Churchill talked England back to life! To beleaguered old men waiting on their rooftops with buckets of water for the fire bombs to fall, to frightened women and children huddled behind sandbags with sirens screaming overhead, to exhausted pilots dodging tracer bullets in the midnight sky, his words not only announced a new dawn but conveyed the strength to bring it to pass.

No wonder Ruskin described a sermon as "thirty minutes to raise the dead."[7] That is the awesome assignment of a Christian pulpit: to put into words, in such a way that those gathered to listen will put into deeds, God's new future that is ours in Jesus Christ our Lord!

NOTES

1. Amos N. Wilder, *The Language of the Gospel: Early Christian Rhetoric* (New York: Harper & Row, 1964), 9–25.

2. Stopford A. Brooke, ed., *Life and Letters of Frederick W. Robertson* (Boston: Ticknor and Fields, 1865), 2:59–60. Cited in Kyle Haselden, *The Urgency of Preaching* (New York: Harper & Row, 1963), 16.

3. Paul Tillich, *Systematic Theology* (Chicago: University of Chicago Press, 1957), three volumes in one. See all references under "ultimate concern" in the Index to vol. 3, p. 442.

4. James Russell Lowell, *Literary Essays: Among My Books, My Study Windows*, Fireside Travels (Boston: Houghton, Mifflin, 1892), 1:354–55.

5. Cited in *Christianity Today* 6, no. 8 (January 19, 1962): 3.

6. Cited in *Time* 98, no. 13 (September 27, 1971): 94.

7. Cited in Donald G. Miller, *Fire in Thy Mouth* (New York: Abingdon, 1954), 17.

PART ONE

——✦——

THE REACH FOR TRANSCENDENCE

. . . we look not to the things that are seen but to the things that are unseen; for the things that are seen are transient, but the things that are unseen are eternal.

2 Corinthians 4:18 RSV

Are there really two realms of reality, or only the one we can see? Do those intangibles that we cherish so much —such as integrity, courage, and love—belong to a higher order of being whose architect goes by the name of God? If so, how do we peer beyond the tangibles all about us to explore what is visible only to eyes of faith? Indeed, if what we are looking for is invisible, how will we know when we have found it?

As the first verse of the Bible makes clear, everything begins with God (Gen. 1:1), so let us start there in our quest for that which is eternal. Because so many different ideas of deity abound in our world today, I offer two sermons as a corrective to popular notions of what an encounter with the divine might be like. What both of them tell us is that God's ways are not our ways, that ultimate reality is beyond our control, therefore that our negotiations with transcendence will be full of surprises.

Once we learn enough humility to let God be God, then we are ready to practice the three classic disciplines designed to cultivate a deeper awareness of the divine presence in life. The sermon on Bible study suggests how to make that unique anthology of the divine-human dialogue called Holy Scripture relevant to our quest for a word from God today. Next is a message on prayer as radical receptivity to the new answers that God wants us to discover if only we are open to them. The final chapter in this section seeks to show how the Holy Spirit makes us secure enough to undertake this breathtaking journey beyond the world of the here and now.

3

SURPRISED BY GOD

———→►•◄———

Moses was keeping the flock of his father-in-law Jethro, the priest of
Midian; he led his flock beyond the wilderness, and came to Horeb, the
mountain of God. There the angel of the Lord appeared to him in a
flame of fire out of a bush; he looked, and the bush was blazing, yet it
was not consumed. Then Moses said, "I must turn aside and look at
this great sight, and see why the bush is not burned up." When the Lord
saw that he had turned aside to see, God called to him out of the bush,
"Moses, Moses!" And he said, "Here I am." Then he said, "Come no
closer! Remove the sandals from your feet, for the place on which you are
standing is holy ground." He said further, "I am the God of your father,
the God of Abraham, the God of Isaac, and the God of Jacob." And
Moses hid his face, for he was afraid to look at God.

Exodus 3:1–6 NRSV

What an unpromising time and place to have a life-
changing experience! Moses was already advanced in
age, eighty years old and fixed in his habits for half that
time (Acts 7:23, 30). A fugitive from the fury of the
Egyptian Pharaoh, he lived in exile among foreigners
called Midianites amid the bleak mountains of the Sinai
peninsula (Ex. 2:15). Once he had feasted in Egypt's
fairest gardens, but now he trudged about the sand and
sage of the wilderness working for his father-in-law with
only a flock of sheep to keep him company. Banished to
the backside of nowhere, he lived a dead-end existence
devoid of hope.

But in this most unlikely setting, the life of Moses
was suddenly transformed (Ex. 3:1–6). A forlorn and
forgotten has-been found a future that turned a lonely
shepherd into his people's savior. Indeed, it is not too

much to say that what happened would one day make him the human founder of biblical religion! Why? For one reason only: because, in the same old places doing the same old things, he was surprised by God in ways that he would never have expected. The scriptural account is dominated by a dramatic interplay of the human and the divine, of the ordinary and the extraordinary, that brought Moses face to face with his ultimate destiny. Let us seek to get inside his experience so intimately that it becomes a part of our experience as well.

Mystery

It all began with a blaze that caught the corner of Moses' eye: an ordinary scrub bush was burning with a flame that would not seem to die. Unknown to him, an angel of the Lord was lurking in its flickering tongues of fire (Ex. 3:2), but he only discovered that secret when he paused to look more closely (Ex. 3:3). Many of us have seen wildfires burning in deserted places without stopping to investigate. During the dry season, fires seem to erupt by spontaneous combustion in Southern California, but nobody expects the resulting inferno to signal a divine visitation. So why did Moses turn aside? Merely to investigate why the bush was not yet consumed? Or was it, as our daughter, Susan, expressed it in a sermon, because

there is a place in my soul that burns, like a flame, and isn't burned up. The flame is desire and longing and passion, and it is holy . . . it is of God. And when I come face to face with the place in me that burns for life and calls out for me to come closer, I am, like Moses, afraid of it, and at the same time compelled by it, compelled by curiosity, finally, to turn and take note.[1]

In any case, it was not until "the Lord saw that he had turned aside to see" (Ex. 3:4 NRSV) that God addressed Moses. Clement of Alexandria quoted Matthias as saying, "Look with wonder at what is before you."[2] Only after Moses engaged the mystery at close range was he ready to be summoned by hearing his name repeated twice for emphasis. The particularity of "Moses, Moses!" (Ex. 3:4 NRSV) meant that this call was for him and him alone. He was the one person at this time and place who had been chosen to do the divine bidding. With a now-or-never urgency, God was saying that he needed Moses for a special assignment and he would not fulfill his intended destiny unless he accepted it.

In this exclusive encounter we see the limits of generic religion-in-general. For forty years Moses had been married to the daughter of Jethro, a priest of Midian (Ex. 3:1), who undoubtedly involved him deeply in the family faith, but those ties were no longer enough. Now, Moses had to realize that his vocation was unique, that God was not just looking for somebody to do a job. His name was on this project, and God was not interested in any substitutes. Not only had God sought him, but God had found him where nobody else would think to look. It is only when we hear God call us by name that we grasp the mystery of the burning bush, namely that, no matter how obscure our lives may be, they can have the dignity of participating in a divine purpose. God has a mission that only each of us can fulfill. We are called to be agents of the Almighty in the great task of setting his people free from the bondage that imprisons them.

Majesty

Once Moses realized that he had been singled out and called by name, this was no time to say, "I will try to find somebody to help you." Instead, he replied, "Here I am" (Ex. 3:4 NRSV), which meant, "You wanted me, and now you have me. I am at your disposal." As a soldier might say when reporting for duty, "I am present and accounted for." God had not asked for something *from* Moses but for Moses *himself,* which is precisely what he got in his three-word response. There was nothing that this poor shepherd could offer God except his very being. But this was the one thing that God wanted, for it meant that Moses had made himself available, open to hear a voice that seemed to come out of nowhere. As the philosopher Gabriel Marcel wrote, "there is a way of listening which is a way of giving."[3] Mark it well: everything that follows was based on the willingness of Moses to respond to God with the whole of who he was.

Now that God had Moses' undivided attention, he needed to prepare him to receive his marching orders. The great danger in any religious assignment is over-confidence. Many persons who suppose that God is on their side soon come to believe that they are empowered to do anything they wish. After all, if the one who had called Moses was able to make a bush burn with unquenchable fire, could he not do as much for him? Is anything more powerful than fire? Moses saw its light and felt its heat. And the very fact that it did not burn out made it the perfect symbol for inexhaustible energy. How easy for him to assume that the God who had kindled such a remarkable fire could also ignite him with unlimited power. From the outset it was crucial to cleanse Moses of any presumption that he could do the Lord's work in his own strength. Even now, he was a desert recluse because, many years earlier, he had slain an Egyptian when his fiery temper blazed (Ex. 2:11–15). Such hotheaded efforts would no longer suffice for the task that lay before him.

And so, in that barren wasteland, God disclosed his mystery in terms of majesty. At first the voice that had called Moses' name seemed to be inviting him to come closer, but now it bade him to stand back and keep his distance (Ex. 3:5). Moses felt simultaneously attracted and repelled by the ineffable greatness of God. His experience was similar to that of Isaiah in the Temple, who experienced both the "woe" of uncleanliness and the "lo" of divine forgiveness (Isa. 6:5, 7). Or, of Simon Peter, who wanted to follow Jesus but also wanted Jesus to depart from him because he was a sinful man (Lk. 5:8, 11). Think of it: Moses was being treated to his own personal theophany, a private audience with the Sovereign of the universe who knew his name and came seeking his assistance; yet, he must not take anything for granted or assume that God was at his beck and call.

To underscore the nature of their relationship, God instructed Moses to slip off his sandals and stand barefooted before him as a little child, vulnerable even to the soles of his feet. Make no mistake: this miserable mountainside, devoid of any trappings of religion, had become "holy ground" (Ex. 3:5 NRSV). In just a moment God would explain to Moses, "I have observed the misery of my people . . . I have heard their cry . . . I know their sufferings, and *I have come down* to deliver them . . ." (Ex. 3:7–8 NRSV). Never did he come down farther than when he occupied that wilderness outpost as his sacred space. If God would condescend to meet Moses on "the backside of the desert" (Ex. 3:1 KJV), then he was willing to meet him anywhere! If Horeb could become holy ground, it meant that majesty was willing to squander its prerogatives on ordinary people, that the most obscure corner of life could be set ablaze with divine glory!

Memory

Standing as a barefoot volunteer in sand that had suddenly become a sanctuary, "Moses hid his face, for he was afraid to look at God" (Ex. 3:6 NRSV). The burning bush no longer fascinated him, because he had met the one who lit its blaze. Humbled by the holiness that surrounded him, it was time not to look but to listen, to wait quietly for God to disclose his will on his terms. All that mattered in this moment was not what Moses saw in God but what God saw in Moses. Some might take his acquiescence as a sign of weakness or insecurity, but those who tremble in awe before the majesty of God learn to face any threat that earth has to offer—even from the mighty Pharaoh of Egypt. If this act of submissiveness contained an element of human passivity, it was a passivity that invited divine activity. As the gospel song says it, "Have Thine own way, Lord! . . . While I am waiting, Yielded and still."[4]

Remember the big picture. Our text is talking about the making of one of history's greatest leaders; yet, the description of Moses with his face hid in fear represents the antithesis of the modern image of leadership. Today, we want leaders to be in the spotlight, their faces filling television screens and magazine covers. We want them to exude the self-confidence that conveys a sense of being in control of every situation. Instead, Moses was cringing in front of a little brush fire because he thought he had heard a voice, even though no sound broke the desert stillness, except for the occasional bleating of sheep.

How quickly would the Donald Trumps of today dismiss this pathetic old man with his head filled with frustrated dreams! But this is where we learn the secret of true greatness. Moses was about to be given enormous power, but only those who tremble before the holiness of God are worthy to be entrusted with such power. Without the acceptance of limits, power corrupts. Moses was about to lead an enslaved people whose wills had been broken by oppression for four hundred years. His own sense of unworthiness, so strong that he wanted to hide his face from God, would enable him to relate patiently to the weaknesses of others.

We might suppose that God should respond to this touching display of humility on the part of Moses by bolstering his self-esteem with a word of encouragement. Instead, he offered him a brief history lesson: "I am the God of your father, the God of Abraham, the God of Isaac, and the God of Jacob" (Ex. 3:6 NRSV). What good would it do to remind Moses of patriarchs who had lived hundreds of years earlier? It was God's way of saying that this was not the first time his people had needed a courageous leader to help them initiate a new beginning. He had guided Abraham from Mesopotamia to Palestine in search of a "city which has foundations, whose builder and maker is God" (Heb. 11:10 RVS). He had spared Isaac from the knife of sacrifice, as if to raise him from the dead, that through him many descendents might be named (Heb. 11:17–19). He had brought Jacob back from Babylon and prepared him for a new future in a midnight wrestling match that changed his name (Gen. 32:22–32).

But more, this tour of memories would remind Moses of promises made to the patriarchs that had not yet been fulfilled: an inheritance to be claimed, a homeland to be settled, a reward to be received (Heb. 11:8, 13–16, 26). His ancestors had been haunted by the mystery of a greater destiny than they could ever imagine and submissive to the majesty of a greater God than they could ever control. It was time for Moses to claim this legacy with the guidance of the One who had been their help in ages past. To be sure, he was about to be asked to attempt something radically new; yet, it would be in profound continuity with what God had been doing for centuries. God was activating the memory of Moses, not as the nostalgic recollection of a hallowed past, but as the gathering of "so great a cloud of witnesses" (Heb. 12:1 NRSV) to surround him every step of the way.

On one occasion, when pressed to defend the idea of a future life, Jesus interpreted this verse in Exodus 3:6 as follows:

> ". . . have you not read in the book of Moses, in the story about the bush, how God said to him, 'I am the God of Abraham, the God of Isaac, and the God of Jacob'? He is God not of the dead, but of the living . . ." (Mk. 12:26–27 NRSV).

What this means is that a God-given memory permits us to enjoy what is called "the communion of the saints," a living relationship with those heroes of faith who have gone before us and blazed a trail that we may follow— prophets and apostles, martyrs and reformers, giants who have faced every spiritual challenge which we might be asked to undertake. Heaven is not a celestial mausoleum where God gathers his people as a collection of corpses turned to dust. Instead, it is a place of companionship with the God of the living, not the dead!

May I invite you to the backside of nowhere in quest of holy ground? Let not age make you linger, for Moses was already in his eighties. Do not be trapped by the fixed routines of habit, for Moses had been doing the same thing at least forty years. Ask not to be excused as one without talent or impressive achievements, for Moses was just a shepherd whose only job was to work for his in-laws. The key question is not what you have to offer God but whether you are willing to be surprised by God. You will never know the answer to that question unless you turn aside and look more closely at the kind of fires that cannot be extinguished. As our daughter, Susan, explained, only after Moses chose to pay attention to the flame that was of God did it call out his name and speak to him. "Which is to say that there are burning bushes everywhere in the wilderness of our souls that never speak, never call, because we do not notice, because we do not draw near and pay attention."[5]

If you are willing to turn aside, to take off your shoes, and to hide your face, then what becomes of the flame lit by God? In the case of Moses, did the bush finally burn up and the fire go out? Or did that flame kindle the heart of Moses until it finally blazed forth to set his people free? Are you willing to become part of an incendiary fellowship[6] that has been ablaze for centuries because, as Augustine put it, "One loving heart sets another on fire"?[7] Susan has recounted a story from the Desert Fathers and Mothers that presses the deepest claim of this passage on our lives.

> Abba Lot went to see Abba Joseph and said, "Abba Joseph, as much as I am able, I keep the small rule, I fast, I keep vigil, I pray. What else should I do?" Abba Joseph then stood up and stretched his hands up to the heavens, and said, "Why not be turned into fire"?[8]

NOTES

1. Susan V. Hull, "Anatomy of a Call," (sermon, Woodfords Congregational Church, Portland, ME, May 8, 1988), 3.

2. Clement of Alexandria, *Stromateis,* Book Two, 45(1), trans. John Ferguson. The Fathers of the Church, vol. 85 (Washington, DC: The Catholic University of America Press, 1991), 189.

3. Gabriel Marcel, *The Philosophy of Existentialism* (Secaucus, NJ: Citadel Press, 1956), 40.

4. Adelaide A. Pollard, "Have Thine Own Way, Lord," stanza 1, *The Baptist Hymnal,* ed. Wesley L. Forbis (Nashville: Convention Press, 1991), #294.

5. Susan Hull, "Anatomy of a Call," 3.

6. Elton Trueblood, *The Incendiary Fellowship* (New York: Harper & Row, 1967).

7. Aurelius Augustine, *The Confessions,* Book 4, chapter 14, section 21, a free translation of *"ex amante alio accenditur alius."*

8. Susan Hull Walker, "Why Not Be Turned Into Fire?," (lecture, Mepkin Abbey Exhibit Artist Talk, Moncks Corner, SC, January 30, 2005).

4

WRESTLING WITH GOD

———➤•◄———

The same night he got up and took his two wives, his two maids, and
his eleven children, and crossed the ford of the Jabbok. He took them
and sent them across the stream, and likewise everything that he had.
Jacob was left alone; and a man wrestled with him until daybreak.
When the man saw that he did not prevail against Jacob, he struck him
on the hip socket; and Jacob's hip was put out of joint as he wrestled
with him. Then he said, "Let me go, for the day is breaking." But Jacob
said, "I will not let you go, unless you bless me." So he said to him,
"What is your name?" And he said, "Jacob." Then the man said, "You
shall no longer be called Jacob, but Israel, for you have striven with
God and with humans, and have prevailed." Then Jacob asked him,
"Please tell me your name." But he said, "Why is it that you ask my
name?" And there he blessed him. So Jacob called the place Peniel,"
saying, "For I have seen God face to face, and yet my life is preserved."
The sun rose upon him as he passed Penuel, limping because of his hip.
Genesis 32:22–31 NRSV

The Jabbok is a twisting, turbulent stream that cuts its
way through the hills of Gilead as if they had been hewn
with a mighty ax.[1] As it rushes westward to join the
Jordan River near Jericho, the great gorge narrows into
an even deeper ravine whose high walls cast shadows
by day and cover the chasm with gloom by night. The
word Jabbok in Hebrew contains the root of the verb
"to wrestle," suggesting that this raging torrent was a
"struggler" because of the difficulty with which it
made its tortuous way through obstructing rock.

Our story opens where the canyon walls widen at
Penuel, spreading the waters enough so that travelers
may safely ford on their journey from Gilead to

Canaan (Gen. 32:22–32). A solitary figure stands beside the restless stream shrouded in utter darkness (Gen. 32:24a). It is our ancestral patriarch, Jacob, caught up in the greatest crisis of his life. As he listens to the wild roar of the waters, they seem to echo the writhing of his own heart. Before the night is over, Jacob will, like Jabbok, become "the wrestler." But more, his struggle anticipates that dark night of the soul through which we, too, must pass before we are ready, with him, to enter the Promised Land.

Anxiety

On that fateful evening, Jacob was hemmed in by more than the high walls of the *Wadi Zerqa* formed by the Jabbok. For twenty years he had worked for his uncle Laban (Gen. 31:38), marrying two of his daughters, Leah and Rachel. After cheating their father out of an entire herd through a breeding scam (Gen. 30:25–43), Jacob gathered up all of his family and flocks and fled from Haran while Laban was away shearing sheep (Gen. 31:19–21). Enraged by this deceptive departure, and by the fact that treasured religious icons had been stolen, Laban hotly pursued Jacob until he caught up with him in the hill country of Gilead where he bitterly upbraided him for secretly carrying off his daughters and grandchildren without so much as a farewell kiss (Gen. 31:25–32). When a careful search failed to turn up the missing household gods because Rachel had hidden them under her skirts (Gen. 31:33–35), Jacob was able to lodge a self-righteous protest of his own (Gen. 31:36–42), pressuring Laban to accept a "covenant" that amounted to little more than a nonaggression pact designed to keep the family from each other's throats (Gen. 31:43–55).

The bad blood between Jacob and Laban, however, was nothing compared to the rift between Jacob and Esau. Years earlier Jacob had tricked his brother into squandering his birthright for a bowl of soup (Gen. 25:29–34), then later had cheated him out of the deathbed blessing of their father Isaac by which he designated his chosen successor as head of the family (Gen. 27:1–29). Seething with hatred of Jacob for twice "supplanting" his rights as first-born (Gen. 27:36), Esau determined to kill his brother as soon as Isaac was dead, a plot that was thwarted by Jacob's hasty flight to Haran (Gen. 27:41–45). But the death-vow had never been revoked, and now Esau was approaching with four hundred men (Gen. 32:6)! Jacob was utterly defenseless, able to meet this veritable army with nothing but women and children and livestock. Cold terror clutched at his heart as he contemplated the prospect of a massacre in which Esau "may come and kill us all" (Gen. 32:11 NRSV).

Outwardly, Jacob was alone in the inky blackness, his back to the wall with nowhere to hide, relentlessly pursued by threats both behind him and before him. Inwardly, it seemed as if the sins of a lifetime had finally caught up with him, despite the legendary cunning that had served him so well. All of us know those who seem to cut corners without ever stumbling, who dance down the sidelines of life without once stepping out of bounds, who bend every rule and exploit every weakness to get their way, only to make a fateful miscue when all of their cleverness catches up with them, when their success is seen to be leveraged by promissory notes that cannot be paid, when smoke and mirrors can no longer conceal a lack of bedrock character.

Jacob had always been a quick study, a fast-start

artist who, at midlife, should have been reaping the rewards of patient labor but instead found himself, not empty-handed, but empty-hearted. His ill-gotten gain was worthless to buy him a good night's sleep beside the surging Jabbok. We join Jacob at the moment of his greatest vulnerability, that fateful evening when he knew that on the morrow he might lose it all. Now there was nothing to keep his conscience company but rampant anguish over what another day might bring. To be sure, he had already launched a last-ditch effort to blunt Esau's raw and violent rage with extravagant gifts that amounted to bribes, but, in the suffocating stillness, Jacob had no way of knowing whether this ploy would suffice to outsmart his brother one more time. No wonder that some early Jewish commentators supposed that Jacob had stayed behind on the other side of Jabbok so as to flee in case his peace offering failed to placate Esau's wrath.

But mark it well: precisely here, during the desperate hours, when frantic with fear, when pain was as palpable as the darkness, when every vestige of security had been shattered, God came to Jacob in the depths of his ordeal, bound himself tightly to his predicament, and entered fully into the abyss of his wretchedness.[2] My pastor, Jim Moebes, often likes to pray that God "meet us at the point of our deepest need." Believe me, we have now reached that point in Jacob's life, where he discovered that God would come when he felt utterly alone, when there was nowhere to turn, when life seemed like an endless struggle. Call it, if you will, the ministry of the midnight watch, which means that when we have *nothing*—absolutely nothing but emptiness and fretfulness and weariness—it is precisely then that we also have God!

Adversity

But how can God help those who are rendered helpless by their own pride and self-sufficiency? All of his life, Jacob had practiced salvation by shrewdness and seduction. He always thought that he could be saved by his wits, but now he was at his wit's end! What Jacob needed to learn more than anything else is that ingenuity is no substitute for integrity, that he did not always have to win at any cost, that the best things in life come from the goodness of God, rather than from his own selfish grasping. How could God help Jacob discover that divine grace cannot be won by human guile? The incredible answer of this story is that God would do it *by wrestling with him!* Jacob had always been able to run from his problems, but now he would have to engage in hand-to-hand combat, entwined in a tortured embrace from which there was no escape. Especially when he usurped Isaac's blessing, Jacob had been able to camouflage himself, but now he would feel fingers dug into his flesh reaching for the bone.[3] Jacob had just prayed his favorite prayer for the blessings of peace and prosperity (Gen. 32:9–12), but God decided that what Jacob really needed was to be shaken to the very core of his being.

The divine adversary began by giving the trickster a taste of his own medicine. Suddenly, the defenseless Jacob felt himself blindsided by a hostile intruder who attacked without warning and refused to identify himself. If the primitive superstitions of that time were to be believed, Jacob might well have supposed that the local river-god had sent a night-demon to thwart his crossing of the Jabbok at dawn. But he quickly realized that this was no nightmare of his imagination, for he was fighting his own kind, "a man" (Gen. 32:24b). Was it Laban, determined to exact revenge before returning to Mesopotamia? Or, even more plausibly, was it Esau, whose army could easily destroy Jacob's family at sunrise after the hairy hunter had first taken care of his "supplanter" in the night? As the fight continued, and Jacob began to realize that his opponent was not intent on slaughter, he may have supposed, as did the prophet Hosea many years later (Hos. 12:2–4), that his striving was with an angel such as he had encountered at Bethel during another anxious moment in his life (Gen. 28:10–17). But when the titanic struggle neared its end at daybreak, the realization finally "dawned" on Jacob that he had, in fact, been wrestling with God himself (Gen. 32:30)!

This discovery was slow in coming because of the startling way in which God condescended to meet Jacob. Not only did he assume human form, but he limited himself to human strength. Here the Sovereign of the universe, who had flung a world into space, who had sent floods to cover the earth and fire to demolish Sodom and Gomorrah, decided, not only to fight Jacob, but to fight him on even terms, to risk a draw or even a defeat. As hard as it is to picture God grunting and sweating and groveling in the dirt, it is even harder to conceive of him with his shoulders pinned to the ground or with his arms held in a hammerlock by a mere mortal. But Jacob needed to learn his limits, to find out what he could do without the benefit of pretense or subterfuge. So God set the ground rules for this midnight wrestling match: "pick on somebody your own size" and "may the best man win!"

Let us admit that we are hardly prepared for the confrontational theology lurking in this little story. We want God to come in the sunshine and give us peace, to offer the blessings of comfort and strength, and so make us feel good about ourselves. But there are times when God decides instead to come in the shadows, not to pat us on the back, but to pick a fight. Sometimes we must contend with God when we do not realize that it is God with whom we struggle but conjecture that we are being hounded by a host of sinister forces or earthly enemies. Often it is after the fact, when the crisis has run its course, before we realize that neither demons nor angels nor humans but God himself has been forcing us to test our limits and plumb our depths as never before. Such is the strange work of the hidden God who condescends to deal with our true condition by ambushing us when we least expect it.

Many years ago, the congregation in Louisville, Kentucky, to which our family belonged offered a series of Sunday evening services in which selected members recounted their pilgrimage of faith. After several weeks I began to notice a consistent pattern according to which those giving testimony always located God in the good times of life. Almost as a refrain, one after another affirmed the reality of God in terms of the success and happiness, the fulfillment and usefulness that they had experienced as a Christian. While this text does not discount for a moment the value of such blessings, it balances them with the reminder that God can also be found in our torments, our anguish, and our struggles. If Jacob had contributed to that series, he might well have said, "God came to me, and I have the battle-scars to prove it!" Ministers sometimes decline a difficult job because they cannot get "a sense of peace" regarding the challenge. Jacob did not find a sense of peace in his Jabbok ordeal, but he found instead what God felt that he needed even more, a good dose of Kierkegaardian "fear and trembling."

We have tried hard to tame God and keep him on a leash, but this telling will not have it. Can we not, with Jacob, learn to look for God *in* our doubts, *in* our fears, *in* our struggles, *in* all the senseless tragedies that threaten to engulf us? God gives us permission to wrestle with him because he first decided to wrestle with us. He lets us beat our fists against the silent vault of heaven when prayers go unanswered, argue with him when the riddles of human existence seem insoluble, even accuse him when he seems to have "stacked the deck" against us. The veteran pastor Carlyle Marney had wise counsel for a young friend broken by tragedy when he said, in effect: "Don't repress your bitterness and hostility just because it is God with whom you are frustrated. Go ahead and 'have at it' with the Almighty. God has much to answer for, but he can take care of himself." Whatever the issue, it is far better to stand and fight *with* God than it is to "throw in the towel" and run *from* God!

Ambiguity

The only thing as strange as the combatants in this struggle was its outcome. Wrestling is so strenuous and even dangerous that we usually look for a verdict in a matter of minutes, but this fight lasted throughout the night as if it would never end. Tension mounts as we wonder who finally prevailed, the mighty God willing to hold his divine power in check and fight like a man, or the wily Jacob trying desperately to survive? But in this bruising conflict there was no winner and no loser. In one sense God and Jacob fought to a draw, each needing what only the other could give, both prevailing because neither prevailed. In another sense we can say that both won something and both lost something as the fearful encounter took its toll. Jacob's victories were at God's expense, and God's victories were at Jacob's expense, yet both emerged from the fray enhanced rather than diminished. Let us look more closely to see how this could be.

As night wore on toward morning, the stranger sought to leave before sunrise only to find himself snared in Jacob's frantic grasp (Gen. 32:25a, 26a). Even though God had succeeded in throwing Jacob's hip out of joint as they wrestled, the wounded warrior refused to release his nocturnal assailant without a blessing (Gen. 32:25b, 26b). Here is one of the profoundest expressions of the tenacity of faith in all of Scripture. If Jacob did not release God, it might prove fatal, for no one could look directly upon God in the full light of day and live (Ex. 33:20). But Jacob now had God so tightly in his grip that he was willing to risk that fearful possibility, rather than miss the blessing that only God could bestow. By this desperate strategy he declared that he would rather die than forfeit God's favor.[4] At last Jacob's ultimate priorities had been defined in life-and-death terms: better not to live another day, better not to face his brother Esau, better not to enter the Promised Land unless he could do so in the strength of God's grace!

Wonder of wonders, as Jacob held on to God for dear life, his audacious request was granted. But first he was asked to disclose his name (Gen. 32:27). Jacob meant "the supplanter," the one who grabs from behind to get ahead of others, who does whatever it takes to end up on top. But now Jacob was given a new name. Henceforth he would be known as "Israel," which meant "the struggler," the one who must strive for what he gets, who must pay the price of pain in order to prevail. Not only did the change of name signal a new identity but a new destiny as well. Now Jacob would become, as Israel, the namesake of a nation, the patriarch of a people who would perpetuate through the centuries his contentious struggle with God, wrestling with the demands of prophets and priests and yet clinging in hope to the covenant of blessing. At the moment, Jacob may have wished for more tangible tokens of divine protection, such as a battalion of soldiers with whom to fight Esau's army! Instead he was given only a promise: that he would initiate a new people called Israel who would forever embody what he had learned in his jousting with God beside the Jabbok.

But this does not mean that Jacob got all that he wanted by grappling tenaciously with God. Even though he had now met God in a face-to-face encounter (Gen. 32:30), he could not penetrate the mystery of his antagonist. God could learn his name, and even change it, but he could not learn God's name or change it (Gen. 32:29). Jacob could scratch and claw for all that he was worth, but only God had the power to bless. God could give him a whole new future, but he could not give God anything. This meant that Jacob "prevailed" in securing from God what he needed to receive, but God "prevailed" in offering to Jacob what he wanted to give.

Furthermore, remember that Jacob gained that blessing only at the cost of becoming a cripple. Wrestling is not a very nice way to negotiate differences, and this was obviously a no-holds-barred fight to the finish. God seemed to get in a lick "below the belt," a punch to the groin that, as Jacob fought on with reckless abandon, threw his hip out of joint (Gen. 32:25b). Another thing that Jacob learned from his Jabbok ordeal is that if you push God to the limit, it will leave you with a limp! Ironically, the very ferocity with which Jacob fought earned him both a blessing and a curse. From now on he would be a new man, Israel, but he would also be hobbled in the hip. His successors, the Israelites, would forever remember the high price that Jacob paid to prevail by refusing to eat the meat of the thigh muscle that contained the nerve that God had damaged in the fray (Gen. 32:32).

We dislike indecisive outcomes, but does not this ambiguity speak to our true condition? On the one hand, we find here an incredible expression of the hidden motions of grace. We, like Jacob, have the chance to "prevail" because God allows himself to be prevailed upon, to be badgered and begged, even to be coerced and, in a sense, captured by our desperate assaults upon his mercy. When novelist Walker Percy was asked why he was religious, he replied: "I take it as axiomatic that one should settle for nothing less than the infinite mystery and the infinite delight, i.e. God. In fact I demand it. I refuse to settle for anything less. I don't see why anyone should settle for less than Jacob, who actually grabbed aholt of God and wouldn't let go until God identified himself and blessed him."[5] When pressed to account for his faith as a gift of God, Percy persisted in saying, "The only answer I can give is that I asked for it, in fact demanded it."[6]

But, on the other hand, this determination to force the hand of God is dangerous business indeed. In the agony of Gethsemane and the terror of Calvary, Jesus learned that even when rescued by God's resurrection, the scars of defeat would still be visible for all to see (Jn. 20:20). Paul pushed his calling to the breaking point, and it got him the stigmata or marks of the Master branded on his body (Gal. 6:17). So with us: Wrestle with the deepest truths of Scripture, and it will leave the mind with a limp. Wrestle with the mandate of God for a worldwide mission, and it will leave the will with a limp. Wrestle with the scandal of an apathetic church, and it will leave the heart with a limp. Paradoxically, it is when we take hold of God by faith and try to wrest from him the greatest blessings that we also receive the deepest wounds. What this text is whispering to us between the lines is that we will never get the best of God without becoming utterly vulnerable in the process.

So, is the prize worth the price? Are you willing to demand the best that God has to offer if, by that very act, your self-sufficiency is forever lost? Are you willing to do it God's way as Israel the struggler if that means you can no longer do it your way as Jacob the supplanter? The central thrust of the story is that we cannot avoid that choice because God may decide to jump us at midnight and insist that we struggle with the deepest issues of our destiny until we decide what really matters most. When the long ordeal is nearly over, and we confront the claims of our self-centeredness, we will either let go of God and run for cover in a frantic effort to save our skin one more time, or we will bet everything on his blessing and head for the Promised Land, confident that God will not let us be destroyed by the foolish mistakes that we have made.

What did Jacob do with his Jabbok experience? When his struggle was finally ended, as he passed Penuel "the sun rose upon him" (Gen. 32:31 NRSV). That shaft of light after so much gloom was the omen of a better day. Jacob's story is not that of long day's journey into night but of long night's journey into day! He crossed the Jabbok, seemingly alone again, but God's signature was upon him for he walked with a limp. The meeting with Esau no longer held any terrors for Jacob, even with that gimpy hip, because he had now fought with God and lived to tell it! Granted he was no longer cocky and self-assured, but to know that he had claimed God's blessing was enough. Renamed and yet lamed, defined and yet diminished, he set out to claim the Promised Land, dragging his leg behind him like a trophy from heaven.

Years before, Jacob had met God at Bethel as friend. Now he had met him at Penuel as enemy: the enemy of his whole bag of tricks, of his shortcuts and deceptions, of his invincible self-sufficiency. But with that blessed limp, God had become what Frederick Buechner called his "beloved enemy."[7] And if we, like Jacob, will go, not only to Bethel but to Penuel as well, we can know the magnificent defeat that comes only when we wrestle with God.

NOTES

1. This description was suggested by Nelson Glueck, *The River Jordan* (Philadelphia: Westminster, 1946), 127.

2. Terence E. Fretheim, "The Book of Genesis," *The New Interpreter's Bible,* ed. Leander E. Keck (Nashville: Abingdon, 1994), 1:567.

3. On the intimacy of wrestling see Gordon Dalbey, "Fingers on the Flesh, Touched to the Bone: Wrestling with God for New Life," *Preaching* (July–August, 1988): 24–26, based on a prize-winning sermon in the Billings contest at Harvard Divinity School.

4. Clyde T. Francisco, "Genesis," *Broadman Bible Commentary,* rev. ed., ed. Clifton J. Allen (Nashville: Broadman, 1973), 1:226.

5. Walker Percy, "Questions They Never Asked Me," *Esquire,* December, 1977, 190.

6. Percy, "Questions They Never Asked Me," 193.

7. Frederick Buechner, *The Magnificent Defeat* (New York: Seabury, 1968), 18.

5

THE LIVELY WORD

—➤•◄—

Indeed, the word of God is living and active, sharper than any two-edged sword, piercing until it divides soul from spirit, joints from marrow; it is able to judge the thoughts and intentions of the heart.

Hebrews 4:12 NRSV

The Associated Press reported the following story from Caen, France, in the summer of 1971:

A shell or mine from World War II blew up yesterday while a farmer was burning brush near here. He was gravely wounded.

Nearly 1.5 million unexploded bombs, shells, mines, grenades and other explosive devices have been defused in the last eight years in France, about half from World War I, half from World War II.[1]

The Bible is strikingly like the millions of unexploded bombs that lie scattered across the European countryside, with one important exception. It is similar in that its truths still retain their explosive power if only they can be discovered and unleashed. Fortunately, it is different in that the contents are life-giving instead of death-dealing. Rather than needing to be defused, they need to be ignited by committed Christians as resources for transforming the human scene.

How may the Bible be used to change lives today? Handled aright, it is the chief weapon of our spiritual warfare, a word from God "living and active, sharper than any two-edged sword" (Heb. 4:12a NRSV). Utilized wrongly, however, it is a collection of ancient curiosities bidding us to offer animal sacrifice, cast out demons,

and speak in tongues. Nothing is as dangerous as a
sword being swung wildly in every direction. The need
of our day is not to sharpen the blade, as if the Bible has
become dull to modern ears, but to learn how to aim its
point so that the word will pierce to the joints that lay
open the marrow of life! (Heb. 4:12b).

Such skill, which uses the scriptural sword as a scalpel
instead of a butcher knife, comes from an intimate
understanding of the nature of the Bible. Let us seek
here to rediscover the reality of Scripture under three
rubrics: the context of the Bible as history, the content of
the Bible as literature, and the concern of the Bible as
theology. From each of these essential dimensions we will
then develop guidelines that enable us to use the word of
God in a way that "is able to judge the thoughts and
intentions of the heart" (Heb. 4:12c NRSV).

Context

The most fundamental fact about the Bible is that it
records what "came to pass" at particular times and
places in the past. The Scriptures understand this
history as a dialogue between God and man in the
language of events. To say that "the Word became flesh"
(Jn. 1:14 NRSV) is to say that God's revelation stepped out
on the stage of history in human form. Therefore,
there is no way to take the Bible seriously without also
taking seriously the context in which it happened.

When divine-human encounters took place in the
events of biblical history, the nature of each situation
determined the form that the revelation assumed and
the way it was interpreted. For example, when the story
of Jesus took root in various Christian centers, it was
shaped into at least four distinctly different accounts,
each an attempt to make the message relevant in the

setting where it was planted. Although there was only one "gospel" from God, it was taken down "according to" various interpreters of its significance, identified as Matthew, Mark, Luke, and John. Again, Paul was determined to preach the only true gospel (Gal. 1:6–9), yet his formulation of the faith in Galatians and Romans differed markedly from that in Colossians and Ephesians. The explanation lay not in a decision by the apostle to change his message but in the creative interaction of his proclamation with different historical situations.

This means that biblical truth is not timeless but timely. The word of God is inescapably time-bound, because it was fused to its own situation in the dynamic of proclamation and response. The same should be true of our message today as it seeks to confront the twenty-first century with the claims of Christ. Therefore, the outward expression of our message may not always be identical to that of the biblical message, since our modern world is not identical to the first century world. The enduring authority of the Bible requires rather that our message should claim lives today in the same way that it claimed lives then. Language and custom continue to change but not the kind of transformation that Scripture seeks to accomplish.

The recently popularized phrase "purpose-driven" well describes the thrust of the interpretative process. Whatever else may be true of Christians in the New Testament era, they were passionately concerned to fulfill a specific mission. We today, who, by faith, accept the authority of the Bible, believe that because those first Christians were privileged to participate in the unique Christ-event on earth, they were thereby enabled to apprehend, and be apprehended by, the ultimate disclosure of God's intentions for his world. As a result, they lived on the frontier of change from death to life, from bondage to freedom, from darkness to light. Because they existed as a transformed and transforming remnant, the literature that was a precipitate of their life together shared this burning sense of mission.

Our task, then, is to grasp the full implications of this biblical intention for our day. We are not simply to say to America the same thing that Paul said to Rome, for modern America is obviously not like ancient Rome. Rather, we are to find in Scripture the gospel that will produce the same kind of changes in America that Paul was contending for in Rome. When we read about washing feet (Jn. 13:14), or veiling women (1 Cor. 11:10), or abstaining from meat offered to idols (1 Cor. 8:7–13), we are not to ask one question, "Must we do all of that today to be true to the Bible?" Rather, we should ask two questions. First, "What life-changes wrought by Christ are reflected in the way the Bible approached its ancient circumstances?" The second is like unto it, "How may we best witness to these same life-changes in our modern circumstances?"

Content

But the word that became flesh and thereby was anchored in history also became literature and thereby was embodied in a book. Profound changes took place when the dynamic event became a written text. For one thing, a moving time line was suddenly stopped, freezing the truth in the way it was being declared then and there. In book form the message could be multiplied and translated for alien cultures that spoke different languages and followed other customs. As time passed and circumstances changed, the content of the writings did not change. Thus, the message was set permanently in its own history, which was not the history of succeeding generations.

Beside that characteristic phrase, "it came to pass," which points to the context of the Bible as history, there is another characteristic phrase, "it is written," which points to the content of the Bible as literature. This formula is used in the perfect tense with the force of "it stands written" and so underscores the permanence of the word of God. What is found in Scripture was composed at a particular point in time but, once composed, it continues in that givenness to the present moment and, indeed, will so continue to the end of time. Thus the fluidity of the word in history is balanced by the fixity of the word in literature. Incarnation means that God is deeply involved in the flux of time, but inscripturation means that he also transcends such temporal contingencies.

There are many advantages to truth in written form. For one thing, it is more easily remembered, even memorized. History can be overpowering in its immediacy but is easily forgotten. Unlike events, books are not necessarily superseded by subsequent developments, partly because they may influence the way in which the future unfolds. Further, the tangible text can be pondered at one's own pace, in contrast to important happenings that may occur too swiftly for their meaning to be absorbed. Again, writing may combine abstract reflections with concrete descriptions and so permit explicit interpretation that was only implicit in the happening itself. We often like to read in the newspaper about some public event which we have attended because the published account includes an indication of what it meant to a trained observer.

But do the liabilities of literature as a channel for truth outweigh its assets? After all, as already hinted, it is precisely this crystallization of revelation in book form at a particular point in history that makes it seem increasingly out of date the longer time marches on. Soon we have to use new languages, with all the tedium of translation. Then, we have to write commentaries explaining archaic historical references. Finally, we resort to archaeology in the hopes of digging up a long-forgotten past. At first glance, "freezing" the gospel in a set of first-century books seems to have trapped it in the tomb of time, fostering a "museum" mentality among those who would search for the secret of life amid such ancient relics.

The writers of the New Testament were aware that many problems would be created by forever defining Christianity in first-century categories, but they also knew how to overcome these difficulties by virtue of their experience with the Old Testament as Scripture. For one thing, they realized that sometimes a provision of God is not understood or accepted for many years, even for centuries. Rather than dismissing it as irrelevant, better to set it down in writing against the day when brave spirits are ready to claim it for their own. That is the way the author of Hebrews viewed the promise of Sabbath rest made so long ago in Psalm 95 but only then coming true for the People of God (Heb. 4:1–10). In like manner we may view the Bible as a bundle of promises that, far from being exhausted in antiquity, still await fulfillment on that day when believers finally find the courage to implement them.

Moreover, the New Testament writers were keenly aware that subsequent events might immeasurably clarify and enrich some vision of truth only dimly foreshadowed at first. For example, descriptions of the righteous sufferer in Psalm 22 and 69, or of the Servant of the Lord in Isaiah 42 and 53, took on incredibly deeper meaning once Jesus had actualized their anticipation in his death. Just so, during the many centuries of church history, the pages of the New Testament have been overlaid with a rich deposit of experience that has deepened our perception of their meaning. Who can read Romans today without thinking of Martin Luther, or the Great Commission without remembering William Carey, or the Beatitudes without seeing Francis of Assisi? The New Testament has not been quietly gathering dust for twenty centuries. It has rather taken on a rich patina from the blood of martyrs, the sweat of apostles, the tears of prophets.

Supremely, as the Upper Room discourses in the Gospel of John make clear, the Holy Spirit has been given to remind us of all that Christ said (Jn. 14:26), to draw out for us the meanings already implicit in that final revelation (Jn. 16:14–15), and so to guide us into all truth as we are able to bear it (Jn. 16:12–13). Thus the givenness of the written word corresponds to the givenness of the incarnate word, so that all that was latent in his definitive life is also latent in the inspired record of what he said and did. Why complain of an ancient, and thereby difficult, source when we have only begun to claim a fraction of all that it has to offer? Admittedly, the well is deep and, with the passage of time, grows deeper yet, but it still gushes with an inexhaustible supply of undiscovered truth whenever we pay the price to let our bucket down!

We have now clarified a second guideline for using Scripture to change the human scene. Already we have seen that, because the context of the Bible is history, we must inquire of its *intentionality* in each of its original life situations. But now we realize that, because the Bible is literature, we must also inquire of its potentiality as each succeeding generation unfolds. The search for intentionality is a very deliberate, rational process in which we utilize the investigative tools of the historian to avoid reading our preconceptions into the past. The search for potentiality, by contrast, is a more spontaneous, emotional process in which we utilize the intuitive tools of the poet to offer our experiences for the enrichment of the present. In the former quest, our objective is careful methodological control so that each successive moment in the past can be seen for what it really was. In the latter quest, however, our objective is an unfettered exercise of the imagination in an effort to grasp the fullest possible implications of the text as it gathers light and strength from centuries of devotion.

Concern

We are now ready to take a final step by pondering the obvious fact that the books of the Bible were not fashioned as ends in themselves but were "written that you may believe . . . and that believing you may have life . . ." (Jn. 20:31 RSV). In a very real sense this literature was recorded not just to be read but, more important, in order to be preached. We come full circle with the recognition that the word first became flesh in order that it might then become book, but that it became book in order that it might again become flesh through the living witness of its heralds.

That being so, we are to understand the Bible not only as history and as literature but also as theology, not

only as revelation and as inspiration but as proclamation as well. Scripture declares what "came to pass"
in the revelatory events of history. It records what
"stands written" through the inspired interpretation of
its human authors. But it also announces what "saith
the Lord" to each new hearer who opens its pages
listening for a voice from the beyond.

This insight, however, raises the last great problem
which we shall seek to solve. For faith, by its nature, is a
unifying reality which brings the truth about God to
bear in reconciling fashion upon the fragmented life of
humanity. Therefore theology, which is the con-
ceptualization of faith, must be coherent in order to be
theology at all. Because faith is a "centering
experience" that deals with "the heart of the matter,"
with the innermost nature of reality, theology which
does not have integrity is a contradiction in terms. This
means that the only way we may approach the Bible as
theology is to define its principle of unity so as to be
able to locate its center.

The magnitude of that difficulty is presented in
tangible form by the reality of the writings included in
Scripture. For the word did not become just one book
but a library of sixty-six books written over more than a
millennium by dozens of authors in a variety of styles.
Once they were collected and codified into a canon, an
external principle of unity was superimposed by
ecclesiastical authority that was foreign to the writings
themselves. Not one of these books was written on the
assumption that it would become "Bible" as we know it,
that it would stand beside sixty-five other writings within
the covers of a single anthology. But once that
happened, any one part could be compared with and
even interpreted by any other part, thus opening the

door to endless diversity of understanding.

The problem is so obvious that it needs little illustration. At the surface level there are innumerable decisions to be made regarding the harmonization of parallel accounts. Shall we follow Kings or Chronicles, Mark or John, Acts or the Epistles of Paul in their presentation of the same events? More broadly, there is the resolution of broad differences between the two Testaments regarding such central features of religious life as the Temple, Sabbath observance, and circumcision. Our difficulties arise not so much from any one writing, which may have a unified perspective, but from its relation to other writings which may take different approaches. Many of the controversial issues that bitterly divide the church—such as homosexuality, the rights of women, and the charismatic movement—root not in a failure to consult Scripture but in the use of one Scripture over another for lack of agreement on a unifying principle.

We have come, then, to the need for a third guideline of interpretation to deal with the essential nature of the Bible as theology. Here, the key problem is *atomization*, which we obviously need to overcome by discovering the unifying center of Scripture. What reality is comprehensive enough to fuse this library of sixty-six originally unrelated documents into a unified whole? I suggest that it is the reality of Jesus Christ who alone is the eternal Word of God heard through all the varied words of Scripture.

How may this guideline be applied to practical problems of interpretation? We may begin with an insight attributed to Martin Luther: let the whole Bible lead you to Christ, then let Christ lead you back to the whole Bible. In other words, take any religious reality found in Scripture, whether it be an idea or an institution or a practice, then trace the unfolding of that reality to its fulfillment in the ministry of Jesus. In the case of the Temple this means spiritualization, in the case of the Sabbath it means supersession, in the case of circumcision it means termination. But all three involve a transformation that preserves the essential reality even when recast in different form. Our faith finds its resting place, therefore, not in what these realities may have meant to some interpreter at an intermediate point in their journey through Scripture, but what they finally meant to Christ who is Lord of all Scripture.

This approach sharpens the recognition that all Scripture is not on the same level; rather, its landscape resembles a mountain range with one Mount Everest towering above all else. There is a different density of light in John and Romans than in Leviticus and Nahum. But the fact that some parts of the Bible do not point to Christ as clearly as others does not diminish the significance of Scripture by suggesting that some of its parts are "inferior." Rather, it enhances the importance of the written word by insisting that all of it exists to pay tribute to him who alone is the living Word, the one in whom "all things hold together" (Col. 1:17 NRSV). Finally, therefore, Christ is our supreme interpreter of Scripture. The Bible best becomes a "lively Word" when understood through the intentionality of his historical ministry, the potentiality of his guiding Spirit, and the centrality of his cosmic Lordship.

NOTE

1. Reported in the *Courier-Journal*, Louisville, Kentucky, August 1, 1971.

6

A REVOLUTION OF RISING EXPECTATIONS

Ask, and it will be given you; seek, and you will find; knock, and it will be opened to you. For every one who asks receives, and he who seeks finds, and to him who knocks it will be opened.

Matthew 7:7–8

On Wednesday morning, June 1, 1792, at the spring meeting of the Northamptonshire Baptist Association in Nottingham, England, a thirty year old shoe cobbler named William Carey stood to preach. Taking his text from Isaiah 54:2–3 (KJV), which contained the ringing challenge, "spare not, lengthen thy cords and strengthen thy stakes," Carey developed two themes, "Expect great things from God" and "Attempt great things for God."[1] As he spoke, the American Revolution was already an accomplished fact, the French Revolution was underway, and a Baptist revolution was about to begin. Up until that time, Baptists had been a tiny minority movement, embattled within a hostile culture, bickering among themselves over fine points of Calvinist theology. But after what came to be called Carey's "deathless sermon" launched the modern missionary movement, they became a poised, purposeful people with a world to win, too busy pursuing their grand mission to quibble over differences with others or among themselves.

What was the secret of this transformation that marked a watershed in Baptist history? It was not a triumph of human ingenuity. Carey had no political clout, financial resources, or organizational support.

All that he could urge was to "*expect* great things," and that is precisely what he launched: a revolution of rising expectations, a sense of new possibilities under divine leadership, a confidence that the future could be better than its past. The great expectations that Carey planted in the hearts of his fellow Baptists that day came straight from Scripture that described what the church of Jesus Christ was meant to be and what God promised to provide so that it could reach its full potential. The boldness with which Carey spoke was based on the conviction that the church in every age has an inalienable right to claim the divine resources promised for the fulfillment of its mission.

The Problem

If we as individuals and as a church wish to participate in that revolution, we need to carefully examine our expectations. Do we really "expect *great things*" as we attempt to do God's will in our world? The answer to that question will come only through prayer. The New Testament spells out the entitlements that every group of believers may claim. But this scriptural evidence does not answer the question of whether we actually expect all of these possibilities to come true for our own church today. Only in prayer can we say to God, "Do for us now all that you did for the churches of the New Testament, all that you have done for churches throughout Christian history, all that you are doing for other churches at the present time." Prayer by its very nature is petition, which is why it breathes the air of expectancy that we so urgently need.

To be sure, we often pray for ourselves that we might receive God's blessings. And we pray for one another in times of personal need, such as illness or bereavement.

But how earnestly *do* we as a church pray *for* our church? The apostle Paul made supplication for the saints a prominent feature of his letters, both at their beginning (Rom. 1:9; Eph. 1:16; Phil. 1:4; Col. 1:3; 1 Thess. 1:2) and at their ending (Rom. 15:30; Eph. 6:18; Phil. 4:6; Col. 4:2; 1 Thess. 5:25). It was his way of saying to struggling, immature congregations: don't rise to the level of your own expectations for yourself—for they are much too low! Don't even rise to my expectations for you—even though they are much higher! Instead, rise to God's expectations for yourself, confident that God will provide whatever it takes to accomplish that goal! Because prayer pleads for the realities of heaven to enter the life of earth, it is by its very nature an expectation-setting activity. As such, it should fill us with a keen sense of how much greater is what God yearns to do for us than what we ever request him to do (Eph. 3:20).

So why do we not pray like this more earnestly? First, for some, it is because of a limited conception of God. Jean Jacque Rousseau once remarked to a friend, "I bless God, but I never pray. Why should I, a weak and finite creature, presume to ask God to change the order of things for me?"[2] Did not Jesus himself tell us that God already knows what we need even before we ask him (Mt. 6:8)? If God is all wise, can he not decide what we deserve better than we can ourselves? Measured by the "job description" of God, which includes governing the entire universe, is not our agenda trivial and unworthy of divine attention? Isn't God too busy to be bothered with our everyday concerns? Has he not regulated our existence by natural laws so that he can devote his attention to more important matters? Some even feel guilty asking God for anything lest it imply that they are not submissive to his will.

A second cause is our own sense of self-sufficiency. The legacy of Frank Sinatra as a singer is summarized in his signature song, "I Did It My Way." Many of us never pray because we want to determine our own priorities. To ask God for help implies the Gethsemane contrast, "not my will but yours be done" (Lk. 22:42 NRSV). Many people in positions of power are accustomed to live the entire day bossing others, which makes it hard to reverse gears and ask God to be their boss when they pause to pray. At times, our lips are sealed by a stubborn pride that pretends we are self-made without need of any help.

A third reason for our reluctance to pray expectation-setting prayers is based on our sense that God's future for us is not very clear. Even if given the chance to plead for a revolution, we cannot pinpoint just how we want our future to be different from our past. Often we get so overcommitted to the status quo that we lack the boldness to imagine a better tomorrow. As long as we are satisfied with life as more of the same, it can seem risky to ask for anything else.

All of us know people whom we genuinely want to help, but they will not let us. Many children grow up not wanting the best that their parents have to offer. Many employees stubbornly refuse to ask a supervisor or colleague to help them improve their work. Many church members are reluctant to invite a minister into their lives, even when they are hurting badly and desperately need support. In such cases, our impoverishment comes, not from the refusal to give, but from the refusal to receive! The Bible states a principle that is too often true in both our human and our divine relationships: "You do not have, because you do not ask" (Jas. 4:2 NRSV).

The Prayer

How may we learn to pray the kind of prayers that embolden us to participate in the revolution of rising expectations in which God wants his people to participate? Nowhere is better guidance given than by Jesus who taught: "Ask, and it will be given you; seek, and you will find; knock, and it will be opened to you" (Mt. 7:7 RSV). Let us explore the implications of approaching God in this fashion.

Here prayer is portrayed as the habitual lifestyle of the Kingdom disciple. All three of the imperatives are in the present tense, which makes their force repetitive: "Keep on asking . . . never weary in seeking . . . continue knocking over and over." In the next verse, the durative force of the present participles strengthens the emphasis: "for it is those who perpetually ask and seek and knock who will be blessed again and again by God" (AT). These words point to no momentary religious impulse but rather describe a way of life lived in the expectant mood.

What is common to all three of these imperatives— ask! seek! knock!—is the inalienable right of God's people to expect more from Him than they have yet received! "Asking" implies that there are many answers already available that we have not yet been given. "Seeking" implies that fresh discoveries are already in place waiting to be found. "Knocking" implies that there are many doors to be opened through which we have not yet walked. What an amazing optimism about God's grace undergirds these promises! According to Jesus, life is bursting with potential to be realized, with opportunities to be accepted, with surprises to be claimed. Reality, in other words, is far greater than we have thus far apprehended. Therefore, we dare not limit our expectations to a perpetuation of the predictable. For the realm of the unknown and undiscovered and unexplored is much vaster than the tiny world of the commonplace that we find comfortable.

If we are to possess the unclaimed treasures offered by God, we must be adventuresome, courageous, and persistent. After all, what good is an extensive library if we never open a book? Or a great symphony if we never listen to a note? Or a rich museum if we never look at an exhibit? The summons to "ask . . . seek . . . knock" is an antidote to apathy; a challenge to overcome fatalism, pessimism, and determinism; a repudiation of the grim surmise that things will always be the same. Instead, Jesus says, take a proactive approach to the promises of God. Overcome your rigidity, seize the initiative, dare to believe that the best is yet to be.

This call to expectant living by Jesus was not a reflection of some kind of success psychology rooted in secular optimism. Rather, his promises were grounded in an unshakable conviction that the Kingdom of God was "at hand" (Mk. 1:15 RSV), that is, that the blessings of God's reign were near enough to be experienced. But his hearers needed to realize that these long-deferred promises were now within reach, that they could be had simply for the "asking . . . seeking . . . knocking." Without readiness and openness and eagerness they would be missed, for God does not force his gifts on anyone. Jesus was convinced that God wants to do far more for us than we could ever imagine, a desire long thwarted by our lack of eagerness to embrace his offer. So, the Master urged, show God just how deeply you desire what he has to offer!

Proof that this is a God-centered rather than a self-centered quest is provided by the very nature of the three imperatives. To "ask" means that we do not need to figure out all of the answers but only to raise truly probing questions. To "seek" means that we do not need to invent any new discoveries but only to find the ones that God has already prepared for us. To "knock" means that we do not need to know how to open doors but only to be persistent in expressing our desire for greater access to God's promises. There is deep humility in all three verbs before the mystery of life: to "ask" confesses that we do not have all the answers, to "seek" admits that we have not found a solution to every problem, to "knock" acknowledges that we must not walk in uninvited. Put simply, God's blessings are available, but they are not automatic.

The Promise

With each of these three descriptions of the kind of praying that nourishes rising expectations Jesus coupled a promised response: those who ask will "receive," those who seek will "find," those who knock will have the door "opened" to them (Mt. 7:8 AT). Notice how the active and the passive are carefully balanced. On the one hand it is imperative that we ask, seek, and knock. But, on the other hand, we can do nothing to provide what is received, found, and opened. In all three instances it takes two persons to complete what Jesus described and, as he immediately made clear, it is the Father in heaven who fulfills his promises to us (Mt. 7:9–11). We do the asking, but God gives what is received. We do the seeking, but God provides what is found. We do the knocking, but God opens the door.

This interactive approach to prayer tells us that ours is a God who wants to work with us in a personal relationship. The heavenly Father has no desire to come crashing into our lives uninvited any more than we would try to do something for another person without knowing whether they will welcome it or not. Only by praying in this fashion do we let God know both that we want something important from him and that we will do something significant with it if only he will provide what we need. When prayer creates a reciprocal relationship between us and God, it results in a divine-human synergy, a dynamic process of cooperation in which both we and God are committed to the making of his promised future.

Ask yourself: Do I regularly tell God what I most urgently want and need from him? Does he know what is important to me, or do I just petition for whatever favor pops into my mind? Have I defined for him my ultimate priorities in life? Have I been persistent in pleading for a future that is different from my past? Have I conveyed to God my confidence that his response will make a decisive difference in my life? Am I as deeply engaged in God's agenda as I want him to be in my agenda?

Another truth embedded in this way of praying is that abounding grace lies at the bedrock of ultimate reality. The God of Jesus is not stingy but generous to the point of extravagance. After all, is it not futile to pray for anything at all unless there is already more of something, or Someone, "out there" not yet claimed? The fundamental premise of Jesus' teaching was that the unfound is greater than the found, the unknown is greater than the known, the unseen is greater than the seen. This conviction was meant to stimulate in his disciples a sense of curiosity, of hopefulness, of wonder. It nourishes in us an intuition that the best is yet to be, a surmise that there is far more to life than we have apprehended that may be ours if only we are eager rather than reluctant to receive it.

This insight points us to what is positive about the doubt that we usually dismiss as dangerous. Honest disbelief is a useful reminder that whatever truth we have already glimpsed is not worthy to be compared with the greater truth that is yet to be found. Doubt is a manifestation of our discontent with inadequate conceptions of reality. It can be destructive as an end in itself but constructive if it provokes us to lead lives of asking, seeking, and knocking rather than absolutizing the status quo as if the quest for truth were finished.

This understanding of grace as the overflow of a bountiful God prepares us to understand the future as an horizon of promise. To receive answers that we did not devise, to make discoveries that we did not invent, to walk through doors that we did not open means that we have no control over what is given. We cannot determine when, where, or how these gifts will be given because they come from God rather than from us. This means that an element of surprise is inherent in the very nature of grace, making us vulnerable to a future that is different from the present. Even in earthly terms, many of our greatest explorers never found what they were seeking. It has been said of Columbus that he did not know where he was going when he set forth, did not know where he had arrived when he got there, and did not know where he had been when he returned home. And yet, what he found was far greater than what he sought. If that was true of one seeking to expand an earthly kingdom, how much more is it true of those seeking the Kingdom of God.

Because seekers seldom find what they think they will find, they must be open to change. This involves a willingness to reconceptualize the future in light of God's new gifts. How sad to find something and not realize its potential. For example, Swiss watchmakers invented the quartz movement but then ignored its application for years because they assumed that clocks worked only by springs.[3] In terms of answered prayer, the incentive to change comes from a realization that what we are given is almost always greater than what we sought. Most spiritual breakthroughs are serendipitous, they seem almost to be accidental. But they come to those willing to risk failure, to lose themselves in a bold venture, to wrestle with new challenges, believing that God will supply every need.

In his poem "The Listeners," Walter de la Mare asks: "'Is there anybody there?' said the Traveller, Knocking on the moonlit door . . ."[4] That is the ultimate question: What is behind the door of the universe, the door to be beyond? Emptiness and silence? Or a God more eager to give than we are to receive? If God is not there, then there is no reason to knock. But if God is there, then there is no reason to ever stop knocking. How can we learn the answer to that troubling question?

In the last book of the Bible, Christ is pictured as the one "who opens and no one shall shut" (Rev. 3:7 RSV). Because of this he can say, "Behold, I have set before you an open door, which no one is able to shut" (Rev. 3:8 RSV). The deepest answer of Scripture is that God is behind every closed door, and Christ can swing it wide open. But that same chapter describes Christ standing at our heart's door and knocking (Rev. 3:20). Christ opens the door to the God of grace, but we must open the door to the heart of faith. Ultimately, we are made bold to knock on God's door because, in Christ,

God comes to knock on our door! If we believe that God seeks us in order to give, and wants us to seek him in order to receive, then we are ready to join the revolution of rising expectations.

NOTES

1. Timothy George, *Faithful Witness: The Life and Mission of William Carey* (Birmingham: New Hope, 1991), 30–33. George traces how the two key watchwords may have been expanded as the story was frequently recounted.

2. Cited in John R. Claypool, "Asking and the God Who Already Knows," (sermon, Broadway Baptist Church, Fort Worth, Texas, June 27, 1976), 2.

3. Joel Arthur Barker, *Discovering the Future: The Business of Paradigms*, 3rd ed. (St. Paul: ILI Press, 1989), 57–60.

4. Walter de la Mare, "The Listeners," *The New Oxford Book of English Verse*, 1250–1950, ed. Helen Gardner (New York: Oxford, 1972), 840.

7

THE SEAL OF THE SPIRIT

---•>•◄•---

Do not bring sorrow to the Holy Spirit of God,
in whom you were sealed unto the day of redemption.

Ephesians 4:30 AT

Thornton Wilder, in *The Ides of March*, portrays Julius Caesar reflecting on those ancient religions that offer "a vague sense of confidence where no confidence is . . .," that "flatter our passivity and console our inadequacy." "What can I do," cries Caesar, "against the apathy that is glad to wrap itself under the cloak of piety . . .?"[1] That is the central question with which to grapple in any search for religious assurance: How may we claim genuine security without becoming spiritually spineless?

On the one hand, our time has well been named "The Age of Anxiety,"[2] the key word coming from the Latin term *angustia* meaning "shortness of breath."[3] Many today are suffocating in the spiritually cramped quarters of a secularized world. In such a bottleneck our phobias multiply in bewilding profusion: one standard medical dictionary catalogues 217 of them.[4] Grim statistics of murder, alcoholism, and divorce reflect an unbearable discontent with life as it is now being lived. As a result, we feed off of our fingernails, a diet calculated to produce acute spiritual indigestion.

On the other hand, religion has responded to the sinisterness of life by creating a cult of reassurance that coddles anxious Americans with promises of inner peace and boundless prosperity. We glibly claim to have a gospel with all the answers by identifying a one-way walk down the aisle with a one-way ticket to glory. In so doing, we cheapen the radical demands of faith, assuring persons that they are acceptable to God when in actuality they are not even acceptable to one another or to themselves. What the New Testament trumpets as a battle cry, we mute into a lullaby! Too many times we use the Gospel to pat the world on the back when it was meant to turn the world upside down!

Our task, therefore, is twofold: We must address the answer of the Gospel to the restless insecurity of the modern mood, yet we must do so in a way that offers at the same time the authentic challenge of responsible discipleship. No finer guidance may be found than in the truth of our text, "Do not bring sorrow to the Holy Spirit of God, in whom you were sealed unto the day of redemption" (Eph. 4:30 AT). Here, the tension between comfort and courage is beautifully balanced so that apathy can no longer "wrap itself under the cloak of piety."

The Spirit

The controlling affirmation about the security of the Christian is that it roots in nothing less than "the Holy Spirit of God." This assertion underscores the truth that ultimate security is not found in anything human or external. Let us be done with misplaced dependence upon public profession, water baptism, or church membership as the anchor against anxiety. Some who cry "Lord, Lord" and "do many mighty works" in his name will one day hear that terrifying declaration, "I never knew you; depart from me, you evildoers" (Mt. 7:21–23 RSV).

Instead, let us grasp the truth that our confidence is exclusively in God! The deities of Greece and Rome were fickle and capricious, leaving their devotees to fret and tremble in uncertainty. By contrast, the chief characteristic of the Christian's God is his reliability. He is always true to his promises though we all be false (Rom. 3:3–4).

The New Testament throbs with this affirmation: "God is *faithful*, by whom you were called" (1 Cor. 1:9 RSV). Because "God is *faithful*, "he will not let you be tempted beyond your strength" (1 Cor. 10:13 RSV). Even when temptation triumphs, "if we confess our sins, he is *faithful* and just, and will forgive our sins" (1 Jn. 1:9 RSV). In this assurance we can "hold fast the confession of our hope without wavering" (Heb. 10:23 RSV), confident that because he is *faithful* "he will finish what he has set out to do" (1 Thess. 5:24 JBP). In short, "if we are faithless, he remains *faithful*—for he cannot deny himself" (2 Tim. 2:13 RSV). As J. B. Phillips translated this recurring refrain, "God is utterly dependable" (1 Cor. 1:9 JBP).

Such precious promises in Scripture set the soul to singing:

A mighty fortress is our God,
A bulwark never failing.[5]
Again:
Great is Thy faithfulness, O God my Father,
There is no shadow of turning with Thee;
Thou changest not, Thy compassions, they fail not;
As Thou hast been, Thou forever wilt be.[6]
Finally:
"The soul that on Jesus hath leaned for repose
I will not, I will not desert to his foes;
That soul, though all hell should endeavor to shake,
I'll never, no, never, no, never forsake!"[7]

God does not take back what he has given, nor does he make any false starts. He always acts permanently, for he is the same yesterday, today, and forever. Therefore, our only hope for help lies in a God who keeps faith with his followers.

In this era of violence, national leaders receive the most elaborate security precautions imaginable. Whenever they step out in public, personal bodyguards stand ready to use their bodies as shields against bullets or bombs. When visiting in a foreign land, public figures have every morsel of food checked and every sewer manhole along their route sealed. Their beds are dismantled and examined in advance. Literally thousands of persons and millions of dollars are committed to keep them safe from harm.

But God has provided each Christian with greater protection than that! The Holy Spirit, who lives in every Christian, is a faithful defender who never departs, who is never deceived or overcome by evil, who is never in doubt about the will of God, who is never dismayed by earthly difficulties. God would not lavish such perfect protection on his children unless he intended for them to experience the fullness of his salvation.

The Seal

At present, it is painfully obvious that Christians are a long way from the goal toward which they press, for "the day of redemption" (Eph. 4:30 RSV) has not arrived. To be sure, our salvation was established by a past event, the death of Christ (Rom. 3:24; 1 Cor. 1:30), and is made effective by a present experience of the indwelling Spirit (Col. 1:14; Eph. 1:7). However, final redemption is essentially a future expectation for which we wait (Rom. 8:23; Eph. 1:14). How are Christians protected during the interim while they journey as pilgrims in an alien land? Our text has the answer: by the seal of the Spirit.

The uses of a seal in the ancient world furnish clues to the threefold significance of this metaphor:

(1) Seals were used to designate *possession* by an

owner. Animals were branded, and slaves were tattooed with the mark of their master. Just so, Christians are not their own, for they have been bought with a price (1 Cor. 6:19–20). As "slaves" of Jesus Christ, they receive the stamp of the Spirit as a badge of divine ownership (2 Cor. 1:21–22). With the awareness that they belong to Another comes deliverance from fretful self-concern. They discover stability in the certainty that "God's firm foundation stands, bearing this seal: 'The Lord knows those who are his'" (2 Tim. 2:19 RSV).

(2) Seals were used to guarantee *protection* from an enemy. Valuable merchandise and documents were fastened with a seal to prevent tampering or falsification. Money bags were sealed before embarking on a perilous journey. The sepulcher of Jesus was made secure "by sealing the stone" (Mt. 27:66 RSV). In like manner, Christians are guarded from harm by the mark of God upon their lives (Rev. 7:3). The Holy Spirit is God's seal guaranteeing that Christians will be safeguarded from their enemies until they receive the full inheritance that is promised them (Eph. 1:13–14).

(3) Seals were used to furnish *proof* of authenticity. They certified the outstanding service of a soldier, attested to the validity of a document, ratified the terms of a covenant, or accredited the credentials of an envoy (Jn. 6:27). In the same way, the presence of the Holy Spirit in the lives of Christians confirms beyond any doubt that they are children of God (Rom. 8:16). Just as the seal of a school upon a diploma places the reputation of that institution behind the degree, so the seal of the Spirit is God's way of authenticating the validity of one's salvation. In the same way that trademarks ensure the integrity of merchandise, the Holy Spirit furnishes the credentials of the Christian gospel, the proof which

corroborates a believer's claim to eternal life.

The Sorrow

Because the Holy Spirit is the source of our ultimate security, nothing must jeopardize the relationship of Christians to their Comforter. This paramount concern is underscored by the imperative that stands at the outset of our text, guarding the precious truths which follow.

The admonition to "grieve not the Holy Spirit of God" (Eph. 4:30 KJV) throngs with important implications for an understanding of Christian security. This phrase bears witness to the personality of the Spirit and to the intense interest that God takes in each Christian's life. It is impossible to speak of grief without speaking of a person, for whatever else may be true of an impersonal force, it cannot be thrown into sorrow. Sin does not merely stifle a moral influence, it injures a living person! Unlike pagan gods, the Holy Spirit is not above the human predicament, aloof and indifferent. Just as Jesus grieved at the hardness of the human heart (Mk. 3:5) and wept over unrepentant Jerusalem (Lk. 19:41), so his Spirit is seared by sin in the Christian's life.

The present imperative verb form used in this passage does not picture one monstrous act by which a person would presume to overthrow the work of God. Rather, it suggests a steady process of spiritual deterioration, a harassing of the Holy Spirit with those commonplace sins of a rebel tongue enumerated in the larger context: falsehood, bitterness, clamor, and slander (Eph. 4:25–32). The entire New Testament bears witness to the possibility of a progressive erosion of one's relationship to the Spirit. It not only warns against "grieving" the Spirit (Eph. 4:30) but also against "resisting" the Spirit (Acts 7:51), "outraging" or "despising" the Spirit

(Heb. 10:29), and even "quenching" the Spirit (1 Thess. 5:19).

This downward drift in one's dealings with the Holy Spirit must be checked, or the Christian will face the most fearful consequences. According to Jesus, those who blaspheme the Spirit will not be forgiven either in this age or in the Age to Come (Mt. 12:31–32). According to Stephen, those who resist the Spirit will destroy those who speak for God (Acts 7:51–53). According to Hebrews, those who harden their hearts in rebellion against the Spirit will never enter into God's rest (Heb. 3:7–15). Ananias and Sapphira falsified (Acts 5:3) and tempted (Acts 5:9) the Spirit, and their tragic fate stands as an unmistakable demonstration of the terrible judgment which falls upon those who sin against the indwelling presence of God.

In the light of these warnings, we cannot proclaim with conviction that Christians are "sealed unto the day of redemption" unless we proclaim with equal conviction that they must "not bring sorrow to the Holy Spirit of God" (Eph. 4:30 AT). The security of the believer is not compounded out of divine coddling and human complacency. God is not an inflexible tyrant but a sensitive Spirit. Christians are not helpless marionettes dangling by divine strings, but are responsible children offered the intimacy of a divine-human relationship that they are to cultivate at any cost.

Those who have been sealed by the Spirit are to "live" in the Spirit (Gal. 5:16), be "led" by the Spirit (Gal. 5:18), and be "filled" with the Spirit (Eph. 5:18). In this day of moral indifference among Christians, it is imperative to remember that the seal of the Lord has two sides: "God's firm foundation stands, bearing this seal: 'The Lord knows those who are his,' and 'Let every one who names the name of the Lord depart from iniquity'" (2 Tim. 2:19 RSV)!

Thus the security of the believer, like every great reality of the Christian life, is still a work in progress. We have been delivered into a new era of salvation but continue to live in an old era of sin. Even though we are set free from bondage to sin (1 Jn. 3:9) and death (Rom. 8:11), we may succumb to their despotic powers (1 Jn. 1:8; 1 Cor. 15:26). We are already glorified (Rom. 8:30), but "it doth not yet appear what we shall be" (1 Jn. 3:2 KJV). In like manner, we are already secure but have not yet entered into our final rest.

How are Christians to live on that boundary between the security of heaven and the insecurity of earth? The only answer is by faith, a faith that fuses complete dependence upon God with a holy determination to grieve not the Spirit. Such robust faith, not complacent apathy, is the gospel's answer to the Age of Anxiety.

Over the fireplace of an old hotel in England hangs this motto:

Fear knocked at the door.
Faith answered.
No one was there.[8]

Ours is a day in which fear stalks the land and knocks on every door. Let us answer with a faith controlled by the truth of our scripture text, and fear will flee from its threshold.

O to grace how great a debtor
Daily I'm constrained to be!
Let Thy grace, Lord, like a fetter,
Bind my wand'ring heart to Thee:
Prone to wander, Lord, I feel it,
Prone to leave the God I love;
Here's my heart, Lord, take and seal it,
Seal it for Thy courts above.[9]

NOTES

1. Thornton Wilder, *The Ides of March* (New York: Harper, 1948), 3.

2. The title of a 1947 book by W. H. Auden reprinted in *Collected Poems,* ed. Edward Mendelson (New York: Random House, 1976), 343–409. Haynes Johnson recently published a book on the past half-century entitled *The Age of Anxiety: McCarthyism to Terrorism* (New York: Harcourt, 2005) in which he suggests that the legacy of fear prompted by the Cold War with Communism has been revived by the advent of global terrorism.

3. Helmut Thielicke, *Nihilism* (New York: Harper, 1961), 188, with a discussion of the modern sense of "cosmic constriction" on pp. 118–147.

4. This reference is to *Blakiston's New Gould Medical Dictionary.* Quoted in "The Anatomy of Angst," *Time* 77, no. 14 (March 31, 1961): 45.

5. Martin Luther, "A Mighty Fortress is Our God," stanza 1, *The Baptist Hymnal,* ed. Wesley L. Forbis (Nashville: Convention Press, 1991), #8.

6. Thomas O. Chisholm, "Great Is Thy Faithfulness," stanza 1, *The Baptist Hymnal* (see note 5), #54.

7. John Rippon, "How Firm a Foundation," stanza 4, *The Baptist Hymnal* (see note 5), #338.

8. The inscription is on the mantle of the Hind's Head Hotel in Bray-on-Thames, not far from London. The inn is more than three hundred years old but an appended comment indicates that the motto was inscribed at the time of Dunkirk (1940). For representative uses of the illustration see Margaret Blair Johnstone, "You're Braver Than You Think," *Reader's Digest* (August, 1955): 122; George A. Buttrick, *Sermons Preached in a University Church* (New York: Abingdon, 1959), 43.

9. Robert Robinson, "Come, Thou Fount of Every Blessing," stanza 3, *The Baptist Hymnal* (see note 5), #15.

PART TWO

—➤•◄—

THE TRANSFORMING ENCOUNTER

Now we look inside, and what we see is that anyone united with the Messiah gets a fresh start, is created new. The old life is gone; a new life burgeons! Look at it! All this comes from the God who settled the relationship between us and him, and then called us to settle our relationships with each other.
        2 Corinthians 5:17–18 MSG

The more we explore the unseen world of the spirit, the more we discover how personal it is. The God at its center is forever taking the initiative to form a relationship with us when we least expect it. Instead of being infinitely remote in the highest heavens, he wants to talk to those who will listen to his word, as well as to listen to our every word as we pray. He fills welcoming hearts with his indwelling Holy Spirit in order to be a constant presence with us on the journey of life. Again and again we intuit a beckoning from the Beyond that calls us to companionship with the Sovereign of the universe. This amazing realization, that we are *wanted* by our Maker, goes a long way toward explaining why the human species is incurably religious.

Then why is it so hard for us to find God, much less to feel accepted by him? Partly because it is easier to cling to the world that is seen than to go looking for a world that is unseen. Before we know it, our sense of security is tied so closely to the material things we have accumulated that we become afraid to depend on anything we cannot control. Pride in earthly accomplishments feeds a self-centeredness that makes us suppose that we are masters of our fate. When challenged by others intent on self-rule, we retaliate, and the awful struggle for domination brings the wreckage that we know so well.

The only way to escape that vicious cycle is to replace self-centeredness with God-centeredness. Our plight requires the kind of cleansing pardon that radically redirects our desire to dominate. The good news is that a person named Jesus of Nazareth lived a God-centered life so consistently that he was utterly free of our destructive tendencies. The sermons in this section seek to show how we can be saved from self-centered futility by letting his presence permeate the core of our being. To know this Jesus is to discover the heart of God and to claim the deepest realities of his realm.

8

THE BITTER HARVEST

—➤•◄—

Do not be deceived; God is not mocked, for you reap whatever you sow.
If you sow to your own flesh, you will reap corruption from the flesh;
but if you sow to the Spirit, you will reap eternal life from the Spirit.
Galatians 6:7–8 NRSV

Consider with me the secrets of a seed. Some of the profoundest truths in Scripture come from pondering this fundamental unit of fertility. The opening chapters of Genesis depict the earth as a garden yielding seed (Gen. 1:11–12) and its inhabitants as God's horticulturists for whom life itself is a sowing and reaping (Gen. 2:8, 15). Nor will this archetypal image ever become obsolete: "As long as the earth endures, seedtime and harvest . . . shall not cease" (Gen. 8:22 NRSV).

On the basis of this presiding biblical metaphor, the apostle Paul frequently developed the symbolism of the seed (1 Cor. 3:6–9; 9:7–11; 15:35–44; 2 Cor. 9:6–10). In Galatians 6, for example, near the end of an earnest appeal to a wayward church, he introduced the harvest motif in order to reinforce the urgency of his concern. "Do not be deceived," the passage begins (Gal. 6:7 NRSV). "Don't kid yourself," we would say, for "God is not mocked" (Gal. 6:7 NRSV). The verb used here literally suggests that we cannot turn up or thumb our nose at God—that we cannot jeer, deride, or hoodwink the Almighty with impunity. Essentially, sin is a sneer in the face of the Eternal, a contempt for the Divine, a mockery of morality grounded in Transcendence. God will not be outwitted by human insults. With categorical finality Paul warned in the language of a law learned from nature: "you reap whatever you sow" (Gal. 6:7 NRSV).

Seldom is our human predicament clarified more candidly than when it is compared with a seed. The metaphor breeds meanings in multiple litters, three of which trace the lifecycle of sin from beginning to end.

Sowing

First, Paul's imagery underscores just how insignificantly sin often begins. The seed is proverbially small. A farmer may carry an entire year's crop in a single sack or even, as with tobacco, in the palm of his hand. In like manner, sin may germinate from thoughts and deeds so tiny as to seem meaningless. Traditionally, evil is depicted in grandiose terms, such as a dragon with pitchfork, horns, and tail; whereas, it ought to be visualized as the sowing of microscopic spores in the soil of life.

Consider a quartet of biblical witnesses. The serpent sought to seduce Adam with the subtle suggestion that he take only a bite of forbidden fruit (Gen. 3:1–5). His temptation was to nibble at an apple, not to cut down the whole tree! Delilah teased Samson until he got a haircut in the devil's barbershop, little more than playful sport on a summer evening (Judg. 16:15–17). Peter wanted to draw his sword and face a Roman legion; instead, he was assaulted by the waspish chatter of a servant girl (Lk. 22:54–56). Judas did not bargain to plot high treason, only to brush the cheek of Jesus with one quick kiss (Mt. 26:47–50). Such little things! Sins no larger than a seed. Yet they had the potency to launch a fateful process that would not be denied.

Drama has impact because it magnifies the issues, heightens the tensions, and telescopes the tedious processes of life. But reality is usually more modest. Seldom are we confronted with clear issues painted in black or white. More often, our decisions are compounded out of innumerable choices, often so small that they go unnoticed. Rarely do we turn a corner or choose a fork in the road at one decisive moment. Sometimes the drift of a life cannot be discerned for decades. How nice it would be to stage a Western-style showdown and "shoot it out" with sin. Instead, we are forced to do daily battle with an almost invisible army of seed blowing on the wind.

If sin does come so often as a seed, falling unobtrusively through the crevices of life, perhaps we should reappraise our strategies and the confidences on which our defenses are built. Many of us suppose that we can easily conquer the "little" venial sins, whereas the "big" mortal ones may prove too hard to handle. I suspect that just the opposite is nearer the truth. Faced with monstrous evils, such as murder or rape, we are seldom tempted, and our choices are usually clear. It is when the gremlin sins begin to infiltrate our defenses that we prove most vulnerable. After all, no one will rebuke us, or arrest us, or cause us any problems. Jonathan Swift saw it so clearly in his savage satire—hardly a children's tale!—of Gulliver at the mercy of the Lilliputians.[1] How often do we pose as moral giants when so easily we can be captured by immoral midgets!

Consider some of the lilliputian sins that immobilize our lives. We tend to assume that the "unfaithfulness" of a partner is grounds for divorce, by which we usually mean one blatant deed of infidelity. Although the seamless robe of marriage may be rent by a single act of adultery, more often it is quietly unraveled by an accumulation of incidentals: suppressed boredom, petty jealousies, carping criticism, arguments over money. Most marriages that collapse are like a great granite shaft being split by a tiny trickle of water. To generalize: alcoholics never set out to become captive to a bottle; they only want to sip on a social drink in order to be congenial. Unwed mothers never intend to become parents without a partner; they only bargain for a fleeting pleasure in a moment of ecstasy. Embezzlers never seek to bankrupt their business; they only "borrow" some needed funds that are certain to be repaid as the company prospers.

So often the minister is asked: Why get excited over a family fuss, a cocktail before dinner, a little petting after midnight, a conveniently forgotten item on the income tax return? After all, are not these such small matters that a preacher would be "puritanical" to condemn them? Is it so bad to peek at *Playboy* magazine, or leer at the latest "art" movie, or renege on a church pledge, or sleep in on Sunday morning, or loaf on the job when nobody is looking? Let us concede the point: these are only minor infractions of the moral code, small matters indeed. But the lesson of the seed is that a small beginning may have a significance all out of proportion to its size!

Dr. S. C. Gilfillan has theorized that one factor helping to explain the collapse of the ancient Roman aristocracy is that it was killed off in part by lead poisoning![2] Exhumed bones tend to confirm the classic symptoms: sterility, miscarriages, stillbirths, mental impairment, and paralysis. Tombstone inscriptions and census statistics indicate that life expectancy among the upper classes was only 22–25 years. Even one milligram of lead per day regularly introduced through mouth and lungs can eventually prove fatal. How did this elite group bring such destruction upon itself? By the trivial practice of eating food cooked in lead-lined pots. Wine, in particular, became highly toxic when warmed in such containers, especially when mixed with a grape syrup that had been boiled down in lead utensils. Ironically, the poor were spared this fate because they cooked in earthenware pots and could not afford much wine.

Confirmation of the importance of little things was provided much more recently in Rome when Clare Booth Luce served as U.S. ambassador to Italy. No sooner had she moved into her spacious seventeenth-century villa than a bone-gnawing fatigue set in, followed by nausea, numbness, and anemia, plus a loosening of hair, nails, and teeth. Exhaustive tests finally located the cause: arsenic poisoning. When security investigations failed to turn up any suspects, further detective work finally exposed the culprit, the ornate, heavy-beamed ceiling of her favorite bedroom. As the servants moved about in quarters overhead, their footfalls jarred loose tiny specks of paint that fell like an invisible white powder into her coffee and cosmetics. Because of the type paint used to decorate roses on the ceiling, Clare Booth Luce was slowly succumbing to a deadly dust with a high content of arsenate of lead.[3] Never underestimate the power of little things!

Growing

Between "sowing" and "reaping" is a vital connecting link that must not be overlooked, the *growing*. A seed is small, but its harvest can be enormous. The farmer who begins with his "crop" in a bag may end with his crop filling a barn. Jesus spoke of seed bringing forth grain, "growing up and increasing and yielding thirtyfold and sixtyfold and a hundredfold" (Mk. 4:8 RSV). Herein is disclosed a second significant truth about sin: not only is it small in the beginning, but it has an enormous capacity to multiply.

Look again at our quartet of biblical characters. Adam took only a bite of forbidden fruit, not knowing that it would destroy his sense of innocence and bring shame to his nakedness, causing him to hide from God (Gen. 3:6–8). Little did Samson realize that one frivolous haircut would sap his strength, deliver him into the hands of his enemies, and chain him like a blind animal on a treadmill to oblivion (Judg. 17:18–21). Peter thought that he could parry the questions of bystanders beside the fire, but suddenly his tongue was tripped, and he was shocked to hear his own lips thrice deny the Lord (Lk. 22:57–60). Judas may have supposed that his kiss would only force Jesus' hand and compel him to use his miraculous power. With mounting apprehension he must have watched the torture and trial unfold, never dreaming that his cohorts could be so cruel or that Jesus would prove so submissive (Mt. 27:3–4). How tragically each man miscalculated the consequences of his "minor" sins!

Are not these biblical examples a mirror of our own condition? Like Adam, we nibble at the notion that we can "know it all," until finally we lose all humility before the great Unknown. Like Samson, we trivialize our sacred vows and make light of the symbols of our spiritual strength, then try once more to summon divine power, only to discover that the Lord has left us and we knew it not. Like Peter, we stop for idle chatter but soon hear from our lips the hollow echo of those blasphemies that swirl about us. Like Judas, we become impatient with God's pace and seek to "prime the pump" with a little coercion. In almost every case, the stalk that shoots up is surprisingly larger than the small seed that spawned it (1 Cor. 15:37–38). How great are the changes that come in life once sin has taken root!

Few characteristics of evil are more crucial than its power to proliferate. A crowd gathers just to grumble about some controversy, and suddenly a riot is underway. Nations watch in alarm as diplomatic "incidents" become the occasions for a world war. Two schools begin a friendly football rivalry only to have it degenerate into pitched battles forcing the series to be cancelled. A "harmless" word of gossip is compounded until a career is ruined. There is a strange undertow of irrationality to evil that sucks its victims out beyond safety. Sin is like quicksand—it takes only one step to fall into the mire, but then each effort to escape demands another move that only makes matters worse.

Think of the strength latent in a seed. Few things have more potential in proportion to their size. Mighty oaks push up through the soil from a tiny acorn. If sin is like that, we need to revise our notions of its basic nature. We like to describe evil as if it were inert, a broken rule or a skeleton in the closet. But the biblical images are more robust: a leaven in the lump (Mt. 16:6), a wolf on the prowl (Mt. 10:16), a voracious bird of prey (Mk. 4:4), an army arrayed for battle (Eph. 6:12). Paul began Galatians 6 with the warning that evil may *overtake* a person like a swift runner relentlessly bearing down upon us from behind (Gal. 6:1). These are vivid ways of insisting that sin is a vital, dynamic power that wreaks havoc when given a chance.

This insight clarifies one of the most crucial questions that can be asked about any decision: *To what does it lead?* We are accustomed to assess each act on its own merits, as if the deed itself is inherently right or wrong. While this is often the case, the really questionable practices lie in a "twilight zone." Young people, in particular, are forever asking, "Is it all right to dance, to wear 'short' shorts, to gamble playing poker . . .?" The answer is confused by the way the question is put, for these behavior patterns are not necessarily right or wrong in themselves. Rather, we must ask: What processes do these acts set in motion? What kinds of thoughts, attitudes, and relations do they foster? In borderline areas, we must look not only at the seed that's sown but also at the crop that's grown to determine the wisdom of a decision.

There are at least three ways to judge right and wrong. (1) Some acts are inherently good or bad by virtue of their *content*. For example, it is always good to love and always bad to hate. (2) But "situation ethics" has taught us that the evaluation of some deeds is determined by their *context*. For example, sexual intimacy may be wrong when practiced by virtual strangers seeking only momentary self-gratification, but the very same activity may be profoundly right when employed to express mature affection by a husband and wife bound to each other in the fidelity of a lifelong commitment. (3) Finally, in some cases, the merit of a course of action is determined by the *consequences* to which it leads. The apostle Paul knew, for example, that meat offered to idols was, in and of itself, neither good nor bad; but he also knew that, while some might eat with impunity, others could have their faith impaired by the practice, and so should avoid it at any cost (Rom. 14:13–23).

In 1884, water hyacinth was brought from South America to the New Orleans Cotton Exposition, where its orchid-like lavender blossom won many admirers.

Tradition has it that a San Mateo, Florida woman took a cutting home for her fish pond and, as it rapidly multiplied, tossed the surplus into the nearby St. John's River. Little did she know that water hyacinth can double in as little as 6–18 days. Eventually it covered 125,000 acres of Florida's waterways with up to two hundred tons of hyacinths per acre. Finally brought under maintenance control at a cost of millions of dollars, it must be constantly watched lest its explosive growth again run wild.[4] Similarly, sin can spread just as rapidly if the seed finds fertile soil. Be not deceived by small beginnings.

Mowing

Finally, we reach the end of that process conceived by a tiny seed, continued by its explosive growth, and completed by the harvest. As surely as there is sowing and growing, there will also be mowing when the reapers appear. The third truth about sin now becomes clear. Locked within the act of evil is an inexorable dynamic of judgment. Paul explained it simply: ". . . he who sows to his own flesh will from the flesh reap corruption" (Gal. 6:8 RSV). The Book of James is more explicit: ". . . each person is tempted . . . by his own desire. Then desire when it has conceived gives birth to sin; and sin when it is full-grown brings forth death" (Jas. 1:14–15 RSV). Lord Byron confirmed this fearful prospect in his own experience:

> The thorns which I have reap'd are of the tree
> I planted; they have torn me, and I bleed.
> I should have known what fruit would spring
>   From such a seed.[5]

Take one last look at our biblical quartet. Adam did

not succeed in hiding from God but instead was condemned to live east of Eden, banished beyond a burning sword that guarded the tree of life (Gen. 3:22–24). Samson eventually regained his squandered strength but by then had become so embittered that he pulled down the wreckage around his own miserable life and those of his enemies (Judg. 16:23–30). Peter finally paid the price to get the campfire crowd off his back only to have the cock crow in fulfillment of his Master's woeful prophecy. At that moment of utter shame, "the Lord turned and looked at Peter" (Lk. 22:61 RSV); there was nothing to do but run out and weep bitterly, a broken man (Lk. 22:60–62). Judas was at last revolted by the tragedy that he had triggered, but it was too late to give the bribe back. In despair, he hurled his wretched life into the void by committing suicide (Mt. 27:5).

To be sure, judgment in many instances is not so dramatic, but it is as devastating. A silly quip has it that "people spend the first six days of the week sowing wild oats, then go to church on Sunday and pray for a crop failure." But the crop will not fail! Judgment may be delayed, but it will not be denied. A single strand of isolated sin may be easy to snap, but at last many strands will weave bonds that cannot be broken. Reciprocity is built into the universe. Physically, we cannot move without affecting distant planets; spiritually, we cannot act without growing a harvest. Judgment means simply that *decisions have consequences*!

While such a judgment is surely inexorable, it is not thereby capricious. The unity of root and fruit guarantees that we shall reap only what we sow (Mt. 7:16–20). In other words, whatever we decide that we *will* be, God decrees that we *must* be. The punishment need not come from without, like a thunderbolt from heaven. God has more important things to do than spank his errant children. Rather, we grow the bitter fruit that sets our teeth on edge. Someone has said that it would be hell enough to live forever with the mess that we know we have made of our lives. Forget the old "fire and brimstone" metaphors if you must. Think instead of harvesting all the shallowness of petty thoughts, all the narrowness of brittle prejudices, all the loneliness of selfish deeds, all the meanness of idle gossip. The mills of God may grind this harvested grain slowly, yet they do grind exceedingly small!

How shall we escape this fearful harvest of evil? Some try to fashion a euphoric religion without judgment, supposing that it can somehow halt the wild toboggan slide at the edge of the abyss, that the seeds of sin will not germinate into the killing fields of the soul. There is not a shred of support for this wishful thinking, either in Paul or elsewhere in the Bible. If anything, the coming of Christ only intensified the certainty that sowing and reaping are inseparable.

The answer of the gospel is not that of crop-failure: "If you sow to your own flesh, you will reap corruption from the flesh" (Gal. 6:8a NRSV). Rather, the gospel offers us the opportunity to sow a different sort of seed: ". . . but if you sow to the Spirit, you will reap eternal life from the Spirit" (Gal. 6:8b NRSV). Paul had just given detailed commentary in the preceding chapter on the "desires of the flesh" and the "fruit of the Spirit" (Gal. 5:16–25 NRSV). The issue is not *whether* seed will grow, given enough soil, sun, and water. The issue, rather, is *which kind* of seed each person will choose to grow.

The best way to choke out the bitter harvest is to grow a better harvest in its place. Look closely at your life: What kind of seed are you sowing? Each act of prayer, Bible study, and worship is a tiny seed indeed, but think of its potential for growth! Deeds of love and mercy are so inconspicuous that we are tempted to view them as insignificant, but, tended faithfully, they can make the heart bloom like flowers opening to the sun. The key is to "not grow weary in doing what is right" for it is as certain as the laws of nature that "we will reap at harvest time, if we do not give up" (Gal. 6:9 NRSV). Take care how you tend the garden of your life!

NOTES

. Jonathan Swift, *Gulliver's Travels* (New York: Oxford University Press, 1977), 1–70.

2. "Lead Among the Romans," *Time* 88, no. 13 (September 23, 1966): 70.

3. "Arsenic for the Ambassador," *Time* 68, no. 4 (July 23, 1956): 11.

4. *Saturday Evening Post* 233, no. 21 (November 19, 1960): 30–31; *Reader's Digest* 84, no. 21 (October, 1964): 253–56. On the "maintenance control" of water hyacinth see http://aquat1.ifas.ufl.edu/hyacin2.html.

5. George Gordon Noel, Lord Byron, "Childe Harold's Pilgrimage," *The Poetical Works of Lord Byron*, canto 4, st. 10, ed. Ernest Hartley Coleridge (London: John Murray, 1905), 212.

9

THE GLORY OF THE GOSPEL

———>•◄———

For I am not ashamed of the gospel; it is the power of God for salvation
to everyone who has faith, to the Jew first and also to the Greek.

Romans 1:16 NRSV

Like spokes converging on the hub of a vast wheel, all roads in the first century led to Rome. The Imperial City was the nerve center of the Roman Empire, the uncontested capital of the world. As a result, it was glutted with gospels from every corner of its conquered lands. To the historian Tacitus it seemed that his city had become an open sewer where "everything sordid and degrading converged from all quarters of the earth."[1]

In describing Rome as a cesspool for the religious refuse of the Empire, Tacitus singled out Christianity as an especially "detestable superstition."[2] To express his utter contempt for the movement he commented: "Though suppressed for the moment" by the execution of its founder, "it broke out again, not only in Judea, the origin of this evil, but even in Rome, that receptacle for everything atrocious of *which one ought to be ashamed.*"[3]

A half-century before these words were written, a harassed Christian missionary paused for three months, probably at Corinth in the midst of a dangerous journey (Acts 20:2-3), to prepare his answer for Rome. Writing to an embattled community whose faith was ridiculed and persecuted on every hand, the Apostle Paul anticipated the challenge of every "Tacitus" who would dismiss his message with the sneering rebuke,

"You ought to be ashamed!" "No," cried Paul, ". . . *I am not ashamed* of the gospel" (Rom. 1:16 NRSV). Far from being an abomination or a scandal, he was utterly certain that "it is the power of God for salvation to everyone who has faith" (Rom. 1:16 NRSV)—even to *you*, its cultured despiser!

". . . I am not ashamed of the gospel . . ."

That opening retort, "I am not ashamed," was no proud boast but a costly confession. Simply for preaching the gospel, Paul had been imprisoned in Philippi (Acts 16:19–24), smuggled out of Thessalonica (Acts 17:5–10), hounded out of Beroea (Acts 17:13–14), laughed out of Athens (Acts 17:32), and driven out of Ephesus (Acts 19:28–20:1). If he was "not ashamed" of his cause, then he was certainly one of the few! His fellow countrymen, the Jews, were so ashamed that they were plotting to take his life (Acts 20:2). The Jewish Christians in Jerusalem were so ashamed that they dogged his steps to undermine everything he did (Gal. 1:6–9). His fellow apostles, Peter and Barnabas, were so ashamed that they capitulated to political pressure from the party of James (Gal. 2:11–14). Many of his own converts and missionary companions were so ashamed that they forsook him completely (2 Tim. 1:15; 2:15–18; 4:10).

The realization that his gospel created a scandal came early for Paul, and he faced the crisis squarely in the opening chapters of 1 Corinthians (1:18–2:5). Because the essential content of that message concerned a crucified Messiah, it would always be folly to the wise and clever (1 Cor. 1:18–19). Both to Jews demanding signs and to Greeks seeking wisdom, the preaching of Christ seemed to be foolishness and weakness (1 Cor. 1:22–25). But Paul was not in the least intimidated. Although his message meant that he would have to minister "in much fear and trembling" rather than "in lofty words or wisdom," paradoxically that very helplessness served to demonstrate that the power of God was working through his life (1 Cor. 2:1–5).

It was this conviction, that divine power is most clearly seen in human weakness, which enabled Paul to resist the strong temptation to become chagrined even when his missionary enterprise seemed on the verge of collapse. Near the end of his life he would tell Timothy, "*Do not be ashamed* . . . of testifying to our Lord . . . but take your share of suffering for the gospel in the power of God" (2 Tim. 1:8 RSV). Or, again: "For this gospel . . . I suffer as I do. But *I am not ashamed*, for . . . I am sure that he is able . . ." (2 Tim. 1:11–12 RSV).

Behind this unabashed confidence of the Apostle lay the terrible warning of his Master, who knew what a stumbling-block the cross would prove to be: "For whoever is ashamed of me and of my words in this adulterous and sinful generation, of him will the Son of man also be *ashamed*, when he comes in the glory of his Father with the holy angels" (Mk. 8:38 RSV). In the showdown, the choice is not between accepting the gospel and bearing its shame, or rejecting the gospel and escaping its shame. Rather, it is between enduring its shame in the present for being faithful, or facing infinitely greater shame in the future for being unfaithful. The bedrock of Paul's position was that it is far better to risk acute embarrassment at the hands of thoughtless critics than to risk ultimate disgrace at the hands of the sovereign Lord. What this clarion cry of the apostle, "I am not ashamed," really meant was that he was willing to be vindicated by the judgment of God, rather than by the culture of Rome!

It is amazing how glibly we glide past Paul's understanding of the gospel as a rock of offense. Uncomfortable with his negative beginning here, some translate "I am not ashamed" to mean "I *am* proud!"[4] But the opposite of shame is not so much pride as it is courage. With his back to the wall, hemmed in by foes on every hand, Paul did not have the luxury of boasting about his gospel. Nor may his words come easily to our lips. With "fear and trembling" (1 Cor. 2:3 RSV) we must fling our "not ashamed" into the face of a skeptical world that has become cynical about whether any power is strong enough to transform human personality. Only when the scandal stands starkly revealed, does it really matter to respond, "but *I* am not ashamed!"

There is no threat of shame in preaching the gospel in our cozy sanctuaries surrounded by sympathetic friends. There is no threat of shame when we offer the gospel as a formula for psychological peace and economic prosperity. There is no threat of shame when we restate the gospel so subtly that we appear to be purveyors of the latest philosophical vogue or spiritual fad. Nor are these risk-free stratagems necessarily wrong in themselves. The problem, rather, is that they do not go far enough, because they do not expose us to the authentic scandal of the gospel where everything is at stake in the defiant assertion, "I really *am* not ashamed!"

The challenge of our time is not to make the gospel so palatable to the modern mood that we bask in crowd approval, but to make the gospel so scandalous that we risk the open contempt of its cultured despisers. That will happen only when our message shatters pride, rebukes prejudices, denounces greed, decries complacency, and condemns aggression. The task will not be easy. All too often, pulpit and pew engage in a conspiracy of silence to keep the radical claims of the gospel from ever surfacing. But the issue must be faced, for we will never grasp the full glory of the gospel until we prove to ourselves that we can endure its deepest offense without becoming ashamed!

"... it is the power of God for salvation ..."

How could Paul maintain such an unwavering confidence in the gospel despite its potential for ridicule and scorn? Supremely, by realizing that his message was not what it appeared to be. Instead of a foolish story of human weakness, it was, in reality, "the power of God for salvation" (Rom. 1:16b NRSV). A few verses earlier Paul had identified the content of his gospel as Jesus Christ, who "was designated Son of God *in power* . . . by his resurrection from the dead" (Rom. 1:4 RSV). A few verses later he will explain that his gospel is a divine revelation "from heaven" (Rom. 1:18 NRSV). The context, therefore, guides us to understand that all of the supernatural power vested in the exalted Lord of glory flows through the scandalous message that proclaims his earthly shame!

Note well: Paul did not say that the gospel is a proclamation *about* the power of God. Rather, he said that the gospel is that very power at work for human redemption (1 Cor. 1:18). The gospel does not merely bear witness to salvation but has within itself the strength to save. Its preaching of the sacred story literally reenacts the Christ-event. When the message is faithfully uttered in the power of the Spirit, Christ actually *happens* again in human affairs. This means that the gospel is both a word and a deed, both an utterance and an occurrence, because it has the potency to bring to pass what it declares. The herald does not review an ancient record or analyze a religious idea but rather calls into being a redemptive event! Ultimately, therefore, the gospel is nothing less than a miracle, because through it, Christ comes again into the world and that coming always was and always will be the supreme miracle of God's visitation.

Proof that the gospel is impelled by a divine dynamic is seen in the fact that it can deliver us from destruction. The power that was present in the person of the Savior (Rom. 1:4) continues to be mediated by the preaching of his gospel, and thereby, becomes effective in the lives of all who accept its claim. The message goes forth as a gale of God's wind blowing in a heavenly direction (Jn. 3:8), a transcendent force propelling persons toward salvation, a kind of spiritual "counter-gravity" that lifts them above every threat of earthbound existence. Although the completion of that safe passage through earthly trials to eternal fulfillment lies in the future, the gospel does not merely *announce* or even *anticipate* the outcome. Rather, it *inaugurates* the pilgrimage of salvation and *actualizes* the experience of its reality here and now, in advance of the end!

The glory of the gospel is seen not only in the way that it conquers shame but also in the way that it speaks to the central issue of our time, the crisis of power. There is deep irony in our present predicament. On the one hand, enormous energy has been harnessed by science and technology to launch both an Industrial Revolution and an Information Revolution with incredible potential for human progress. But at the very moment when human power is in such great supply, much of it is being used to wreck havoc in human life. All over the world, ethnic groups engage in genocide while, at home, handguns blaze even in the hands of children intent on wanton destruction.

Our human dilemma is that we have so much power that shatters, so little power that saves! It was the same way in the first century as in the twenty-first. Caesar's legions were everywhere, ready to butcher any who resisted their advance. To be sure, there were nonviolent alternatives as well. Paul knew all about the benevolent power of Jewish law, of Greek culture, and of Roman justice. But he also knew, in contrast to every earthly power, that only his gospel had the power to save! So with us: we may pay our respects to military might, to the rule of law, to education, and to culture, but still ask of them the ultimate question: Do you have the power to save humanity from destruction? Paul had actually seen lives changed, hopes awakened, purposes redirected, and relationships established. He knew what his gospel could do. His own transformation on the Damascus road was living proof that it was, indeed, "the power of God for *salvation*" (Rom. 1:16 NRSV).

The church lives or dies by the truth of that claim. Unless there is a regenerating, redeeming, reconciling power at work at the center of our common life, we will not flourish as an instrument of God's will. But if there stirs within us a divine dynamism that freshens the wellsprings of our honored traditions with living water, that infuses our bureaucratic inertia with prophetic boldness, that energizes our evangelistic complacency with holy zeal, then there is no limit to the ways that God can use us in the perilous days ahead. Such power will come, not from our strategies or our structures, but from the consistency and integrity with which we embody the gospel of Jesus Christ in word and in deed. The ultimate test of our fidelity is whether the gospel given to us is proclaimed with such power that it leads others "unto salvation." The issue to ponder is not, "are we increasing in popularity or in prestige with our neighbors?, but is anybody around here being *saved* these days? To answer in the affirmative is not to engage in self-congratulation. For salvation, by its very nature, comes only from God. To claim that our every endeavor is directed toward the redemption of the world is to confess that we are attempting what is humanly impossible, that we are risking everything in the awareness that unless God intervenes all is lost. Paul put it well: ". . . that your faith might rest not on human wisdom but on the power of God" (1 Cor. 2:5 NRSV).

". . . to everyone who has faith . . ."

Complete reliance on the sufficiency of God is demanded not only by the divine aspect of the gospel as "the power of God unto salvation" but also by the human aspect of the gospel as effective "to everyone who *has faith*" (Rom. 1:16c NRSV). In its biblical definition, faith is not some human activity that would base salvation on our religious works, but is a *re-*action to the divine action declared in the gospel (Eph. 2:8–9). It is the absence of self-assertion that makes room for the divine initiative. As a commentator on this passage, C. H. Dodd, explained, "It is an act which is the negation of all activity, a moment of passivity out of which the strength for action comes, because in it God acts."[5] Faith is emptying life of its earthly clutter to make room for God. It is our readiness to hear the divine summons (Rom. 10:14–17), our willingness to answer the divine knock (Rev. 3:20), our eagerness to receive the divine gift (Jn. 1:12).

In the eyes of the world, it is utter nonsense to cry,

"In my hand no price I bring, simply to Thy cross I cling."[6] That smacks of ultimate irresponsibility, a cop-out of which we should be "ashamed." And such would be the case if deliverance depended upon our works instead of on the gospel, if there were nothing there for the asking when we stand still to see the salvation of God. But because divine power is given in the gospel, the scandal of faith as the opposite of religious works is fully vindicated. Through simple trust we discover that our emptiness is his filling, our weakness is his strength, our abdication is his coronation, our humiliation is his exaltation. The issue is really very simple: Can we save ourselves better than God can save us?

The glory of a gospel received by faith alone is that it makes salvation available "to everyone" (Rom. 1:16c NRSV). We cannot all share the same citizenship, for national boundaries divide us; or the same culture, for social classes divide us; or the same prosperity, for economic differences divide us; or the same culture, for social classes divide us; or the same prosperity, for economic differences divide us. But, thank God, we can all share the same salvation, because the capacity to believe is common to every person made in the image of God. When the gospel defines faith as our "nothing" in the face of God's "everything," it offers each person a second chance regardless of the first chance provided by heredity, environment, or attainment.

Such an understanding protects the offer of salvation from any narrowly inhibiting restrictions. The overriding issue in the ministry of Paul was his contention that the gospel could not be for *any*-one, whether "Jew or Greek," unless it was for *every*-one alike. He was aware that Rome was the most pluralistic city in the world when he wrote that all-embracing phrase, "to *everyone* who has faith" (Rom. 1:16 NRSV). Just so today, we can traverse every continent however distant, enter every ghetto however wretched, and penetrate every culture however sophisticated in the conviction that saving faith is not limited by racial, sexual, or social barriers.

Think of it! The most powerful force in the world is available "to everyone who has faith" (Rom. 1:16 NRSV). Statesmen cannot say that about their country. Politicians cannot say that about their party. Tradesmen cannot say that about their union. Scholars cannot say that about their academy. Salesmen cannot say that about their product. But Christians *can* say that about their gospel! "To *everyone* who has faith." Let us lift that banner above all that we do as a church. Let it be the burning conviction behind every invitation that we extend, every piece of literature that we distribute, every sermon that we preach, every program that we plan, every class that we teach, every conference that we convene. Nothing less than an enthusiastic willingness to share the whole gospel with the whole world is worthy of our high calling!

What would it mean for us to grasp the true glory of the gospel as it shines from our precious text? If we really believed what Paul did about the gospel, would it not reorder our priorities, causing us to place highest importance on the saving rather than the losing of human life? If we really believed the truth of our text, would we not be eager to share the gospel with any and all of those in need of its power? If we really believed that the gospel can still do in the twenty-first century what the Apostle was certain it could do in the first century, would we not allow God's salvation to work much more fully in our own lives?

In the spirit of Paul, I would plead for renewed confidence in the gospel of Jesus Christ: "I am not ashamed"—undaunted by the courage which it demands; "the power of God for salvation"—unmatched by the change which it produces; "to everyone who has faith"—unlimited by the compassion which it expresses (Rom. 1:16 NRSV). May its greatness grip our hearts and guide our steps so that the glory of Christ, proclaimed in his gospel, may change us "into his likeness from one degree of glory to another" (2 Cor. 3:18 RSV).

NOTES

1. Cornelius Tacitus (c. A.D. 55–120), *Annals* XV. 44.

2. The Latin phrase is *exitiabilis superstitio* which may be translated "dangerous superstition" since *exitiabillis* means "destructive, fatal, deadly."

3. The actual wording, *atrocia aut pudenda,* is translated rather literally to bring out its stark contrast with our text. The key term *pudendus* was from *pudere,* "to be ashamed," and meant "shameful, scandalous, disgraceful, abominable." This connotation is retained in the use of the word "pudenda" in English to refer to external genitalia.

4. The wording of the text is actually changed to "I am proud" in the translations of Moffatt, Montgomery, and Barclay. Behind this paraphrase lies the unwarranted supposition that "I am not ashamed" is a deliberate understatement for emphasis.

5. C. H. Dodd, *The Epistle of Paul to the Romans* (London: Hodder and Stoughton, 1932), 16.

6. Augustus M. Toplady, "Rock of Ages, Cleft for Me," stanza 2, *The Baptist Hymnal,* ed. Wesley L. Forbis (Nashville: Convention Press, 1991), #342.

10

THE URGENCY OF THE HOUR

—➤•◄—

From that time Jesus began to proclaim,
'Repent, for the kingdom of heaven has come near.'
Matthew 4:17 NRSV

In 168 B.C., the Syrian ruler Antiochus IV Epiphanes led his forces against Egypt only to encounter Roman legions with similar designs. In a climate of looming confrontation, the competing commanders met to confer. Antiochus badly wanted control of Egypt, but not at the cost of open warfare with Rome. When he requested time to ponder his alternatives, the Roman commander took his sword, drew a circle in the sand around the Seleucid King, and said, "Decide before you leave this circle."[1]

It was with that same sense of decisiveness that Jesus burst upon the scene in ancient Galilee to deliver God's ultimatum to Israel. His first public act was to identify with the conviction of John the Baptist that the long-awaited Kingdom of God had at last drawn near (Mt. 3:2; 4:17). No insistence was more characteristic of everything that he said and did. He streaked through a world of jaded hopes like a comet in the skies. From the beginning, his message bristled with a sense of finality. The dominant note was nearness, the immediacy of the issues about which he spoke.

This does not mean, however, that Jesus was a religious fanatic like the escapist visionaries in Jewish apocalypticism who pointed away from the actual world to some catastrophe in the heavens. Rather, by means of parables, which were simple slices of everyday existence, he showed how momentous crises lurk just beneath the surface of the most commonplace experiences. If Jesus was right, a dimension of urgency pulsates at the heart of ordinary life to which we all must respond.

Let us test the validity of his concern by listening afresh to those familiar stories, discovering for ourselves the note of exigency that they contain, then asking whether this depiction faithfully mirrors our situation. A close look at all of his parables suggests that the urgency of Jesus was rooted in three dominant convictions about the looming hour of crisis.

Sudden

Jesus was convinced that the great issues of life confront us with startling swiftness. His stories were full of examples of unexpected developments that changed everything at a moment's notice:

- A household slumbered peacefully when *suddenly*, during the night, a thief broke in to steal (Mt. 24:43/Lk. 12:39).
- A wedding party awaited the bridegroom who *suddenly* arrived at midnight when some had no oil for their lamps and so could not see to meet him (Mt. 25:1–13).
- A group of servants worked for an absentee master who *suddenly* returned expecting to find them faithfully discharging their duties (Mt. 24:45–51; Mk. 13:33–37; Lk. 12:35–48; Mt. 25:14–30/Lk. 19:12–27).
- A house rested secure on its foundations when *suddenly* it was lashed by a deluge and swept away in the resulting flood (Mt. 7:24–27/Lk. 6:47–49; Mt. 24:37–41/Lk. 17:26–27).

As a shrewd observer of the human scene, Jesus knew that life is punctuated with interruptions as immediate as a flash of lightning across the sky (Lk. 17:24). Woven into the fabric of events are instant intrusions, such as snares that trap the unwary animal (Lk. 21:34), creditors who demand a settlement before sunset (Mt. 5:25–26/Lk. 12:57–59), and armies that swiftly encircle a city (Mt. 22:7; Lk. 21:20). By reminding his hearers of these everyday occurrences, Jesus was asserting that we cannot keep our crises at arm's length; that they often come when we least expect them; therefore, that the time to get ready for them is *now*!

We have confirmed the wisdom of the Master in our daily experience. If we were free to deal with God in leisurely fashion, it would be one of the few momentous decisions that is not thrust upon us with almost blinding unpredictability. We casually sort the morning mail and out pops a job offer altering the vocational course of life. We open the newspaper and stare at a headline that revolutionizes the way our children attend school. The telephone jangles with the message of a fatal accident or death that in a moment changes everything. How suddenly parents discover that a son is on drugs, or that a daughter is pregnant by a boy she scarcely knows. How savage is the swiftness with which we stumble onto a raging fire, or the indiscretion of an unfaithful spouse, or the suicide of one who seemed so well-adjusted.

Nor, can we distance ourselves from this dimension of breathtaking instancy even with our most careful planning. As American citizens, we marvel at the vast intelligence apparatus available to our national leaders. Despite maximum capability to control events, however, President Kennedy suddenly found himself embarrassed by the Bay of Pigs fiasco, President Johnson suddenly found himself mired in the quicksand of Vietnam, President Nixon suddenly found himself enmeshed in the web called Watergate, and President George W. Bush found his victorious armies in Iraq engulfed by sectarian religious strife. None of these presidents wanted to make hasty decisions about any of these disasters, but they were helpless to do otherwise because of the speed of onrushing events. In fact, as the memoirs of many statesmen attest, truly momentous issues have a way of thrusting themselves onto the agenda without warning, demanding decision at a moment's notice.

Curiously, all significant crises retain this element of suddenness even when they unfold slowly and seem to move toward an inevitable climax. Precisely because they are the decisive encounters of life, we are never really prepared for them as we would like to be. A courtship ripens into love, and the relationship almost comes to be taken for granted; yet, when he finally "pops the question," the proposal takes her breath away. An expectant mother patiently waits for the period of gestation to be completed; yet, when the spasm of release finally comes, she suddenly finds new life in her arms for which she could never quite prepare. Desperately ill loved ones may linger near death for days; yet when the passing comes, they seem to be gone in a twinkling. My best friend was told that his leukemia-stricken daughter had eighteen months to live; yet, when the end came, right on schedule, he was utterly dismayed by its "terrible swift sword."[2]

The point is that we cannot hold reality at bay while we patiently negotiate with God! We may want to analyze theology and clarify morality and evaluate denominations before deciding to confess our faith, but life is too unpredictable for all of that. We can never know at what moment we may be swept off our spiritual feet by a flood of tragedy, or blown off our course by a fierce gale of circumstances, or required to give immediate accounting of the ultimate values by which we live. There are so many contingencies in every person's situation that no one has the luxury of setting a private timetable to get right with God. Forget about applying for fire insurance after the house has begun to burn!

In the old revival tradition, every evangelist had his stock of "deathbed stories"—one variety telling how some indifferent or reluctant soul was suddenly confronted with eternity before his or her affairs were in order. "Modern" men and women have come to abhor these stories as excessively emotional and manipulative, prompting a new generation of preachers to repudiate them as "scare tactics." I certainly share the desire to be drawn by love rather than driven by fright into the arms of God. But I wonder if an inescapable facet of reality has not been forgotten in our fastidious avoidance of "deathbed stories"? Tragedy can fall with sledgehammer swiftness on the most unsuspecting of victims. Almost every day as a pastor, I sought to help someone floundering through an ordeal simply because it had erupted with such suddenness. The best way to be free of fear is not to forget deathbed realities but to remember that we are all vulnerable, hence the need to get ready *before* the unpredictable strikes. The Boy Scout motto effectively summarizes this concern of Jesus: Be prepared!

Surprising

A second conviction of Jesus was that the great issues of

life are not only sudden but also *surprising*. The basic reason for this lay in his conviction that our standing in heaven is fundamentally different from our standing on earth, that human status in the sight of others has no bearing on eternal status in the sight of God. The Lukan Beatitudes tersely describe a Great Reversal: those who are poor now shall receive the kingdom then, those who hunger now shall be satisfied then, those who weep now shall laugh then, those who are hated now shall rejoice then (Lk. 6:20–23).

Jesus liked to express this topsy-turvy transformation in the language of paradox: the first will be last, and the last will be first (Mt. 19:30; 20:16/Mk. 10:31/Lk. 13:30). The exalted will be humbled, and the humbled will be exalted (Mt. 18:4; 23:12/Lk. 14:11; 18:14). The great will become servants, and the servants will become greatest of all (Mt. 20:26–27; 23:11/Mk. 10:43–44/Lk. 22:26). Those who save their life will lose it, and those who lose their life will save it (Mt. 10:39; 16:25/Mk. 8:35/Lk. 9:24; 17:33). The rule is constant: in dealing with God, always expect the unexpected.

This dramatic turnabout was vividly depicted in the parables of Jesus. He told of a rich man clothed in purple and fine linen who feasted sumptuously every day while at his gate lay a beggar who ate scraps from his table as the dogs licked his sores. When both men died, however, the rich man was consigned to the fiery torment of Hades, while the poor man was transported to the bosom of Abraham (Lk. 16:19–31). He told of a Pharisee who prayed like a virtuoso in contrast to a lowly publican who dared not pray at all, except to cry for mercy. The shocking verdict on their efforts, however, was that the sinful publican, rather than the pious Pharisee, was justified in the sight of God (Lk. 18:9–14).

He told of tenants entrusted with a vineyard who supposed that they could inherit it simply by killing off the claimants of an absentee owner. To their dismay, however, they discovered that the landlord's patience had been pushed too far, and he personally came to destroy them (Mt. 21:33–46/Mark 12:1–12/Luke 20:9–19).

Perhaps the most vivid illustration of this truth by Jesus was his depiction of the last judgment, which we may call the Parable of Great Surprises. The shocker was not that a process of sifting would occur, but that *both* groups would be startled by its results. Sheep and goats alike incredulously confessed that they were oblivious to those opportunities that had determined their destinies. Those so certain that they would be favored found themselves excluded, while those with no hope of inclusion found themselves accepted (Mt. 25:31–46). It reminds us of Jesus' incredible guest list to the messianic banquet at which outsiders from every quarter will be welcome to sit down and eat with the patriarchs, while "the sons of the kingdom will be thrown into the outer darkness" (Mt. 8:12 RSV). Or of that equally astonishing climax to the Sermon on the Mount when those who had called Jesus "Lord, Lord," and in that name had both prophesied and done many mighty works, would hear the chilling declaration, "I never knew you; depart from me, you evildoers" (Mt. 7:21–23 RSV).

In defining eternity as one big surprise, Jesus was not seeking to shatter religious assurance or destroy hope for a better future. Rather, he was insisting that our confidence must rest, not in earthly securities, but only in God. If we dare to trust in our ancestry, our nation, our denomination, our baptism, our public decency, or our personal piety, then we may be in for a rude awakening! Why? Not because these things have no human importance, but because they do not matter ultimately to the God whose thoughts are not our thoughts and whose ways are *not* our ways (Isa. 55:8).

As my ministry nears its end, I am frankly surprised at how many things have turned out differently from anything that I might have expected. In childhood, I was involved in three of the largest and strongest Baptist churches in Birmingham, Alabama; now, all three have virtually disappeared from those communities. The high school I attended was widely regarded as one of the best in Alabama; now, after years of academic decline, it has closed. I spent a quarter-century at a theological seminary that has changed so drastically in a few years that I would not recognize it today. Some of the most powerful leaders in Shreveport, Louisiana, when I arrived were discredited by the time I left twelve years later. Then after a few more years, casino gambling made the city very different from the place that I once knew. To be sure, there have been some continuities and predictabilities in my life, but for the most part, it has been one long surprise. Jesus was right: we never know what may happen next!

This is especially true in the realm of the spirit. How often we drift along through life content with a thin veneer of religion. Then suddenly, the façade is shattered by a blow to our very being, and—surprise! surprise!—our flimsy faith is not adequate for the crisis. We thought we would be ready when the time of testing came. We had completed a good education, earned a good living, enjoyed a good reputation, and joined a good church, but none of it was enough. How determined we are to surround ourselves with human security systems, but Jesus calls the bluff. Come up against the divine demand, he warns, and these puny defenses will collapse. Hence the urgency of his plea: if you would be ready for the great reversal, and not be dumbfounded by its decrees, then deal decisively with God on his own terms and do it *now*!

Soon

A third conviction of Jesus is also disturbing in its import, that the great issues of life are not only sudden and surprising but that they are sure to require resolution very *soon*. We are tempted to complain that if one cannot evade either the swiftness of crisis or its startling demands, then at least God should stay his hand until we can get ready for such an ordeal. But Jesus would not have it so. For him, a showdown was already looming on the horizon. Events were rushing to their intended consummation. A new day was dawning. The reign of God was about to burst upon the scene (Mk. 1:15).

Everything in the proclamation of Jesus breathed this note of immediacy. Already the seed was sprouting; hence the harvest could not be far behind (Mk. 4:26–32). Already the fig tree had burst forth with spring foliage; hence, the summer fruit was soon to follow (Mt. 24:32–33/Mk. 13:28–29/Lk. 21:29–31). Already the power of the Spirit was evident in the casting out of demons; hence, the days of Satan were numbered (Mt. 12:28/Lk. 11:20; Mk. 3:27). Already the disciples were seeing the promises of the Old Testament take flesh (Mt. 11:2–6/Lk. 7:18–23; Mt. 13:16–17/Lk. 10:23–24); hence, the age of fulfillment was beginning to dawn (Mt. 5:17).

As a result, time was quickly running out in which to tend a fruitless vineyard (Lk. 13:6–9), or to accept a banquet invitation (Mt. 22:1–10/Lk. 14:15–24), or to build bigger barns (Lk. 12:13–21), or to bid goodbye to those at home (Lk. 9:61–62)! Indeed, so near was the impending crisis that each person would have to take sides *now* (Mt. 10:34–36; Lk. 12:51–53). Neutrality was an impossible option when the very foundations were being shaken. The disciples were bidden to get the word out quickly to any who would listen, but to shake the dust from their feet and move on when any refused to hear (Mt. 10:23; Mk. 6:10–11). A mood of decisiveness settled over all that Jesus said and did. Without ever once becoming frantic or impulsive, he nevertheless precipitated a spiritual showdown without delay.

At first glance, it might seem impossible to sustain that incredible intensity for two thousand years, but experience teaches otherwise. Perhaps our most frequent failing in spiritual affairs is to misjudge the amount of available time. The Southern church thought that it could delay dealing with the slavery issue only to find itself in the bloodbath of a national conflagration. For too long Christian leaders dodged the evolution controversy, hoping that those nasty theories of Darwin would simply fade away, only to discover that once-sympathetic universities had left the faith to embrace a new scientific secularism. History has a rude way of rushing past those who suppose that God will let the clock stand still!

J. P. Marquand captured this truth at the personal level in his novel, *So Little Time*.[3] The story tells of a playwright with the best intentions of being a good parent while pursuing his literary career. One day, when the oldest son put on a uniform and prepared to go to war, the father suddenly realized that life for his boy might be briefer than anticipated. Feverishly he sought to overcome years of neglect while the son was at home, only to discover, in the tragic lament of the title, that there was "so little time." How often is that our anguished realization! *Before we know it,* the children are gone, the job is stale, the marriage is empty. Certainly, we were going to do something about it one day, but why did the problem have to come to a head *so soon?*

To recover the urgency of Jesus is not to ignore the virtues of prudence and patience. We may grant that long slow years are needed to fashion a solid character. But to those who contend that "Rome was not built in a day," I would counter that it was begun in a day, and that, precisely because it may take so long to complete the job, there is no better time to get started than *now*!

Prudence and patience certainly have their place in life, but these virtues must be balanced by a healthy awareness of the perils of procrastination. A modern parable tells how three devils met to discuss their strategy for conquering the world.

> The first devil went around proclaiming the message, "There is no God!" But even though some people acted as if there were no God, they knew in their hearts that this message was not true. The second devil announced, "There is no sin!" And again, although many people acted as if that message were true, they knew deep down that it wasn't. The third devil was smarter than the other two. He didn't attempt to change people's beliefs. He made no attempt to argue against their deepest convictions. He simply said, "There is no hurry."[4]

Some overconfident souls may suppose that they can either sidestep, delay, or avoid the crises of life, but such wishful thinking overlooks the ultimate truth that

Jesus himself prompts the unavoidable crisis that every person must face. He suddenly appears from nowhere to herald the dawn of a new day. His description of that upheaval surprises even the religiously secure. He pushes the hands of destiny's clock beyond the eleventh hour and announces that soon the bell will toll for me. Talk about crisis! We shall never know any crisis like that of being addressed by him who cries, "*Come*; for *all* is *now* ready" (Lk. 14:17 RSV)!

Accordingly, my plea to you is this: If you need to get right with God, do it *now*! If you need to repair a relationship, work on it *now*! If you need to risk a brave new venture, begin it *now*! If you need to spend more time with your children, start doing so *now*! Don't look back, don't wait for things to change at home, don't gamble that tomorrow may offer better opportunities. Remember, the offer of God's Kingdom has already been made. In that confidence, seize this moment to claim every promise that God wants to fulfill in your life. Yesterday is in the tomb of time, tomorrow is in the womb of time, only today is yours in which to begin life anew!

NOTES

1. On the ultimatum of Gaius Popilius Laenas to Antiochus IV, see Polybius, *The Histories*, XXIV, 27.

2. See John R. Claypool, "Life is Gift," *Crescent Hill Sermons*, Crescent Hill Baptist Church in Louisville, Kentucky, vol. 7, no. 32, February 8, 1970. At the outset of this sermon, the first preached following the death of his ten-year-old daughter, Claypool confessed that for eighteen months he had lived with a double agenda: "With my mind I faced up to the fact that our daughter's situation was very serious, and I did everything in my power to cope with it realistically. But at the feeling level I had abounding hope. In fact, I did not realize just how hopeful I

really was until that Saturday afternoon as I knelt by her bed and saw her stop breathing. You may find this incredible, but I was the most shocked man in all the world at that moment" (p. 2). Revised and reprinted in *Tracks of a Fellow Struggler* (Waco: Word Books, 1974), 70.

3. John P. Marquand, *So Little Time* (Boston: Little, Brown, 1943).

4. Cited by Martin E. Marty, *Context* 23, no. 8 (April 15, 1991): 1.

11

STOP – LOOK – LISTEN!

—▸•◂—

Therefore, since we are surrounded by so great a cloud of witnesses, let us also lay aside every weight and the sin that clings so closely, and let us run with perseverance the race that is set before us, looking to Jesus the pioneer and perfecter of our faith, who for the sake of the joy that was set before him endured the cross, disregarding its shame, and has taken his seat at the right hand of the throne of God.

Hebrews 12:1–2 NRSV

Early in the twentieth century a major problem arose because railway lines were beginning to crisscross America just as the automobile was becoming popular. Signs reading "Look out for the trains" were erected where roads intersected tracks, but the wording was too tame to prevent a rapidly rising number of disasters as careless motorists lost their lives to the onrushing iron horse. A new slogan was needed that would overcome the distractions, compel the decisions, and direct the actions needed to halt this senseless carnage. And so, a contest was held in 1912 offering a reward for new wording that would promote the watchword of the railway industry, "safety first." The winner was Ralph R. Upton, a Seattle school-teacher and safety lecturer, who contributed the now famous guidelines, "Stop – Look – Listen!"[1]

These three terse imperatives well summarize the essential ingredients needed to avoid tragedy when we face dangers of any kind. Because they are indelibly etched on the American memory, anyone can instantly recall them in a time of testing. Each word is clear and simple, even to a child. Taken together they require no difficult theory to understand or complicated formula to follow. Therefore, I suggest that we adopt them as our motto for practicing spiritual safety first as we come to the crossroads of destiny.

To do this we shall need to clothe each term with biblical meaning, a relatively easy task because "stop" is a key concept in the Prophets, "look" in the Gospels, and "listen" in the Epistles. Moreover, we shall discover that "stop" points primarily to God the Father, "look" to God the Son, and "listen" to God the Holy Spirit. This means that these three tiny terms offer us a fresh approach to the fullness both of Scripture and of Deity.

Stop!

Our first imperative falls like a dull thud on modern ears. Its negativity smacks of a grim puritanism that we left behind in our rush to be rid of inhibitions and embrace a permissive mood. Life has become a race where success belongs to the swift, so why should we pause even for a moment and let others get ahead of us? Any religion that does not have all of its lights set on green is in danger of being viewed as legalistic and repressive. And yet, is not "stop" exactly the word we would shout if we saw a child about to run in front of a speeding automobile or a friend about to step on a coiled rattlesnake? As Ralph Upton realized, when dealing with life-threatening danger, calling a halt to unnecessary risk is the most sensible way to begin.

This raises the key question of just how precarious is the human predicament? When we take stock of our tragedies, whether a destructive addiction, a ruined marriage, or a compromised character, the problem is almost always judged to have begun so small and grown so slowly that we were overwhelmed before realizing its seriousness. There is a cunning to the way in which evil insinuates itself into our lives. Beginning so inconspicuously that we shrug it off as harmless mischief, sin soon gains a foothold, becomes a habit, and attaches its tentacles so gently that we seldom notice its presence. A key reason why we fall for this seductive strategy is that we stay too busy to inventory our true condition. Like the tiny cancer that metastasizes until it becomes inoperable, perhaps because we put off a thorough medical examination, sin ignored or denied can spread decay until it results in a terminal illness of the soul.

A keen sense of the relentless momentum of evil led the Hebrew prophets to emphasize repentance, a term that meant to "turn" from wickedness back to God (Ezek. 33:18–19). Bound up in this spiritual about-face were at least three components: halting the most casual flirtation with sin, considering the wondrous works of God (Job 37:14), then reorienting one's life to God's will for his people. Both John the Baptist and Jesus made repentance the foundation of their message, the necessary way to get ready for the long-awaited Kingdom of God (Mt. 3:2; 4:17). How simple, yet profound! What Scripture is telling us is that the only way to quit running from God is to stop! The only way to confront the long-term consequences of our spiritual compromises is to stop! The only way to explore new options offered by the gospel is to stop! Only in the cessation of self-centeredness is there the possibility of beginning a new life with God at its center.

The importance of making a stop was seen clearly in the tragedy that befell Columbia University teacher Charles Van Doren. Brilliant young intellectual, scion of a distinguished literary family, he was attracted to the television quiz programs that were the rage in the mid-1950s. Accepted to appear on Twenty-One, a new program with high stakes, Van Doren was approached by a producer who insisted that he be given the questions in advance, that he memorize a script containing their answers, and that he receive coaching in the use of mannerisms designed to make the contest more dramatic. To justify these compromises, the producer argued persuasively that Van Doren would create new respect for the teaching profession, that help for quiz contestants was a common practice, and that—after all—the show was merely entertainment. Succumbing for a few weeks to this "small" seduction, Van Doren soon found himself perpetrating a national hoax that earned him more than $129,000 but deceived thirty million viewers in the process.

After only two years, secrets buried like seeds began to send their sprouts above the soil. "I had been living in dread," Van Doren said of those years. When a disgruntled contestant exposed the coverup, he became panic-stricken. Pursued by reporters and the District Attorney of New York, the idol of millions repeatedly perjured himself, haunted lest he destroy the trust that so many had placed in him. At last he "simply ran away," driving aimlessly through New England with his wife, unable to face what he had done. His boyish face became drawn, his eyes bloodshot. He could not sleep for weeks; his attorney feared for his health and sanity.

Then on November 2, 1959, judgment day came for the man whom the press had labeled the "Cinderella of 1957." Appearing before a subcommittee of the United States Congress, Charles Van Doren read a ninety-minute "soul-searching confession" that began:

I would give almost anything I have to reverse the course of my life in the last three years. I cannot take back one word or action; the past does not change for anyone. But at least I can learn from the past. I have learned a lot in those three years . . . about good and evil . . . I learned that things are not always the way they appear to be.

What were the lessons learned when Van Doren finally stopped long enough to face reality? His voluntary confession reflected the kind of self-understanding that comes only in times of deliberate detachment from every form of distraction.

I was involved, deeply involved in a deception . . . I was of course very foolish and . . . incredibly naïve . . . In a sense, I was like a child who refuses to admit a fact in the hope that it will go away . . . I engaged a lawyer . . . In my folly I did not even tell him the truth . . . My life and career, it appeared, were being swept away in a flood . . . I could not face the situation . . . I was completely confused and dismayed . . . I simply ran away . . . Most of all, I was running from myself.[2]

Look!

In the prophetic plea to repent, motivation to stop going in a dangerous direction was provided both by avoiding the consequences of sin and by claiming the promise of the future. No matter how bleak present circumstances might be, what we now call messianic prophecy defined a horizon of hope based on the conviction that God would do a "new thing" to rescue his beleaguered people from tragedy (Isa. 43:19 NRSV). The last of the prophets, John the Baptist, saw in Jesus the fulfillment of those expectations and so cried, "*Behold*, the Lamb of God" (Jn. 1:29, 36 RSV). Careful analysis suggests that this word was part of a revelatory formula according to which "a messenger of God sees a person and says, 'Look!' This is followed by a description wherein the seer reveals the mystery of the person's mission."³ When the disciples of John asked Jesus where he was staying that they might visit with him, the reply was, "Come along and see for yourself" (Jn. 1:39 MSG).

Throughout his ministry, Jesus attached the greatest importance to what others saw in him. When John the Baptist was languishing in prison under threat of death, he became discouraged and sent disciples to inquire if Jesus really were the coming Messiah (Mt. 11:2–3). After treating this delegation to a typical day's work, Jesus responded, "Go and tell John what you hear and *see*" (Mt. 11:4 NRSV), namely: "the blind receive their sight, the lame walk, the lepers are cleansed, the deaf hear, the dead are raised, and the poor have good news brought to them" (Mt. 11:5–6 NRSV), a summary of prophetic expectations for the messianic age (Isa. 29:18–19; 35:5–6; 61:1). Later Jesus would tell his own disciples, "Blessed are the eyes that see what you see! For I tell you that many prophets and kings desired to see what you see, but did not see it . . ." (Lk. 10:23–24 NRSV). Their failure to perceive and understand the meaning of his miracles brought forth the lament, "Having eyes do not you see . . .?" (Mk. 8:18 RSV). In his acts of compassion, the salvation of God had become visible if only they would look with eyes of faith.

If the great word of the Prophets is "stop!" in the sense of repenting from sin, the great word of the Gospels is "look!" in the sense of beholding the claims of the Savior. The theological concept undergirding this emphasis is called incarnation, which means that God stepped out on the stage of history and let us look at him in a human life. The Johannine writings magnify this theme. The prologue to the Gospel declares that "the Word became flesh" as a result of which "we have *seen* his glory" (Jn. 1:14 NRSV). The prologue to the First Epistle asserts that "the word of life" is what "which we have *seen* with our eyes, what we have *looked at* and touched with our hands" (1 Jn. 1:1 NRSV). So deeply was this experience of gazing at God, up close, embedded in the memory of early Christians that the exclamation "behold" became a characteristic way of introducing a story in the Gospels, being used sixty-two times in Matthew and fifty-seven times in Luke with the force of "pay close attention" or "be sure to look at this."

Now that the palpable Jesus of history is no longer with us, we must discover him afresh through the accounts of his life and work in the Gospels. But this does not lessen the need for a discerning eye. As philosopher Mircea Eliade implored his fellow scholars, we all need to look at Scripture "with the concentrated attention, the disciplined sympathy, the spiritual openness that artists evince. . . . How can one understand a thing if he does not even have the patience to look at it attentively?"[4] Just as true stopping provides us with an opportunity to turn inward and inventory our spiritual condition, so true looking permits us to turn outward and ponder what Jesus offers those who follow him.

The ministry of Charles Haddon Spurgeon, hailed by many as the greatest preacher in the second half of the nineteenth century, was inseparable from our second imperative. It all began on a snowy day in January, 1850, when, as a fifteen-year-old lad, he sought shelter in a Primitive Methodist chapel at Colchester, England, where only fifteen people had braved the storm. The preacher took as his text, "Look unto me, and be ye saved, all the ends of the earth" (Isa. 45:22 KJV). After expounding on its simplicity and urgency, he spied Spurgeon under the gallery and, stooping down, addressed him directly: "Young man, you are very miserable, and you will always be miserable if you don't do as my text tells us, and that is, Look unto Christ." Then he called out strongly, "Young man, *look*; in God's name *look*, and *look* now. *Look! Look! Look!* You have nothing to do but *look* and live."[5] It was the turning point. For the rest of his life Spurgeon would testify of that moment, "I looked and I lived!"

In October, 1857, during his twenty-third year, Spurgeon preached to 23,654 persons by turnstile count, said to be the largest crowd ever gathered to hear the gospel. A few days earlier he had gone to the Crystal Palace to test the acoustics since he would be speaking without benefit of a sound system. Standing on the platform he cried out in the empty chamber, "Behold, the Lamb of God that taketh away the sins of the world." Unknown to him, a workman was busily painting high up in one of the galleries where the words seemed to reach him as if from heaven. Moved to deep conviction, he went home and did not find rest until he beheld that Lamb for himself.[6]

With such a bountiful harvest from an overriding passion to show people the Savior, is it no wonder that when Spurgeon's body lay in state at the Metropolitan Tabernacle, where sixty thousand persons filed past to pay tribute, on the coffin lay a Bible open to his signature text, "Look unto me, and be ye saved, all the ends of the earth" (Isa. 45:22 KJV).[7]

Listen!

But no matter how carefully we look at Jesus, whether in the flesh or in the gospels, what we see was long ago and far away. How do we build a bridge spanning two thousand years and reaching halfway round the world? The Christian movement faced that challenge in its first generation by spreading far beyond Palestine just as the original eyewitnesses were beginning to die. Jesus had anticipated the problem before his departure and promised that, even in persecution, his disciples would know what to say because the Holy Spirit would speak through them (Mk. 13:11). In the Upper Room he explained that this divine presence would not only re-mind them of what he had said and done on earth (Jn. 14:26) but would also contemporize truth that they had not been able to bear, thereby helping them to face "the things that are to come" (Jn. 16:12–13 NRSV). Rather than living in the past with a museum mentality, Chris-tians are empowered to face whatever the future may bring with the Holy Spirit as a reliable personal guide.

Which brings us to our third imperative: not only are we to open the eye-gate and "look" but also open the ear-gate and "listen." The prophet had pled in God's name, "Incline your ear, and come to me; listen, so that you may live" (Isa. 55:3 NRSV), but the people were tone-deaf to his entreaty (Isa. 42:20). Jeremiah declared God's diagnosis that Israel had been hard of hearing throughout its long history: "From the day that your ancestors came out of the land of Egypt until this day, I have persistently sent all my servants the prophets to them, day after day; yet they did not listen to me, or pay attention . . ." (Jer. 7:25–26 NRSV). The only hope was for God to waken ears that were sleeping so that they could listen attentively to his voice (Isa. 50:4b NRSV).

Like the prophets, Jesus taught many whose ears were "heavy of hearing" (Mt. 13:15 NRSV). Yet, he worked constantly to overcome both physical and spiritual deafness (Mt. 11:5; Mk. 7:32–37). Indeed, his whole ministry was one long miracle of helping people listen to God, which is why the verb for hearing occurs 230 times in the Gospels. After Jesus ascended into heaven, his followers were able to hear God even better due to the interpreting work of the Holy Spirit in their hearts. Pentecost, for example, was a miracle of hearing that transcended the limitations of earthly languages (Acts 2:6, 8, 11). Now, the apostles could speak boldly, because they were listening to God rather than to the threats of their enemies (Acts 4:19–20). Paul explained that "faith comes by hearing" (Rom. 10:17 AT); that is, listening is a necessary link between the message being proclaimed and its being believed.[8] This is why the story of the early church in Acts ends by saying that the salvation of God has been sent to those who "will *listen*" (Acts 28:28 NRSV).

Only when we worship, pray, and read the Bible listening for a voice does the "old, old story" lay a personal claim upon our lives. George Macleod of the Iona Community in Scotland once told of a young man who would enter a Roman Catholic church at lunch time, kneel before the altar for a moment, and then depart. When asked by the priest why his devotions were so brief, he explained that he had only a short time before he was due back at work, thus he knelt just long to say "Jesus, it's Jimmie!" before going on his way. Later the priest was called to the bedside of the boy as his life ebbed away. Standing nearby as the lad turned to face eternity, the priest was certain that he heard a voice saying, "Jimmie, it's Jesus."[9] Thus does he come to call us by name if only we will listen (Jn. 10:3; 20:16):

"John, Mary, Tom, Betty—it's Jesus."

> Softly and tenderly Jesus is calling,
> Calling for you and for me . . . [10]

Each part of our slogan is undergirded by the broad sweep of Scripture, but if a single text is needed to focus its truth, let it be Hebrews 12:1–2. First we are to stop long enough to "lay aside every weight and the sin that clings so closely" (Heb. 12:1b NRSV); that is, end those dalliances with evil that distance our lives from God. Second, we are to "run with perseverance the race that is set before us, looking to Jesus the pioneer and perfecter of our faith" (Heb. 12:1c–2a NRSV). Third, we are to do this *listening* for the Spirit of him who, despite enduring the cross and its shame, is alive forevermore "and has taken his seat at the right hand of the throne of God" (Heb. 12:2b NRSV). Can you think of a better way to overcome those dangers that pose a threat to your spiritual security? If not, practice "safety first" for your soul by obeying the biblical mandate to stop, look, and listen!

NOTES

1. Helen Falls, "Stop, Look and Listen," *Royal Service*, June, 1955, 24–25.

2. The entire episode was reported extensively by The Associated Press on November 2, 1959, from which this account and quotations are drawn. The incident was popularized by the 1992 television documentary "The Quiz Show Scandal" and the 1994 movie "Quiz Show" directed by Robert Redford.

3. Raymond E. Brown, *The Gospel According to John* (i–xii), The Anchor Bible (Garden City, NY: Doubleday, 1966), 58.

4. Mircea Eliade, *No Souvenirs: Journal, 1957–1969*, trans. Fred H. Johnson, Jr. (New York: Harper & Row, 1977), 230–1.

5. Ernest W. Bacon, *Spurgeon: Heir of the Puritans* (Grand Rapids: Baker, 1982), 22–23. Italics added.

6. Ernest W. Bacon, *Spurgeon*, 59–60.

7. Ernest W. Bacon, *Spurgeon*, 168.

8. On this understanding of the original language, which is nearer the King James Version than some recent translations, see C.E.B. Cranfield, *A Critical and Exegical Commentary on the Epistle to the Romans, The International Critical Commentary* (Edinburgh: T. & T. Clark, 1979), 2:537.

9. Reported from a broadcast by George Macleod in John Short, *Triumphant Believing* (New York: Charles Scribner's Sons, 1952), 122.

10.Will L. Thompson, "Softly and Tenderly," stanza 1, *The Baptist Hymnal*, ed. Wesley L. Forbis (Nashville: Convention Press, 1991), #312.

12

THREE CHEERS FOR LIFE

—➤•◄—

And, behold, they brought to him a man sick of the palsy, lying on a bed: and Jesus seeing their faith said unto the sick of the palsy; Son, be of good cheer; thy sins be forgiven thee. Matthew 9:2 KJV

For they all saw him, and were troubled. And immediately he talked with them, and saith unto them, Be of good cheer: it is I; be not afraid.
Mark 6:50 KJV

These things I have spoken unto you, that in me ye might have peace. In the world ye shall have tribulation: but be of good cheer; I have overcome the world. John 16:33 KJV

These are tough times in which to live. The new millennium was greeted with a surge of optimism caused primarily by the collapse of Communism as a global threat abroad and by a soaring stock market that promised boundless prosperity at home. But to our dismay, we soon learned that religious fanaticism can be just as terrifying as atheistic materialism, particularly when it chooses to kill civilians by ramming the planes on which we fly into the buildings where we work. Excursions into Afghanistan and Iraq have taught us that even the most decisive military victories are no guarantee of peace but may instead unleash endless chaos beyond our ability to control.

Unfortunately, we have not been able to assuage our frustrations in the Middle East with affluence on the domestic front. The early years of the new century brought a sharp recession from which we recovered with the help of record debt, both public and personal.

As China and India flex the economic muscle of their huge labor force, the outsourcing of jobs, which even our strongest companies seem helpless to resist, results in a mood of uncertainty regarding the future. Trapped by pressures not of their making, individuals feel increasingly helpless to grapple with those problems that threaten their sense of security. We feel hemmed in by increasingly complex movements and machines that we can neither understand nor control. Freed from transcendent constraints, our society becomes increasingly unpredictable and unreliable, leaving us with that sort of anguish about which André Gide wrote "at not being able to rely on anything durable, definitive, anything *absolute.*"[1]

Jesus came into a world much like ours. Brute force had left those to whom he spoke subjected to military occupation eking out a meager existence at the subsistence level. And yet, at the core of his message was a note of strong encouragement compressed into a recurring imperative that came readily to his lips. The Greek word *tharsei* is translated as "Have courage!" or "Take heart!" Most commonly it is rendered "Be of good cheer!" in order to capture its bold, resolute thrust. On three occasions Jesus prefaced a pronouncement with this refrain almost as if he were saying "give three cheers for life!"[2]

Pardon

The first occasion on which Jesus offered cheer (Mt. 9:2–8) began grimly enough: "And, behold, they brought to him a man sick of the palsy, lying on a bed" (Mt. 9:2 KJV). Twitching ceaselessly on his pallet prison, this pathetic, shriveled shadow of a man was a misery to himself and a burden to his friends. On seeing such a sight, we would think immediately of sending him to a physical therapist or consigning him to a nursing home. But Jesus moved swiftly in an unexpected direction. "Be of good cheer!," he cried. Why? Because "your sins are forgiven" (Mt. 9:2 RSV). Our first cheer for life springs from the assurance that Jesus provides pardon.

On the surface this response appears to be laughable if not contemptible. In what sort of mischief could one so afflicted engage? He had no livelihood to squander in riotous living. His wasted legs could hardly chase the women! He was not villain but victim. He had not been brought to Jesus as a moral reprobate but as a physical invalid. The crying need was clearly for bodily strength, not for spiritual cleansing. Was the pronouncement by Jesus a cruel evasion, as if to say, "I cannot do anything really useful to overcome your predicament, so I will just send you on your way with a warm feeling of absolution in your heart"? Do we have here that exasperating tendency of some religionists to deal in pious words rather than practical deeds, retreating to the ethereal sweet-by-and-by rather than grappling with the painful here-and-now?

On deeper pondering, however, we discover that Jesus gave priority to pardon because of his profound insight into the human condition. The paralytic lived in a culture that construed illness as divine punishment for sin (Jn. 9:2). Throughout his sickness he had overheard whispered innuendoes that speculated on what grievous evil he must have committed to deserve such retribution. Nor was that reaction limited to ancient superstition. When shattered by disease or disability, the instinct is deep within all of us to cry, "What have I done to deserve this?" Our whole outlook on life is shaped by whether we view God as vindictive, hence attributing our bodily frailties to divine vengeance for real or imagined failures.

Yet the issue goes deeper than that. Because of his paralysis, this man could not journey to the Temple to offer sacrifice, stand in the synagogue to pray, or find fulfillment by providing help to others. His physical handicap was, in itself, a spiritual handicap. He had no opportunity to nourish his spirit through religious activities as did those with healthy bodies. Jesus recognized that God often seems remote to anyone living with such restrictions. And we have found it so. Desperate illness can make us functional atheists, not only because it isolates us from the community of faith, but because pain saps the energy to pray, drugs deaden the desire to study the Bible, suffering sows the seeds of doubt. Ironically, God may prove hardest to find, at least in accustomed ways, for the physically ill who need him most!

At the deepest level, Jesus realized that, even if he cured the man's affliction, relief would prove temporary. Before this encounter ended, the paralytic was enabled to walk (Mt. 9:6–7), but a day came when his legs collapsed under him again. Indeed, every person, no matter how healthy or how religious, sooner or later reaches the point where the body completely fails. Physicians may delay that inevitability and ease the agony of its arrival, but the hard fact is that doctors finally lose every patient. We cannot witness the inexorable finality of that process without asking what remains when we lose our frail scaffolding of flesh. Therefore, Jesus began by addressing the ultimate issue that we must face in negotiating the ups-and-downs of our bodily existence.

By announcing the gift of divine forgiveness, he was affirming that God is "*for* us" and not "against us" (Rom. 8:31 NRSV) even when we are helpless. One can "take heart" in the assurance that the heavenly Father is not vengeful but merciful. He has not sent disease to punish his errant children. Rather, he has sent his son to share with us the choicest blessings of life. The very word "forgive" means the removal of barriers to unhindered fellowship with God. Beside our beds of pain, without benefit of religious ritual, Jesus can make God disarmingly real as friend instead of foe.

Rather than assuring his hearers that, if only they believe in God, the body will always be strong, Jesus moved in the opposite direction by assuring them that, even when the body is weak, God will gladly welcome them! The Father accepts in loving mercy those who cannot lift a finger to give him anything. God will have us, not only when we are robust but when we are infirm (Mk. 2:17). Thus, to set the sequence straight, we do not find pardon because we are healthy; rather, we can face health or illness because we have been pardoned! This is why London pastor Leslie Weatherhead could say, "The forgiveness of God, in my opinion, is the most powerful therapeutic idea in the world."[3]

Major General Courtney Whitney, personal aide to Douglas MacArthur, tells how the day finally came at the climax of World War II when the Pacific Commander-in-Chief returned to the Philippines and made his way toward Manila. Through guerrilla intelligence reports MacArthur had learned that, as his troops advanced on the capital city, the Japanese guards at the prisons were increasing their savagery. The thought of such torture and possible death for these gallant captives after so many years of waiting struck him to the quick; thus, a special operation was devised to capture the prisons ahead of schedule by surprise. As soon as this was done, even while shells were still falling, MacArthur paid a personal visit to the prison at Bilibid. At first he was greeted by civilian prisoners who wildly mobbed him, shouting, crying, trying to embrace him or touch his sleeve. In contrast to this pandemonium was the scene as he entered the military section of the prison. As Whitney described:

> Here, instead of shrieking mobs, were lines of silent men—emaciated, unkempt, but nearly every one standing at attention beside his cot. The only sound was the occasional sniffle of a grown man who could not fight back the tears. Here was what was left of MacArthur's men of Bataan and Corregidor. As he passed slowly down the scrawny, thin column, a murmur accompanied him as each man greeted him with, "You're back," or "You made it," or "God bless you." MacArthur's reply, hoarse with emotion, was: "I'm long overdue. I'm long overdue."
>
> Near the end of the column a man in dirty long drawers and a torn undershirt hobbled forward. He introduced himself as a major who had fought at Bataan. "Awfully glad to see you sir," he said. "Sorry I'm so unpresentable."
>
> MacArthur stopped and shook his hand. "Major," he said, "you never looked so good to me." [4]

Someone has said that the soul stands at attention when Christ passes by. Imprisoned by our fears, paralyzed by our weaknesses, dressed out in the rags of our failures, we nevertheless reach out to greet the conqueror of all those dark forces to which we have succumbed. In contrast to his purity, we seem so unpresentable, but before we can stammer an apology, he takes us by the hand and says, "You never looked so good to me!" And in that affirmation of acceptance, we can face whatever life may bring, knowing that God himself is on our side.

Presence

Divine forgiveness as Jesus understood it was not some instant absolution but an enduring relationship. Because God accepts us as we are, however vulnerable, he will not forsake us regardless of the circumstances. That truth was dramatically illustrated by our second incident (Mk. 6:47–50) when the disciples were overtaken by a storm while crossing the Sea of Galilee in the middle of the night (Mk. 6:48a). Realizing their distress, Jesus came to them through the gale and got into their boat with these words, "Be of good cheer: it is I; be not afraid" (Mk. 6:50 KJV). The God who declares that he is for us in the divine pardon offered by Christ also determines to be with us in the divine presence of his Son.

As in the first account, Jesus did not begin by dealing with the outward, earthly difficulty that confronted his followers. Just as he did not start with a more hopeful medical prognosis for the paralytic, so he did not come with a more encouraging weather report for the disciples. To be sure, later on the storm was stilled (Mk. 6:51), even as later on the paralytic was made to walk, but this was not to be the basis for their encouragement. Rather, they were to take heart from the fact that he was there with them. The simple "It is I" was a way of saying: Winds will rise and fall, storms will come and go, but whatever happens we will face it all in the same boat together and that is enough to calm your panicked hearts.

Throughout his earthly ministry, the physical presence of Jesus made all the difference to his disciples. For example, when he went away to the mount of transfiguration, the disciples who had been left behind were unable to help an epileptic boy until their Master returned (Mk. 9:14–29). When Jesus delayed responding to the illness of Lazarus until after his friend had died, he was chided by Martha, the sister of Lazarus, with the lament, "Lord, if you had been here, my brother would not have died" (Jn. 11:21 RSV). Even after the resurrection, the closest followers of Jesus were afraid until he came and showed himself to them (Jn. 20:19–20). The climactic promise that would enable them to carry out their world mission was "lo, I am with you always. . ." (Mt. 28:20 RSV).

How often are our words and deeds symptomatic of what might be called the "Martha complex" as we fantasize about how different everything would be if only Jesus were here on earth as in the days of his flesh. Where, pray tell, do you think he is save where he said he would be, namely with his own in every time and place (Mt. 18:20)? The Protestant reformer Martin Luther was subject to periods of deep depression when he despaired of life itself. On one occasion when in the grip of melancholy, his wife appeared dressed in the black of mourning. Taken by surprise, Luther asked who had died only to have her reply, "From the way you have been acting I supposed that God had died."[5] How often do our listless spirits suggest that we are going to God's funeral rather than celebrating Christ's resurrection!

In John Masefield's play, *The Trial of Jesus*, the Roman centurion Longinus is depicted talking to Procula the wife of Pilate after the crucifixion. Evading her question of what he believes about Jesus, Longinus reports that "when we had done with him, he was a poor broken-down thing, dead on the cross." But a troubled Procula presses the deeper issue, "Do you think he is dead?," to which the centurion replies, "No, lady, I don't." "Then where is he?" she persists, to which Masefield has him make this magnificent reply:

Let loose in the world, lady, where
neither Roman nor Jew can stop his truth.[6]

If that soldier's reluctant surmise is nothing less than eternal truth, then we who by faith embrace its reality not only follow the footprints of the historical Jesus in the sands of time but also listen for the footfalls of the risen Lord who walks beside us as our ever-present contemporary.

Power

Just before the darkest hour of Calvary, Jesus gathered his closest disciples in an upper room to prepare them for his departure. Surrounded by enemies on every hand, he dared to describe how they would soon weep, lament, and be sorrowful (Jn. 16:20) when powerful opposition scattered them to the safety of their homes, leaving him alone (v. 32). Reaching for the most sinister word in their religious vocabulary, Jesus warned that in their kind of world they would have "tribulation," that dreaded eruption of sheer chaos expected as the final onslaught of evil. And yet, against that darkest possible background, he immediately added, "but be of good cheer, I have overcome the world" (Jn. 16:33). Just as a woman giving birth experiences the anguish of travail followed by joy when her child is born, so the hearts of the disciples would rejoice when they experienced his power to defeat every foe (Jn. 16:21–22).

Is such a claim credible on the lips of one who, in

only a few hours, would endure rejection, humiliation, suffering, and death? At first glance it looked as if he could not conquer any of the forces arrayed against him. As the fickle crowds, the cunning politicians, and the brutal soldiers each had their way, he seemed helpless to counter the escalating treachery that engulfed him. Yet, look more closely at this apparent weakness that so quickly cost him his life. He could not be seduced by popularity or intimidated by power. No matter how frenzied the hatred heaped on his cause, he would not stop loving. No matter how many escapes were offered, he refused to compromise. There were no price tags on his purposes—he could not be bought at any cost. And all of this took power, a hidden inner power that protected his integrity when those around him were covering themselves with shame. It was a power that would not stay buried but, with his resurrection, filled the lives of those who were open to his presence.

There was once a village in the State of Washington that lacked access to electricity until a dam was built some fifty miles away that would eventually provide current to every home. In preparation for that service, the buildings were wired and fixtures installed several months before the dynamos were ready to generate power. One evening the electricity was turned on unexpectedly and entered a house at the far end of town where the switches had been left open causing lights to burn in every room. Immediately the man of the house went running down the main street of the village shouting at the top of his voice, "The power's on! The power's on!"[7] That is an apt description of what happened in the Book of Acts as early Christians ran up and down the Graeco-Roman world crying at the top of their voices to all who would listen, "The power's on! The power's on!"

Nor was this an idle boast. Like their Lord, they would soon confront mob violence by the crowds (Acts 16:19–24), wholesale rejection by the synagogue (Acts 17:1–9), and temptations to compromise by the politicians (Acts 24:24–27). Despite threats of constant danger and overt persecution (2 Cor. 11:23–28), they could cry with the Apostle Paul, in words remarkably reminiscent of Jesus' third cheer, that tribulation would not separate them from the love of Christ. "No, in all these things we are more than conquerors through him who loved us" (Rom. 8:37 RSV). Echoing the imagery used by Jesus in the Upper Room, they knew what it was like to groan inwardly in travail (Rom. 8:22–23) till Christ be fully formed both in themselves and in others (Gal. 4:19). But in their testing by many trials, they also knew how to "rejoice with unutterable and exalted joy," because they were obtaining the eternal salvation of their souls (1 Pet. 1:6–9 RSV).

Is not this the kind of power that we most urgently need today? Consider the shocking contrast between our increase in manpower and our decrease in godpower. Technology has harnessed the machine to multiply our physical prowess. With radar our eyes become so powerful that they can see through a fog. By use of the telephone our tongues can talk and ears hear around the world. The automobile and airplane enable our legs to step miles every few minutes. With our fingers on the gears of a bulldozer, we can literally move mountains. But where is the spiritual stamina to resist the drunkenness and drugs that enslave many of our youth before they finish school? Or where is the transparent integrity to renounce the greed and graft that topple leading business titans? Or where is the stubborn courage to attack the violence and hunger that kill millions of innocent children in Africa? Without the kind of power that Christ bequeathed to his followers, we are destined to become physical giants and spiritual midgets.

Here, then, are three cheers to make life worth living in the toughest of times. In the face of helplessness, Christ mediates God's pardon. In the face of loneliness, he offers God's presence. In the face of weakness, he shares God's power. A trio of tiny prepositions says it well: we can take heart in a heartless world because God is for us, he is with us, and he is in us. Unlike the endless quest for human happiness, none of this is what we do through self-help. Instead, Christ does it all on our behalf. He forgives and accepts us even before we ask. He comes to us in the darkest hours as a complete surprise. He energizes us for service when we are immobilized by fear. "Be of good cheer," he cries and, if we take him at his word, life will never be the same again.

NOTES

1. André Gide, *The Journals of André Gide*, vol. 3:1928–1939, trans. Justin O'Brien (New York: Alfred A. Knopf, 1949), 74.

2. This application was suggested to me by Louis Evans, "It's Your World Now," *The Baptist Student*, March, 1956, 2–5, 41–42.

3. Leslie D. Weatherhead, *Psychology, Religion and Healing* (New York: Abingdon-Cokesbury, 1951), 334.

4. Courtney Whitney, *MacArthur: His Rendezvous with History* (New York: Alfred A. Knopf, 1956), 188–9.

5. Based on the telling by Harry Emerson Fosdick, *The Meaning of Faith*, reprinted in a new edition as part of *The Three Meanings: Prayer, Faith, Service* (London: SCM, 1956), 218–9; and by Carl F. H. Henry, "The Resurrection Is No Sham," *Christianity Today*, March 27, 1961, 20.

6. John Masefield, *The Trial of Jesus* (London: William Heinemann, 1925), 95–96.

7. G. Ernest Thomas, *The Holy Habits of The Spiritual Life* (Nashville: Tidings, 1951), 21.

PART THREE

——•✦•——

THE QUEST FOR MATURITY

God wants us to grow up, to know the whole truth
and tell it in love – like Christ in everything.

Ephesians 4:15 MSG

The apostle Paul put it as plainly as possible: "God wants us to grow up" (Eph. 4:15 MSG). Every living thing in creation—whether plant, animal, or human— requires a process of maturation to reach its intended potential. Nothing is exempt from this developmental challenge. We spend a lifetime training our bodies to be strong, teaching our minds to think, cultivating our relationships with others, sharpening our vocational skills, reaching for a maturity that exceeds our grasp. To state the issue in its starkest terms, we either grow and flourish or we wither and die.

The beginning of the Christian life is often likened to a new birth (Jn. 3:1–7), which imagery underscores the imperative of spiritual growth to accompany physical, mental, and emotional growth. This nurturing process has two primary aspects, a believing side and a behaving side. The former is what Paul called knowing the whole truth, while the latter he described as being able to tell that truth to others in love (Eph. 4:15). We often refer to the former as doctrine or theology, to the latter as morality or ethics. Some Christians emphasize faith while others emphasize works, but the Letter of James insisted that they are both essential and inseparable (Jas. 2:14–26). Rather than choosing certain areas of growth on which to concentrate, the New Testament defines spiritual adulthood in terms of that comprehensive maturity exemplified by Christ (Eph. 4:13–14).

The sermons in this section speak to our quest for a faith that never stops growing by staying focused on the goal of Christlikeness. Particular attention is devoted to how God, the master artisan, is reshaping our affections so that authentic love will be expressed in all the relationships of life. This does not mean, however, that our concern for maturity is limited to self-improvement. The God who created human nature with an amazing capacity for growth also calls us to learn how to fulfill our social, economic, and political obligations in ever more responsible fashion. No area of life is exempt from the mandate to mature if Christ is to fill "all in all" (Eph. 1:22–23 NRSV).

13

A GROWING FAITH

—➤•◄—

The apostles said to the Lord, "Increase our faith!"
                                                    Luke 17:5 NRSV

When I was a teenager, our family lived across the street from a house where I began to hear strange noises. At first I assumed that the source might be a caged pet, such as a parrot, since the cry resembled the cawing sound of some exotic bird deep in a tropical jungle. On a warm summer day, however, I caught a fleeting glimpse through the front screen door of the creature emitting these guttural screams. It was no animal but a human form that I later learned belonged to a twenty-five year old woman who, because of some fetal deformity or massive brain damage at birth, had never been able to progress beyond the functioning of an infant.

The longer we lived in that neighborhood the more I learned of her story. She could not be left alone for a moment, virtually imprisoning her parents in their home. They never took a trip or invited guests to dinner. They had no social life, no church life, no contact with neighbors. The father was engaged in a family business nearby, but his daughter could never learn to work or even go to school. She would never make friends or get married or have children of her own; for, no matter how long she lived, her life had already reached its limits.

As I began to grasp the enormity of the unspeakable tragedy that had engulfed that home, I realized ever more forcibly that it all rooted in her inability to grow up.

Every time I heard that bleating screech, it was like a forlorn wail of frustration, a plea to escape the limitations imposed by the brain in her body and claim the maturity that is the birthright of every baby. Her incoherent cry became, for me, a call to grow up, *grow up!*

Unlike that tragic life, most of us have enjoyed a generous measure of physical, mental, and emotional growth. But what about our spiritual growth: has it kept pace with other areas of maturation? Sometimes, when I listen closely, I wonder if I hear the baby-cries of an infantile or childish faith struggling to live in an adult body, mind, and heart. Let us look more closely at why cases of what might be called arrested spiritual development are all too common among Christians who claim to have been born again.

Fixed Faith

Strange as it may seem, one of the reasons why faith fails to grow is that, in the view of many religious people, it is not *supposed* to grow! After all, if faith puts us in touch with God, and if God is ultimate reality, then what else is there to grow toward? If ours is a "faith which was once for all delivered to the saints" (Jude 3 RSV), then does it not have a dimension of finality to which we should ever hold fast? Put simply, if our faith has already saved us, what more can we ask it to do? Lurking behind these formulations of the issue is the assumption that growth involves change; whereas, God, and the faith he inspires, is changeless. In a world full of ambiguity, faith seeks to lay hold of the Absolute, which, by definition, has no need to grow.

This absolutist understanding of faith is reinforced by three great systems of authority developed over the centuries to protect and perpetuate the Christian religion. The one with which we are most familiar from the Evangelical tradition is the authority of Scripture, which defines the Bible as "a perfect treasure of divine instruction," "the supreme standard by which all human conduct, creeds, and religious opinions should be tried." Terms such as inerrancy and infallibility imply that the Bible is completely sufficient as it now stands because it has "truth, without any mixture of error, for its matter." Since every word is "divinely inspired," we may turn anywhere within its contents for "totally true and trustworthy" guidance from God.[1] Preachers with this view of the Bible often insist that their sermons be accepted as an authoritative word from the Lord because they are based on Holy Writ. An absolutist approach to Scripture leaves little room, or even need, for growth because all of the answers are already there in the Good Book if only we will bother to look.

A second system with which we are familiar from the Catholic tradition stresses the authority of the church. Since the Bible can be interpreted in many different, even contradictory, ways, the true teaching of the faith may be known only from the testimony of the church, carefully clarified by councils and creeds and enriched by the successors to the apostles for two thousand years. But since differences of understanding emerge even within the church, there must be a hierarchy capable of settling unresolved disputes and compelling assent on the part of the faithful. In the case of Rome, the ultimate arbiter of dogma is the Pontiff who, when ruling in the full exercise of his ecclesiastical powers as Vicar of Christ on earth (*ex cathedra*), is viewed as infallible. Knowledgeable Catholics are painfully aware that not all Popes have been worthy of this responsibility, but they are persuaded that the church is finally "indefectible." That is, God will never allow the church to use its authority to require its members to assent to any claim that is false. To be sure, one can grow in the knowledge of the church's teaching, just as in the first instance one can grow in the knowledge of the Bible, but in both cases the answers have already been determined, needing only to be accepted and obeyed.

A final approach, familiar to us from the Pentecostal tradition, stresses the authority of the Holy Spirit in the experience of the believer. By practicing such simple pieties as prevailing prayer, one may gain, not only a new understanding of Scripture and be able to discern what is true in the preaching and teaching of the church, but be led through a process of sanctification and second blessing to a state of holiness that approaches sinless perfection. The intensity of emotion that often accompanies these heavenly visitations comes to a climax for those called charismatics in the gift of glossolalia; whereby, revelations are given in an unknown tongue that must then be interpreted so that others will understand. The ecstasy accompanying such utterances is so overwhelming that it tends to become an end in itself, leaving little room for the encore of further growth.

With this threefold typology of scriptural, ecclesiastical, and experiential authority before us, let us note the features that they share in common. All are absolutist in the sense of offering the Bible or the Church or the Holy Spirit as the source of final truth. A tendency to stress the totality of the divine revelation offered by each source tends to foreclose the need for a quest to discover more truth. To state it differently, these dominant models are more transactional than developmental. They clamor for assent rather than encourage adventure. They are more interested in giving answers than in raising questions. They cherish unassailable certitude and discourage healthy skepticism, making doubt a foe rather than a friend of faith. In such an atmosphere where faith is defined as a willingness to embrace unconditionally whatever the Bible says, or the Church teaches, or the Spirit discloses, then growth is no longer a goal or even a need to be pursued as a Christian imperative.

Flourishing Faith

It might seem that we have decisively settled the issue of growth in the negative since, for many believers, there is nothing to which we can appeal with greater authority than the Bible, the Church, or the Holy Spirit. But I would point out that there is a higher source than any of these, one to whom "All authority in heaven and on earth has been given" (Mt. 28:18 NRSV). I refer, of course, to Jesus Christ, the Lord of Scripture (Lk. 24:37), the head of the Church (Col. 1:18), the one to whom the Spirit testifies (Jn. 16:13–14). Now the key question becomes: Did Jesus himself view faith in an absolutist sense as assent to a fixed and final body of truth mediated either by Scripture, Church, or Spirit? Or was faith for him a dynamic, developmental reality that challenges even the committed believer to a life of ceaseless growth? Does the paradoxical plea of the epileptic's father to Jesus, "I believe; help my unbelief!" (Mk. 9:24 NRSV), imply an open-ended adventure of faith?

In search of insight on this pivotal issue we begin with Jesus' distinctive way of describing degrees of faith as either "little" or "great." In the passage just cited, after Jesus had healed the father's epileptic son, the disciples asked him why they had been unable to effect a cure. The reply, "because of your *little faith*" (Mt. 17:20 NRSV) uses a word (*oligopistos*) found five times in the teaching of Jesus but nowhere else in the literature of that day. In every case this term is used to describe believing disciples, hence it does not imply an absence of faith but rather a deficient or immature faith limited by such things as anxiety (Mt. 6:30), fear (Mt. 8:26), doubt (Mt. 14:31), confusion (Mt. 16:8), or impotence (Mt. 17:20). In none of these passages did Jesus reject "little faith" as such. Rather, by comparing it to the proverbially small mustard seed (Mt. 17:20), which "grows up and becomes the greatest of all shrubs" (Mk. 4:31–32), he was urging a similar enlargement in the dimensions of faith.

This emphasis on explosive growth is seen in his use of the contrasting term "great faith." When a Roman centurion displayed total confidence that, if Jesus would only say the word, his servant would be healed, Jesus marveled at his attitude and remarked to the multitude that "not even in Israel" had he found *such* faith (Lk. 7:7–9 NRSV). Here the modifier "such" means "so great" in the sense of "so much, so strong, such a high degree of quality." Similarly, his response to the Syrophoenician woman who begged on behalf of her distraught daughter, elicited the verdict, "great (*megalē*) is your faith! Let it be done for you as you wish" (Mt. 15:28 NRSV). Gradually, the disciples began to realize that faith is not just something that one either has or does not have. Rather, one can have either micro-faith or mega-faith. Furthermore, their Master had such penetrating insight into the size of one's faith that he could tell whether it was great or small. No wonder they began to entreat the Lord, "*Increase* our faith!" (Lk. 17:5 NRSV).

Near the end of his earthly life, as Jesus prepared the disciples for his departure from them in physical form, it became obvious that their faith still needed to grow (Jn. 14:1–11). In response, Jesus promised that his Holy Spirit would continue to guide them into truth that they were not yet ready to grasp (Jn. 16:12–15). This promise was abundantly fulfilled as the disciples, in less than one generation, moved beyond the most revered institutions of their ancestral faith, substituting baptism for circumcision as the rite of initiation into the people of God, substituting Sunday for Saturday as the day of worship, and substituting a host of local congregations scattered over the Graeco-Roman world for the one Temple in Jerusalem as the unifying center of their faith. These incredible changes could never have taken place so quickly, or even taken place at all, had not the earliest followers of Jesus received from him both the mandate and the freedom to grow.

This transformation wrought by Jesus forever defined his moment as a religion of growth. The earliest Christians dared to assert that their Lord himself set the pattern by *increasing* "in wisdom and in stature, and in favor with God and man" (Lk. 2:52 RSV). What an amazing claim: even the divine Son of God needed to grow! As his many seed parables testify, Jesus saw the world as a place where God makes things grow (Mk. 4:8, 28, 32). Paul recognized that, in the spiritual realm, we may plant and water but God gives the increase (1 Cor. 3:6–7). The church, like each of its members, "grows with a growth that is from God" (Col. 2:19 NRSV). The goal of this growth is Christian adulthood, a maturity that Paul defined as "the measure of the stature of the fullness of Christ" (Eph. 4:13 RSV). The overriding imperative of Christian existence is "to grow up in every way . . . into Christ" (Eph. 4:15 RSV). It is no wonder that the last verse of what

153

may be the latest writing of the New Testament calls on us to "grow in the grace and knowledge of our Lord and Savior Jesus Christ" (2 Pet. 3:18 NRSV).

Focused Faith

These urgings raise for us an important question: How may I have a growing faith? Here let me offer a half-dozen practical suggestions for your consideration.

First, realize that when you are born again (Jn. 3:1–7), you are but a babe in Christ. In Roman mythology, Minerva sprang fully grown from the brain of Jupiter, but we begin the Christian journey as spiritual infants. At first, "Like newborn infants, long for the pure, spiritual milk, so that by it you may grow into salvation" (1 Pet. 2:2 NRSV). But as we develop, we no longer depend on milk as do those "unskilled in the word of righteousness" (Heb. 5:13 NRSV) because they are children. Rather, we need "solid food" that is for the mature "whose faculties have been trained by practice to distinguish good from evil" (Heb. 5:13–14 NRSV). Do not absolutize any stage of your faith but believe that the best is yet to be.

Second, adopt some spiritual giants as your heroes of faith. These may come from Scripture, such as are recounted in Hebrews 11. Paul realized the importance of his neophyte converts serving an apprenticeship in the workshop of Christian living when he said to the confused Philippians, "join in imitating me, and observe those who live according to the example you have in us" (Phil. 3:17 NRSV). The story of the church through the centuries is full of towering figures who, by their lives, show us the meaning of Christian maturity. But our selection of inspiring pacesetters is not limited to those "celebrity Christians" about whom we read because of their brilliant insight or heroic courage. You can find in any congregation a number of wise mentors who are much farther down the road to maturity than you have thus far traveled. Using a "buddy-system" approach, ask one or more of them to share with you the secrets of their spiritual growth.

Third, once you have tapped the wisdom of your spiritual elders, set your specific goals for growth. Inventory both your dreams and your discontents. What attitudes and actions do you want to discard as unworthy of your highest potential? What hungers of the spirit do you want to feed because they have been starved for nourishment? What aspirations will bring you the greatest sense of fulfillment as you are able to achieve them? Make some lists that you can look at and brood about in prayer. Seek to prioritize your purposes in a developmental sequence and set yourself some deadlines for their accomplishment. Share these plans with trusted soul mates, asking them to help you be realistic in attempting the art of the possible. Most important, repudiate low expectations and let yourself be challenged by the promise of growth in God's tomorrow.

Fourth, translate your aspirations into action. Commit yourself to a new pattern of conduct for each challenge you are seeking to meet. Stated simply, there is no growth for couch-potato Christians! Merely sitting in church will not lead to spiritual growth any more than sitting in front of the television will lead to physical or mental growth. The key is to enlarge your fund of experience by doing something that you have never done. If you want to "grow in grace" (2 Pet. 3:18 NRSV) by becoming a more giving person, then decide to tithe. Should that change be too great to make in one leap, then resolve to increase your giving by one percent per year until you get to ten percent. Or if you want to "grow in . . . knowledge" (2 Pet. 3:18 NRSV) of how to apply the Bible, agree to help lead a Sunday School class.

Fifth, once you have begun to make real progress with the encouragement and reinforcement of your fellow Christians, then you are ready for the tougher challenge of taking on the enemies of our faith. Some may want to practice by engaging in armchair combat with the likes of Karl Marx, Charles Darwin, Sigmund Freud, and Friedrich Nietzsche, but the real battle is joined, not with these intellectual heavyweights, but with the ordinary folk whom we see every day. There are more than a hundred million Americans who, regardless of their spiritual heritage, make no claim of religious affiliation. Can you counter their objections to the Christian church? Or answer their questions about Christian doctrine? Here, the point is not so much to defeat their position as it is to persuade them of your position. Can you commend your faith so winsomely that unbelievers will embrace it as their own? You will never know until you try, and you will grow only if you learn by trying!

Sixth, be patient in your efforts to grow, realizing that the achievement of maturity is the quest of a lifetime. Expect progress to be slow and setbacks to be frequent. Think how often we go on a diet to lose weight, or embark on an exercise program to become physically fit, only to neglect these commitments once we tire of the disciplines that they impose. Even so in the spiritual realm, we are easily distracted from our goals, frustrated by our failures, wearied by our opponents, causing us to backslide and regress into patterns of immaturity, as did those addressed in the Epistle to the Hebrews (2:1; 3:12–13; 5:11–12). The only answer is to approach the Christian life with the relentless tenacity of an athlete determined to go the distance regardless of the effort required. Because all of our life on earth is but preparation for the life to come, we must constantly ask ourselves at every stage of the journey, Am I still seeking "to grow up in every way . . . into Christ" (Eph. 4:15 RSV)?

If that description of the Christian life seems too daunting in its demands, remember that God gives the growth (1 Cor. 3:6–7), and Christ is his gift! To be sure, there is a "race that is set before us" that we must "run with perseverance" despite "every weight, and sin which clings so closely." Yet we can run that race, not only "surrounded by so great a cloud of witnesses" to cheer us on, but we can run it by "looking to Jesus" who pioneered the path which we are called to follow (Heb. 12:1–2 RSV). Even though he was God's Son, this Jesus "learned obedience through what he suffered" (Heb. 5:8 RSV). Enduring a cross of shame, he stayed the course until he perfected our faith and took his rightful place in heaven. We are not asked to do anything for Jesus that Jesus has not first done for us. So let the heart kneel before him and whisper with the disciples of old to their Lord, "*Increase* our faith!" (Lk. 17:5 NRSV).

NOTE

1. All quotations in this paragraph are found in the 1963 Baptist Faith and Message Statement with 1998 Amendment, Article I. The Scriptures, as adopted by the Southern Baptist Convention on June 14, 2000. See "Report of the Baptist Faith and Message Study Committee to the Southern Baptist Convention," *SBC Life*, June/July, 2000, 9.

14

A PASSION FOR THE PRIZE

——→>•◄←——

. . . this one thing I do: forgetting what lies behind and straining forward to what lies ahead, I press on toward the goal for the prize of the heavenly call of God in Christ Jesus.

Philippians 3:13–14 NRSV

The Apostle Paul lived what we are learning to call "the purpose-driven life."[1] When comparing his calling to a race he said, as the New Living Translation puts it, ". . . I run straight to the goal with purpose in every step" (1 Cor. 9:26 LB). His strategy for winning that race is best described in our text (Phil. 3:13–14) where he described the four practices that he followed to keep purpose in every step. Let us look at each of these factors in turn so that we may learn how to live "the purpose-driven life" as well.

Unify the Center

After delivering a string of negatives designed to correct false understandings of the Christian faith (Phil. 3:12a, 13a), Paul suddenly cut through the clutter and riveted his attention on a single focus: "this *one thing* I do . . ." (Phil. 3:13b NRSV). Here is what Thomas Kelly would call his "centering" moment[2] when all of life was brought under the mastery of an overarching sense of mission. Paul would not be denied a place to stand, a distinctive niche in the universe that was his alone to fill. Nor are we in doubt as to the thrust of that controlling purpose. With single-minded passion he lived out a "calling" to make Christ available to every person regardless of race, gender, nationality, culture, or ideology. Paul knew exactly where he was going, and he never wavered from that course. It was his reason-for-being, his manifest destiny, his strategic imperative. The meaning of his entire life was grounded in that one magnificent obsession!

We are just beginning to grasp the cruciality of a singular sense of mission to define our identity and integrity. Unless we know *why* we are here, we will never fully understand *what* we are to do. Paul's opponents, the Judaizers, became a mere footnote in history because they tied their mission to a tradition-bound culture on the point of collapse; whereas, Paul realized that his mission must transcend the Jew/Gentile impasse if it was to survive. Many religious movements are waning today because their mission is tied to historical legacies, regional identities, and ideological polarities that are fast becoming relics of the past.

How did the Apostle achieve this breakthrough that forever defined the Christian faith in universally inclusive terms? By not allowing his gospel to be trapped on either side of the culture war of his day that was fast escalating into armed conflict. Instead of identifying with those on the right or the left, Paul determined to accomplish only one thing: so to know Christ, and be known by Christ, that he would be in Christ and Christ would be in him (Phil. 3:8–12). And why did this driving aspiration provide the ultimate solution to the burning issue of his day? Because the welcoming spirit of Christ enabled Paul to transcend the bitter polarities that soon led to bloodshed in the Jewish war against Rome.

At the center of your reason-for-being, is everything you do animated by the ever-changing swirl of circumstance or by the "surpassing value of knowing Christ Jesus" as Lord (Phil. 3:8a NRSV)? Do you want to "gain Christ" (Phil. 3:8b NRSV) merely as an ally to help you achieve your own goals, or as the living Lord who gives you his goals to fulfill? Are you trying to resurrect your life "from the dead" (Phil. 3:11 NRSV) in your own wisdom and strength, or are you willing to obtain this end (Phil. 3:12) by knowing Christ, "the power of his resurrection and the sharing of his sufferings" (Phil. 3:10 NRSV)? Until you can say, "this *one thing* I do" (Phil. 3:13 NRSV), you are not ready to do anything else!

Forget the Past

Suppose that you had the opportunity to reinvent your life. You could start with a clean slate: make new decisions about where to live, what work to do, who to marry. If you could redesign the life that might have been, how would it differ from the life that you are living today? Let the disparity between the ideal and the real prompt a troubling question: Why is it so hard to reengineer the status quo? The answer is immediately obvious: because of the fateful legacy of the past.

There are two primary problems bequeathed to us from the past. First, the road out of yesterday is littered with the wreckage of our defeats. We collect bitter memories of angry confrontations, painful ruptures, cowardly betrayals. Left to fester, these haunting recollections choke the heart with frustration, resentment, and self-pity. An immense sadness settles upon the soul that may eventually descend into the depths of melancholy and depression, immobilizing the will to act. But equally dangerous is a string of unbroken successes that may fill the heart with complacency and pride. Gradually, we come to assume that we know the best way to do things and so succumb to a sense of self-sufficiency. How may we avoid the peril of Lot's wife (Lk. 17:32) so that, having put our hand to the plow of a steadfast purpose, we will not look back and prove unfit for the kingdom of God (Lk. 9:62)?

The answer of the Apostle was radical indeed. Having just recited his conspicuous achievements both as a Hebrew (Phil. 3:4–6) and as a Christian (Phil. 3:7–11), Paul quickly added, "But I forget it all!" (Phil. 3:13b AT). The force of his negation is captured in the paraphrase, I am determined never to be distracted by my attainments, no matter how impressive they may be. Every success or failure slipped into oblivion the moment it was past. This was not, however, an effort to practice spiritual amnesia. For example, Paul was constantly remembering his Philippian converts with gratitude to God (Phil. 1:3), but he refused to clutter his mind and heart with either the grudges or the boasts of a bygone era. In life as in sport, what matters is not who may be ahead after a few laps, but who is in front at the finish line!

We know that Paul was constantly embroiled in controversy with his enemies (2 Cor. 11:23–28), just as he was often praised as "already perfect" by his friends (Phil. 3:12a RSV); yet, he never let either failure or flattery affect his ministry. What was the secret of that contentment by which he knew "how to be abased" as well as "how to abound" (Phil. 4:12 RSV)? The answer is that Paul had been freed from the tyranny of the past to claim a new future, not just because he had made Christ his own, but because Christ Jesus had made Paul his own (Phil. 4:12b). Paul felt no need to grasp at such things as status or reputation or vindication because he had already been grasped by the Lord of the universe!

So for us: no matter how much we may achieve, with Christ we can say of the past that what ultimately matters is not what we did for him, but what he did for us!

Are you trying to reinvent your life out of your past attainments however great or small (Phil. 3:4–12)? Or are you, with Paul, willing to forget what you worked so hard to achieve, putting behind you both the victories too easily won and the defeats too bitterly lost? Can you learn to retell your story, not as a recital of your various accomplishments but as a witness to the ways in which Christ has claimed you for himself and taught you to be sufficient in his strength? Only as we learn to live out of *his* past rather than out of *our* past are we ready to discover the purposes that he has prepared for us to fulfill.

Live with Intensity

The journal *Leadership* carried a cartoon that depicted a rather traditional church building with an enormous sign out front identifying it as "The Lite Church: 24 percent fewer commitments, home of the 7.5 percent tithe, 15-minute sermons, 45-minute worship services. We have only eight commandments—your choice. We use just three spiritual laws and have an eight-hundred-year millennium. Everything you've wanted in a church . . . and less!"[3] This parody of laid-back religion points to the growing casualness with which many congregations practice what has been called our "little churchiness." If the problem of the past is one of despair or pride, the problem of the present is one of blandness and trivialization.

Against this deliberate reductionism there is a growing hunger for true greatness in every area of American life. More than four thousand colleges and universities dot the landscape, but applications pour into the few, such as Harvard or Stanford, that seek to excel. Hundreds of football games are played on a fall weekend, but the stadiums fill to see teams that give an extra effort, such as the Crimson Tide under Bear Bryant or the Green Bay Packers under Vince Lombardi. Most cities of any size have a symphony orchestra that can make beautiful music, but we listen for the edge of excellence achieved by conductors such as George Szell in Cleveland or Eugene Ormandy in Philadelphia.

The Apostle Paul applied what automaker Lexus calls "the relentless pursuit of perfection" to the religious realm in a single phrase: "straining forward to what lies ahead . . ." (Phil. 3:13c NRSV). The picture is that of a runner in a race, every nerve and sinew taut, bearing down upon the finish line. Note the contrast between past and future as they impinge upon the present. It is as if Paul was saying: *behind* me lies a past which I have relinquished in order to be able to run in unfettered fashion; *before* me lies a future which I strive to possess with every ounce of energy at my command. This is not the analogy of an athlete running a few laps each day merely to stay in shape, what we would call the "another day/another dollar" philosophy of life. Rather, this is the depiction of that radical intensity which enables Christians to pursue their mission with utter abandon in the present because they have divested themselves of every distraction from the past.

What are the wellsprings of urgency that give such drive to daily living? First and foremost is the overriding conviction that, because we have been claimed by Christ (Phil. 3:12c), we can run hard with empty hands because Christ already has us in his hands every step of the way! Second, we are impelled to redouble our efforts when we realize how far short we have fallen both in fully knowing the Christ who first knew us (Phil. 3:12a) and in experiencing his power that is mighty enough to raise the dead (Phil. 3:11). Finally, the realization that life leads to a goal, that decisions matter, that there is a prize to be won or lost, should fill us with a new seriousness to live intentionally every step of the way. The *whence* of yesterday and the *whither* of tomorrow give a new dynamic to the *wherefore* of today!

How much intensity is at work within your life today? Does anything dead that was buried deep within your heart come alive when you worship? Are you standing flat-footed doing business as usual with God, or are you running eagerly as one "bound for the Promised Land"? Are your hands at your side in complacency, or are they outstretched in eager anticipation of what is yet to come? Is there a holy boldness, a determination to "go for the gold" animating the decisions that you make? We must begin with a purpose, then proceed with a plan, but it will all be in vain without a passion!

Set New Expectations

Once every four years the eyes of the world are focused on the Olympic games as athletes gather to test the outer limits of human achievement. In a sense they do not compete against one another as much as they do against established standards of excellence. What they want most of all is to set a new record, to redefine the limits of the possible, to achieve a breakthrough that will challenge those who come after them to achieve higher goals than ever before. To set new expectations is to shape a new future.

Just so, the Apostle Paul had the capacity to fill his

horizon with a compelling picture of "what lies ahead" (Phil. 3:13c NRSV). So vivid was that vision that, even when hemmed in by prison walls, he could write, "I go for the goal where God's prize awaits" (Phil. 3:14a AT). The "not yet" of his disclaimer regarding the past was balanced by the "but then" of his confidence regarding the future. It was not just that his life would eventually reach an end, but that the finish line offered a fulfillment that he defined as "God's call to the life above" (Phil. 3:14b AT). What this prize offered Paul was the opportunity to be exhilarated, rather than exhausted by the race that he had run on earth. The end of all his exertions would be but the beginning of an upward journey stretching across the infinite reaches of eternity.

In Christ Jesus, Paul had seen the outer limits of what the human spirit can become. In response, he defined his ultimate goal as Christlikeness that called him ever onward and upward toward the God who filled the life of his Lord. This gave Paul a vision of what he wanted to become, of how he wanted his life to end, of the prize that he wanted most to claim. Christ filled the horizon that defined his future so compellingly that he pressed on despite every adversity (Phil. 3:14).

His sense that the finish line could be crossed at any moment was the Pauline equivalent of Jesus' conviction that the Kingdom of God is always "at hand" (Mk. 1:15 RSV). Those who experience the overwhelming immediacy of God's tomorrow, as if it lies just beyond their outstretched fingertips, discover the secret both of creativity and of courage. They become catalytic agents no longer content with the terrible tyranny of the status quo. Instead of forever talking about "what *is*," they begin to talk about "what *if*." Theirs is the credo attributed to Robert Kennedy by his brother, Edward: "Some men see things as they are and say 'Why?' I dream things that never were and say 'Why not?' "[4] The willingness to make room for change is not based on an easy confidence that "someday everything will work out fine," but on the sturdy conviction that "he who began a good work in you will bring it to completion at the day of Jesus Christ" (Phil. 1:6 RSV).

What the elder George Bush taught us to call "the vision thing" is still of critical importance today. Asked, "How are you able to play the cello with such magnificence?," master artist Pablo Casals replied, "I hear it before I play it." Golfer Jack Nicklaus said that vision "gives me a line to the cup just as clearly as if it's been tattooed on my brain."[5] Likewise, leaders of any organization are able to move it forward only if they see in advance the potentialities of what it can become and are able to share that vision with others. This is what management consultant Stanley Davis calls the ability to live in the future perfect tense, acting today as if tomorrow had already started to happen, viewing the present as the past of the future.[6]

The poet Rilke once said that "the future enters into us, in order to transform itself in us, long before it happens."[7] Is the essence of the Christian life for you, as for Paul, not attainment but aspiration, not possession but pursuit, not security but serendipity? Do you really believe that "it doth not yet appear what we shall be" (1 Jn. 3:2 KJV)? Do you really want God to "do a new thing" in your life (Isa. 43:19 NRSV)? Like Dietrich Bonhoeffer, are you "tossing in expectation of great events"?[8] Are you certain that you can become more than you have ever been before? Ibsen once said that he valued above all else that person "who has allied himself most closely with the future."[9] Do you have your nose pressed in childlike wonder against the windowpane that separates today from all of God's tomorrows? Unless we keep our eyes riveted on the goal of all our strivings, we shall never be able to reach them.

Let us summarize in four terse imperatives what we have learned from Paul about how to live the purpose-driven life: (1) *Stay focused!* Do not let anything keep you from claiming a Christ-centered life. (2) *Travel light!* Do not let either the gains or the losses of yesterday burden what you do today. (3) *Run hard!* Do not let complacency compromise your passion for living. (4) *Aim high!* Do not let discouragement cause you to look down but keep looking up to those goals that will finally be gained on higher ground. This is how Paul actually lived a purpose-driven life. And with his guidance we can live it too!

NOTES

1. The phrase owes its popularity to the best-selling book of Rick Warren, *The Purpose-Driven Life: What on Earth Am I Here For?* (Grand Rapids: Zondervan, 2002).

2. Thomas R. Kelly, *A Testament of Devotion* (New York: Harper & Row, 1941), 112–24.

3. Gerry Mooney and Jim Berkley, *Leadership: A Practical Journal for Church Leaders* 4, no. 3 (summer, 1983): 81.

4. Adapted from George Bernard Shaw, *Back to Methuselah*, Act I, in *Bernard Shaw Complete Plays with Prefaces* (New York: Dodd, Mead, 1962), 2:7, spoken by Edward M. Kennedy at the funeral service for Robert F. Kennedy in St. Patrick's Cathedral, New York City, June 8, 1968.

5. George Laud and Beth Jarman, "Future Pull: The Power of Vision and Purpose," *The Futurist*, July–August, 1992, 25.

6. Stanley M. Davis, *Future Perfect* (Reading, MA: Addison-Wesley, 1987).

7. Rainer Maria Rilke, *Letters to a Young Poet*, trans. Stephen Mitchell (New York: Random House, 1984), 84.

8. Dietrich Bonhoeffer, "Who Am I?" *Letters and Papers from Prison*, 3rd ed. edited by Eberhard Bethge (London: SCM, 1967), 197, stanza 2, line 7.

9. Henrik Ibsen, "Letter to Georg Brandes," January 3, 1882, cited in *Letters of Henrik Ibsen*, trans. John Nilsen Laurvik and Mary Morison (New York: Fox, Duffield, 1905), 350.

15

THE POETRY OF GOD

—→►•◄←—

*We are God's work of art, created in Christ Jesus to live
the good life as from the beginning he had meant us to live it.*

Ephesians 2:10 JB

One of the most breathtaking descriptions of the
Christian life is compressed into a single word found in
Ephesians 2:10. Since that word came from another
language, let us consider it first in the Apostle Paul's
Greek tongue: "For we are his [God's] *poiēma . . .*" The
traditional translation is "workmanship" (KJV, RSV), an
altogether adequate rendering since this noun is built
from a verbal stem (*poieō*) meaning "to make, produce,
create" plus a suffix (-*ma*) indicating the result of that
action. So the simplest etymology yields the idea of
"that which is crafted or fashioned"—the thought being
that Christians are the finished product of God's divine
handiwork. Such a connotation is very compatible with
the context. As the preceding verse indicates, even
saints could not be saved by their own works (Eph. 2:9)
because they are themselves a work of God (Eph. 2:10)—
a new creation, a masterpiece of the divine Artisan, the
expression of his age-long plan.

When we search more deeply and broadly into the
non-biblical usage of this word *poiēma*, we discover that
the basic idea of a "work of art" was quite naturally
applied to a variety of creative compositions, especially
to poetry. In the ancient world, *poiema* and related
terms came to be used for anything poetical, such as a
verse or even a metrical line. Indeed, the word passed

through Latin (*poema*) and Middle French (*poeme*) to become the basis for our English word "poem."[1] Because of this unique historical connection between the Greek and English languages, we may allow a specialized translation of our text: "For we are the poetry of God . . ."[2]

What a suggestive thought: when God saves us by grace through faith (Eph. 2:8), we become like a poem. At its best, religion is to life as poetry is to prose! Grace is not some celestial substance that we swallow like medicine in order to be saved. Rather, it is the offer of rhythm and rhyme and even rhapsody to an otherwise prosaic existence. The faith that embraces this gift is not stolid submission to some creedal absolute but is the catalyst for a creative response to all of the aspirations that haunt the human imagination (Acts 2:17).

Building on this clue, let us consider what it means to think of God as the divine artist and of ourselves as his intended masterpiece. The basic analogy has many applications: we could view our lives as a musical score composed with many notes, or as a painted canvas brushed with many colors, or as a stone sculpture chiseled with many strokes, or as an intricate tapestry woven with many threads. I have chosen to pursue the comparison with poetry both because it is suggested by the biblical language and because it sheds much light on the creative act of true conversion.

Poetry is Built

We begin where the poet must begin, with that tedious process of carefully constructing a poem. Normally, we are so fascinated with the charm of the finished product that we forget the toil which it required. In fact, a good poem is deliberately designed to conceal the marks of its own composition. If successful, its every word will seem to be the only one that the poet could have chosen. Likewise, the rhythm will flow so naturally that it seems inevitable, as if no other sequence would be appropriate. If we are left with a feeling that the creation is contrived, that its words have been manipulated, that its structure has been superimposed, then the poem is a failure. Good art never calls attention to its own nuts and bolts!

But we dare not forget that the underpinnings are always there, paradoxically no more so than when every effort has been made to efface them. The poet John Ciardi told of an evening at a Bread Loaf Writers Conference when Robert Frost was reading his poems and talking about some of his "technical tricks." After reading one poem, Frost paused to ask the audience in what meter it was written; then he had fun scolding those who did not recognize that it was in hendeca-syllabics. Before he could move on a sweet elderly lady was on her feet: "But Mr. Frost," she cried, "*surely* when you are writing one of your *beautiful poems, surely* you can't be thinking about"—and here her voice slurred the dirty words—"about *technical tricks!*" Frost put his hands together, the spread fingers touching tip to tip, looked owlish for a moment, then leaned into the microphone and said with playful exaggeration, "I *revel* in 'em."[3]

Every artist knows that the secret of true spontaneity is vigorous devotion to the disciplines of one's craft, that the price of simplicity is a mastery of the complexities of the chosen medium, and that the visible result is but the tip of an enormous iceberg of toil that inconspicuously undergirds the finished product. The poetry of Edgar Allen Poe, for example, is an enthralling experience of sheer beauty that seems to have gushed without effort from the depths of his creative imagination. Yet, Poe delighted in dissecting his own work in cold blood and to show with faultless logic and mathematical precision how he had weighed and balanced each syllable, calculated the precise effect of each sound, and related each part to the others with deliberate design.[4] This does not mean that the finished work was merely the end result of some algebraic formula. Rather, it means that true poetry is always a fusion of the originality and inspiration of the poet with those enduring principles that are rooted in the very structure of reality.

Careful attention to the intricate complexities of design requires an almost boundless patience in the creation of a true masterpiece. In *The Art of Poetry*, Horace advised Piso, when he had written something, to keep it beside him for nine years before publishing it. Virgil's *Aeneid* occupied the last ten years of his life and would have been destroyed by him at death because of its imperfections had not friends intervened. In Plato's manuscript of *The Republic*, there are no fewer than thirteen alternate versions in his own handwriting of the simple opening sentence.[5] In 1742, Thomas Gray began a poem that he did not complete until 1750 after going through three major revisions in multiple drafts, the lovely "Elegy Written in a Country Churchyard."[6]

Just so it is with those who become "the poetry of God." Their lives are the result of the most careful planning, patient shaping, and complex relating that could be imagined. Nowhere is this emphasized by Scripture more than in Ephesians. Our text compresses this truth into one Greek word which we translate variously as that which God "beforehand/already/from the beginning" had prepared/ordained/predestined/ planned/designed." The idea is that the poetic life is not something that we try to rhyme as we go along, writing a timeline each day, as it were, without knowing what the next line will be. Rather, the entire path down which we are led by Christ is part of a grand design mapped out by God from all eternity. We can be certain that God has lavished as much attention on the building of each Christian life as any poet has devoted to his or her greatest masterpiece!

Although the entire theological argument of Ephesians concentrates on this assurance, we have been slow to share it with others because any hint of divine initiative smacks of coercion or control. Rather than taking the trouble to understand Paul's concept of predestination, we have told silly jokes on Presbyterians and supposed that we were thereby emancipated to seek our own destiny. But in so doing, we have succeeded in shutting ourselves up alone in a capricious universe with more privacy than we know how to handle. This turns our times into an "Age of Aimlessness," a generation drifting from one fad to another, passing out "fickle finger of fate" awards and pretending that it is all in jest. How many lives lack any depth and rootage in that which endures. Not only has our sense of the sweep of history shriveled, but more crucial, we seem not to be anchored in anything eternal.

Contrast, if you will, the Apostle Paul. Here was a man with a burning sense of mission, possessed by a great purpose that could not be deflected even by tragic circumstances. Remember that Saul of Tarsus had been just as aggressive before his conversion. The difference was that earlier he had been a hotheaded zealot for the traditions of his people, defending the religious status quo against any change (Gal. 1:13–14). After his conversion, he saw clearly what God had set him apart to do even before he was born (Gal. 1:15), as well as the ultimate goal toward which he would press until his race was won (Phil. 3:14). Because Paul knew what he was meant to be and to do, and because he saw God guiding his life from the womb to the tomb, his earthly existence became an episode between two eternities. This sense of divine destiny gave a dimension of depth to the daily round that is still available to all who are "the poetry of God."

Poetry is Beautiful

A second insight follows closely from the first. Because poetry is so carefully built, it is, as a result, intrinsically beautiful. Somerset Maugham said it this way: "The crown of literature is poetry. It is its end and aim. It is the sublimest activity of the human mind. It is the achievement of beauty."[7] We hear so much cant and bombast that, when tired old words are made to bear fresh new meanings, it takes our breath away.

What is the secret of this beauty? Not the subject matter of the poem, which may be utterly commonplace. In fact, poems usually fail when they require some sensational theme that calls attention to itself. The most ordinary human experiences are the stuff from which poetry is made. Again, the words used as raw materials to express the matter of the poem are not in themselves the source of beauty. Often they are the monosyllables found in the vocabulary of children. The poem that dresses itself in ornate terms is on the road to ruin. In a successful poem, the reader glides effortlessly through the structure without pausing to admire its design. No, the true beauty of a poem is more unobtrusive than all such stratagems to which amateurs must resort.

There is a positive lesson to be learned from these negative observations. If the subject, speech, and style of a good poem are unexceptional in themselves, if its beauty comes not from outward embellishment but from inward harmony, then that means that our ordinary lives, without surface adornment to attract attention, are candidates for the kind of beauty that belongs to the poetry of God. We do not have to be like "Richard Cory," who "glittered when he walked,"[8] in order to be beautiful. For it is the vocation of art to transfigure the commonplace. The poet's words, the musician's notes, the painter's colors are all around us in profusion, waiting for that careful selection and creative combination and controlling vision that gives a dimension of beauty to what otherwise would be commonplace or even ugly.

God works exactly like that in fashioning human poetry. First, he chooses each individual with loving care, which is what being "prepared beforehand" is all about (Eph. 2:10 RSV). Then, he sets all of those so chosen into a right relationship with one another, which is what it means to say that Christians are "members"—also a poetic term![9]—of the "Body of Christ" (Eph. 5:30). Finally, he provides a high calling for our lives that is integral to the overarching purposes in his "plan for the fullness of time" (Eph. 1:10a NRSV). Such are the ingredients of true beauty, whether in a poem or in a person.

Paul acknowledged this by affirming that "our way of life" is to be one of "good works" (Eph. 2:10 NRSV). The word for "good" (*agathos*), far from having the shallow connotation implied in our term "do-gooder," actually refers to those gracious expressions of love that are always fitting because they spring from a mature character concerned for the well-being of others. The deeds themselves may be modest, but they take on a beauty because they are so "right" for the kind of person doing them. It is this same congruity between what the poem is and what it does that is the secret of its beauty.

Poetry is Biographical

In one sense, our final suggestion is the sum of the first two. Because poetry is carefully built to be beautiful, it is also inescapably biographical. In the very process of conception and combination, the mind and heart of the poet are stamped on every syllable. The almost infinite number of choices required are guided by the poet's genius and judgment. Into the agony of creation are poured the poet's sweat and tears. Indeed, we may wonder if anything pierces to the very marrow of a person's spirit and style as does the fashioning of a work of art?

And yet, we need to be careful in describing a process that is more complex than it first appears. For one thing, the poet uses words that already have a life of their own. Language is not ours to invent but is fashioned out of inherited words that we learn by being "present" to what they "*sign*-ify." The very impulse to sort these word-symbols into some meaningful configuration of reality often arises because the meaning has already been "given," not from within but from Beyond. The testimony of many poets is that they are being "used" as the servant of what is sometimes called the Muses, or the literary imagination, or even divine revelation. Indeed, the torment of trying to be a poet arises from the fact that a poem is never finished until it is "right," as measured by an elusive but ever-present standard of rightness that is beyond the control of the poet.

Ultimately, therefore, poets create something that is a passionate part of themselves, yet stands on its feet with an independent existence. This explains why poet T. S. Eliot, in correcting those critics who supposed that he simply wrote whatever poetry he wished to write, pointed to the phenomenon of the poet's quarrel with his own poem.[10] There would be no quarrel if a poem expressed only the life of the poet. But, in his poetry, Eliot offered his own life—what he had seen and heard and felt and dreamed—as one channel for the expression of something infinitely larger than himself, which we may call "Life" that is the source of all our lives. That is why I suggest that poetry is more properly "*bio*-graphical" than it is "*auto*-biographical." The vocation of the poem is to say something true about that "Ground of Being" which is the foundation of existence itself.

It is with this clarification that we come to understand more fully what it means to be the poetry of God. There are two complementary aspects to the truth underscored here, one divine and one human. From the side of God, the Master Poet, we learn that we are not simply fragments of divinity scampering about on planet earth. It is pantheistic to view Christians or anyone else as a projection of the mind and heart of God. Paul was quite clear that everything human is "created," standing in sharp contrast to the Creator. In Romans 1:20 (the only other place where *poiēma* is found in the New Testament), Paul referred to the "made things" of the created order as visible pointers to the invisible realities of God. In Ephesians 2:10, he affirmed that we are "created" both in a natural and in a supernatural sense. When God fashioned us as physical beings, and then refashioned us as spiritual beings, he was dealing with a reality other than himself. Because the poet and his poetry differ, God may even quarrel with us, as the prophets of Israel understood so well (Hos. 4:1; Mic. 6:2; Jer. 25:30–31).

From the human side, this difference and distance from the divine does not mean that, as God's poetry, we are to reflect only our own experience. Rather, we are to live our lives bearing witness to Life itself. God has made this possible by creating his poetry "in Christ Jesus" (Eph. 2:10 NRSV). Because Christ is "the life" (Jn. 1:4; 14:6 NRSV), we may relate to him as the one who bridges the gap between heaven and earth, who resolves the tension between poet and poem. In union with him our lives become biographical of his life. True to the poetic calling we sing, "Let others see Jesus in you!"[11]

Now, our lives become beautiful with the beauty of his spirit. Now, our works become "good" because he works through us. Now, God's will for our lives becomes purposeful, because his age-long plan has been summed up in Christ. As we become "conformed to the image" of God's Son (Rom. 8:29 NRSV), we more and more "fit" that full measure of humanity that is still beyond us but also now within us. When that happens, the Great Poet is satisfied with his handiwork. Because then we are on the way to becoming what he intended us to be from the beginning: "the poetry of God."

NOTES

1. Philip B. Gove, ed. *Webster's Third New International Dictionary* (Springfield, Mass.: G & C Merriam, 1965), 1748. J. A. Simpson and E.S.C. Weiner, *The Oxford English Dictionary*, second ed. (Oxford: Clarendon Press, 1989), 11:1116.

2. This rendering is suggested in a footnote, though not adopted in the text, by Helen Barrett Montgomery, *The New Testament in Modern English* (Philadelphia: Judson Press, 1924), 515.

3. John Ciardi, *Dialogue with an Audience* (Philadelphia: J. B. Lippincott, 1963), 19–20.

4. Charles Cestre, "Edgar Allen Poe," *Encyclopaedia Britannica*, ed. Walter Yust (Chicago: Encyclopaedia Britannica, 1953), 18:105.

5. These and other illustrations of artistic patience are conveniently collected by William Barclay, *The Gospel of Matthew* (Philadelphia: Westminster Press, 1959), 1:283–4.

6. R. W. Ketton-Cremer, *Thomas Gray: A Biography* (Cambridge: University Press, 1955), 97–110, 271–3.

7. Quoted on the front cover of *Saturday Review*, July 20, 1957.

8. Edwin Arlington Robinson, "Richard Cory," stanza 2, line 4. Quoted in Louis Untermeyer, ed. *Modern American Poetry*, sixth edition (New York: Harcourt, Brace, 1942), 141.

9. *Webster's Third New International Dictionary*, 1408, defines "member" both as "one who forms part of a metaphorical or metaphysical body" and as "a syntactic or rhythmic unit of a sentence."

10. For a discussion of this dialectic see Henry Rago, "Faith and the Literary Imagination – The Vocation of Poetry," *Adversity and Grace*, ed. Nathan A. Scott, Jr. (Chicago: University of Chicago Press, 1968), 244–48.

11. B. B. McKinney, "Let Others See Jesus in You," refrain, *The Baptist Hymnal*, ed. Wesley L. Forbis (Nashville: Convention Press, 1991), #571.

16

THE THREE LOVES

————➤•◄————

*One of the scribes came near and heard them disputing with one
another, and seeing that he answered them well, he asked him, "Which
commandment is the first of all?" Jesus answered, "The first is, 'Hear,
O Israel: the Lord our God, the Lord is one; you shall love the Lord
your God with all your heart, and with all your soul, and with all
your mind, and with all your strength.' The second is this, 'You shall
love your neighbor as yourself.' There is no other commandment
greater than these."*

Mark 12:28–31 NRSV

Love is at once the most desired reality in human
experience, and yet, the most difficult to express.
More than anything else, we want to love and be
loved, for love sets the heart to singing with an ecstasy
sublime. In a famous tribute to 1 Corinthians 13,
Henry Drummond called love "the greatest thing in
the world,"[1] and his verdict has been affirmed by
universal acclamation. And yet, how hard it is to love
in mature and sustained fashion. The most intimate of
human devotions are often wrecked by divorce when
we see tender affection become angry bitterness, as if
love and hatred are conjoined as Siamese twins in the
human heart. Even our highest religious affections
often prove fickle when we are seduced by the allure
of careless trifles. How may we protect true love from
the pathologies that so easily beset it?

Jesus set love at the center of his understanding of
life and made it the hallmark of true religion. When
asked to identify the core convictions of his ancestral
faith, he responded by citing two commandments that

unify the three great loves in triadic fashion: (1) the upward love of God, (2) the outward love of others, and (3) the inward love of self (Mk. 12:30–31). As we achieve mutuality and reciprocity among these three expressions of love so that each shapes and supports the others, we learn to live the life of love in all of its splendor and fullness. Let us examine each of these loves with that goal before us.

Love of God

Jesus was certain that love must begin with an undivided adoration of the one true God strong enough to claim the whole person. The imperative to love God, implied by the command "Thou shalt!", is based on one making a radical decision to renounce all unworthy infatuations—such as with materialism, the rapacious desire for earthly gain (Mt. 6:24); or with egotism, using religion to pursue the vainglory of human adulation (Mt. 6:1–2). In uncompromising fashion, Jesus insisted that to love God is to exist for him exclusively, to value him supremely, to make his sovereignty the compelling aspiration of one's life. The totality of this commitment is expressed by the fourfold "all" that claims "heart . . . soul . . . mind . . . strength" (Mk. 12:30 NRSV), which Eugene Peterson translates as loving God "with all your passion and prayer and intelligence and energy" (Mk. 12:30 MSG).

Why did Jesus stress that love to God must always be first and foremost, the essential prerequisite to other loves? Because God is the only one who never uses our love to his own advantage. All of us know that selfish, manipulative, and exploitive desires can masquerade as love, such as when a teenager whispers in the moonlight, "I love you, I love you," but really means, "I love me and I want you!" Even spouses and parents use love to smother or control their beloved, but God never misuses our affections. Our love for him is not vulnerable to abuse, because God is utterly free of fickleness. Thus, we begin by offering him our unworthy human love that it may be purified and enriched before we offer it to anyone else. Unless we begin by loving God, we will never learn what it means for passion to be guided by purpose, for devotion to be infused with discipline, and for impulsiveness to be based on integrity.

The enemy of love is a self-centeredness that resists our every effort to be rid of it. Because we are mortal, insecurity asserts itself as a self-preservation instinct that clamors for the kind of domineering control that is incompatible with love. By contrast, God is our sovereign Lord (Mk. 12:29), and therefore secure, the one and only utterly unselfish person in the universe whom we can love without fear of having our relationship misused. By definition, love seeks the best for the beloved, but only God can define the highest good without a trace of self-aggrandizement. When we begin by loving others, we are immediately drawn into the many little games that love plays in seeking its own advantage. When, instead, we begin by loving God, we immediately confront one who plays none of our little games, but rather bids us to renounce subtle strategies and love him with all the abandon of which we are capable. Only in communion with the divine do we discover the true nature of single-minded love that cleanses our duplicity.

How far have you gone in loving God with every fiber of your being? Jesuit priest Father Edward Collins Vacek noticed how "many contemporary Christians subscribe to Jesus' second great commandment, but not to his first." That is, "almost all of them talk approvingly about love for others, some talk confidently about God's love for us, but few are willing to talk about their love for God."[2] We often sidestep the imperative of loving God by emphasizing his great love to us, as if he never wants or needs our love to him. Yet the Bible portrays God yearning to receive our love, welcoming our love with his forgiveness, suffering to win our uncoerced love because he honors human freedom (Hos. 11:1–4, 8–9). By adopting the language of family and friendship, Scripture is telling us that God is not content to live in splendid isolation but cherishes intimate relationships. Indeed, the pathos of Jesus weeping over Jerusalem mirrored the anguish of his unrequited love (Lk. 19:41).[3]

Love of Others

When asked to identify the *one* commandment that is greatest of all, Jesus replied by citing *two* commandments, one from Deuteronomy 6:5 and the other from Leviticus 19:18. Although these verses were not normally connected, Jesus made them inseparable from each other (Mk. 12:29–31). To identify the latter imperative as "second" (Mk. 12:31 NRSV) did not mean that it was of secondary importance. Rather, both commandments together were set above all other requirements in the law as constituting the essence of true religion. Here the two parts were not being ranked in value but were being listed in sequence as components of equal importance.[4] By concluding that "there is no other commandment [singular] greater than these [plural]" (Mk. 12:31 NRSV), Jesus was clearly distinguishing between love in two very different relationships, yet holding both of them to be integral parts of a larger whole.

Why is this linkage and sequence so crucial? Because the act of loving God first completely redefines how we are to love others. In Luke's account, the admonition to love one's neighbor prompted the further question, "And who is my neighbor?" (Lk. 10:29 NRSV). Originally, the Old Testament injunction was directed toward "your people" (Lev. 19:18), that is, to fellow-Israelites. When Jesus responded by telling the story of the Good Samaritan (Lk. 10:30–37), he shifted the issue from the question, "Who is my neighbor?" to the question, "How can I be a neighbor?" His answer was that love for others is no longer based on their qualifications to be loved but on the concrete actions that I take to express my love.

In revolutionary fashion, Jesus radically redefined love for others in terms, not of its object, but of its subject; and neighbor in terms, not of kinship, but of anyone in need who is near enough to be helped. Now it is clear why the second commandment is bound so tightly to the first. Only in relation to God do we learn to express our love without calculation, with no trace of self-interest, no trading of favors, no hint of possessiveness. God created every person with whom I will ever come in contact, and he seeks the best for each of them as his children. Jesus commanded to love them all: not as one loves God, for they are certainly not godlike, but as God loves them, which is utterly without partiality. As nature itself discloses, the "Father in heaven . . . makes his sun rise on the evil and on the good, and sends rain on the righteous and on the unrighteous" (Mt. 5:45 NRSV). But as the gospel of forgiveness reveals even more clearly than does nature, God relates to all with a pardoning love for the many, rather than a preferential love for the few. We are not merely to love those who love us in order to win their approval (Mt. 5:46a); rather, we are to love everyone as God does in order to meet their needs.

The Jews, Greeks, and Romans had elaborate definitions of friend and enemy that fixed a gulf between the two groups "as though the relation of enmity was natural and permanent . . ."[5] Jesus transcended this dichotomy by including enemies among the neighbors to be loved. After all, "if you greet only your brothers and sisters, what more are you doing than others? Do not even the Gentiles do the same?" (Mt. 5:47 NRSV). Love of enemy was the most daring advance that Jesus made over the prevailing ethic of antiquity, an incredible breakthrough accomplished by linking the second commandment to the first. Eugene Peterson captures the thrust of Jesus' thought in the climactic Matthew 5:48. "In a word . . . *grow up*! Live generously and graciously toward others, the way God lives toward you" (Mt. 5:48 MSG).

Here we see even more clearly just how dangerous it is to love God with the totality of our being. For only in that fateful embrace do we grasp just how indiscriminately God loves every person. After all, God has no "neighbors" defined as his "own kind." If he loved only his equals, he would not have anyone on earth to love, for we all stand in need of his boundless mercies. That is why God changed the ground rules by which we are accustomed to love: he does not love those who *deserve* him but those who *need* him. Now comes the question that cannot be avoided: how can we love a God like that with all of our being and not love others as he does? Indeed, in the Parable of the Last Judgment

(Mt. 25:31–46), Jesus taught that loving needy neighbors—not our "own kind" but those who are hungry, thirsty, lonely, naked, sick, or imprisoned—is precisely the way that we love God himself (v. 40)!

Love of Self

The deeper we dig into our text the more dangerous it becomes. We began on the safe side by being told to love a God who will never take advantage of our affections. But then we were told to love any and all who need our love even if they are enemies who may slap our faces, or sue us for the coat on our back, or demand that we carry their burdens an extra mile (Mt. 5:39–41). Jesus loved his enemies and look what it got him—a cross! So are we setting ourselves up for grief by following what appear to be counsels of perfection? I think of two groups with whom I have struggled endlessly over this dilemma.

The first group is drawn from my fellow clergy, what one psychotherapist has called "the overhelpers." They give themselves so relentlessly to serving others that they seek nothing for themselves. As one analyst put it, "These people are pathological givers . . . and they can even be good at it, to a degree, but they become impoverished after a while. They have given so much that they finally run out of spiritual and nervous energy, and what remains is the underlying resentment." A lot of anger and bitterness may hide behind a façade of benevolence and contentment on the part of those who "give too much without knowing how to take . . . They are into loving their God and loving their neighbor, but they forget that little, crucial, additional thing: 'as thyself.' "[6]

The second group are devout Christians who struggle so long with hostile relationships, particularly within the family circle, that they themselves are broken by the very problems that they are trying desperately to solve. I shall never forget a luncheon date that lasted all afternoon with one of the finest church leaders it has been my privilege to know, a deacon who for years had been attempting to pacify the furies of an utterly egotistical wife. Hour after hour we reviewed the extraordinary lengths to which he had gone to meet her exorbitant demands, only to be rewarded with screaming fits of rage that threatened his very sanity and had clearly driven him to the brink of despair. At no point in this grim recital did he seek to justify himself or to convince me that he deserved a divorce. Quite the opposite, his whole purpose was to find out if I could possibly think of anything else he might do to save a marriage that had long been shattered beyond repair.

All of us can multiply stories like this which illustrate the way in which many deeply religious people risk the destruction of their own selfhood in a frenzied effort to love God and others ever more completely. Indeed, there is a very strong tradition in Christian ethics that insists on defining love exclusively in terms of *self*-denial, *self*-sacrifice, *self*-renunciation, *self*-crucifixion. In its extreme form, the demand is that love be so radically free of any form of self-interest that one would even be willing to be damned if it were for the glory of God.[7] In the most prominent theology of love written in the twentieth century, Lutheran theologian Anders Nygren argued that any notion of self-love "is alien to the New Testament commandment of love . . . Self-love is man's natural condition, and also the reason for the perversity of his will. . . . So far is neighborly love from including self-love that it actually excludes and overcomes it."[8]

Notice how differently Jesus addressed this issue
(Mk. 12:31). After pairing the two commandments in
careful sequence, it would have seemed logical for him
to say "Love others *as you love God*" or, even better, to
say, "Love others *as God loves them.*" But instead he stuck
to the formulation in Leviticus and said, "Love others
as you love yourself." Does that final phrase somehow
compromise the dual love commandment by
corrupting it with self-interest? No, for it is impossible
to love oneself in a selfish fashion if that self has first
loved God with utter abandon and then has loved
others with sacrificial service. Elsewhere, Jesus clearly
taught us to renounce self-centeredness (Mk. 9:35;
10:43–44), but here he is being completely consistent in
teaching us to love self as well as others since we, like
them, are made in the image of God. Just as love
impels us to meet the needs of others for human
support, so it also impels us to meet our own needs for
growth, enrichment, and the fulfillment of all that God
meant us to be.

Why did Jesus select these two biblical texts as the
hallmark of his ethics? Was it not because he
understood love in relational terms as the building of
true mutuality through the reciprocity of sharing? We
not only need to love; we also need to *be* loved. We grow
in godliness as we *give* love, but we also grow in
godliness as we *receive* love because God made us for
community with a "will to belong." To renounce all
concern for self in the name of love, as if my selfhood
had no intrinsic value or inalienable rights, comes
perilously close to implying that God cares for everyone
in the universe but me! Moreover, it gives a blank check
to the enemies I am seeking to love that allows them to
trample on my most cherished values without fear of

protest, which is not good for them or for me.

For us to love the self that also loves God and others in balanced fashion is the most unselfish thing we can do. Such love values the self as God values it, it builds the kind of self-respect that merits the respect of others, and it takes seriously the development of the self's highest potential. Conversely, to neglect or reject the self in the name of love is to depreciate the image of God with a low self-image. It is to divorce love from faith and hope and risk depression or despair. It is to view love as a source of personal weakness rather than of strength. Eric Hoffer, the longshoreman philosopher, insightfully observed:

> The remarkable thing is that we really love our neighbor as ourselves: we do unto others as we do unto ourselves. We hate others when we hate ourselves. We are tolerant toward others when we tolerate ourselves. We forgive others when we forgive ourselves. . . . It is not love of self but hatred of self which is at the root of the troubles that afflict our world.[9]

What have we learned from this engagement with the teaching of Jesus? That true love is triadic, with upward, outward, and inward dimensions that require most of all to be kept in dynamic equilibrium. Some love only God as the source of every blessing, feeling inviolable within the divine caress, but their spirituality becomes otherworldly and finally irrelevant. Some love only others, feeling that the best chance for security this side of heaven is to scratch every back and please every friend. Some love only themselves, content to live like a sponge soaking up all that they can from those about them. But Jesus calls us beyond a narrow focus on unilateral love, whether it be God-centered, others-centered, or self-centered. When each of the three loves extends and enriches the other two, we begin to attain that moral maturity perfectly expressed by the God who loves each of us, and every other one of us, and himself with all the fullness of his being (Mt. 5:48).

NOTES

1. Henry Drummond, *The Greatest Thing in the World*. Centennial Edition (Birmingham: Samford University Press, 1997).

2, Edward Collins Vacek, "The Eclipse of Love for God," *America* 174, no. 8 (1996): 13.

3. Stephen G. Post, *A Theory of Agape: On the Meaning of Christian Love* (Lewisburg: Bucknell University Press, 1990), 52–66.

4. Victor Paul Furnish, *The Love Command in the New Testament* (Nashville: Abingdon, 1972), 25–8.

5. Lionel Pearson, *Popular Ethics in Ancient Greece* (Stanford: Stanford University Press, 1962), 87. For a summary of the evidence see Furnish, *The Love Command in the New Testament*, 46–7, 65–6.

6. Thomas Maeder, "Wounded Healers," *The Atlantic Monthly*, January, 1989, 41–42.

7. For details see Post, *A Theory of Agape*, 36–51.

8. Anders Nygren, *Agape and Eros* (London: S.P.C.K., 1954), 100–101.

9. Eric Hoffer, *The Passionate State of Mind and Other Aphorisms* (New York: Harper & Brothers, 1954), 64.

17

LEARNING THE LESSONS OF SLAVERY
—➤•◄—

Were you a slave when called? Do not be concerned about it. Even if
you can gain your freedom, make use of your present condition now
more than ever. For whoever was called in the Lord as a slave is a freed
person belonging to the Lord, just as whoever was free when called is
a slave of Christ. You were bought with a price; do not become slaves
of human masters.

1 Corinthians 7:21–23 NRSV

Slavery has long been the most challenging moral issue in the history of the United States. It prompted secession, which threatened to split the Union into competing nations. It precipitated the most costly war that we have ever fought, drenching our soil in the blood, not of enemies, but of fellow Americans. Its aftermath gave rise to enforced segregation which poisoned the soul of the South for at least a century.

The existence of slavery posed the supreme challenge to Southern religion, a challenge that our ancestral faith failed miserably to meet. As nowhere else, White Evangelical Protestantism in the antebellum South was tried and found wanting at the judgment bar of history. Its response to the problem of slavery provides an insightful case study of misdirected faith. For this was not an instance of timidity or cowardice, as if the pulpit muted its denunciation of a monstrous evil out of fear. On the contrary, Southern clergy in one voice went to the opposite extreme, vigorously defending slavery as divinely sanctioned. Now that contemporary southern Christianity has reached a consensus that slavery should be condemned, let us ask how our forebears could come to the opposite conclusion.

The Cruciality of Biblical Interpretation

Then, as now, for Southern evangelicals, the Bible was the supreme source of religious authority; hence, the final arbiter of the slave question. As preachers and theologians poured over the sacred text, they found slaveholding by the godly patriarch Abraham (Gen. 12:5; 14:14; 24:35–36; 26:13–14), a practice that was later incorporated into Israelite national law (Lev. 25:44–46). Slavery was never denounced by Jesus, who made servanthood a model of discipleship (Mk. 10:44). The Apostle Paul supported slavery, counseling obedience to earthly masters (Eph. 6:5–9; Col. 3:22–25) as a duty in agreement with "the sound words of our Lord Jesus Christ and the teaching that is in accordance with godliness" (1 Tim. 6:3 NRSV). Because slaves were to remain in their present state unless they could win their freedom (1 Cor. 7:20–24), he sent the fugitive slave Onesimus back to his owner Philemon (Philem. 10–20).

The abolitionist North had a difficult time matching this biblical evidence passage for passage. They could only point out that biblical slavery was more benevolent and, in some cases, more temporary than its modern counterpart. They argued that neither Jesus nor his apostles legislated slavery but only sought to make it more humane. At best, they had to appeal to the overall spirit of the Bible rather than to specific texts, buttressing this appeal with general principles of justice drawn from moral philosophy. But they could not shake the fact that Israelite masters considered their slaves to be property that could be sold (Ex. 12:44; 21:20–21, 32), that they often used female slaves for reproductive purposes and claimed the offsprings as their own (Gen. 16:1–4; 30:3–4, 9–10; 35:22), and that they were permitted to punish slaves by beating them to the point of death (Ex. 21:20–21).

The debate over the biblical teachings on slavery was based on a method of interpretation that viewed Scripture as an infallible authority for life to be understood literally using common sense.[1] The South won the theological debate over slavery because both sides followed a static approach, which assumed that, if the Bible permitted slavery, it must also be permitted by all who believe the Bible. This victory gave to the institution of slavery a transcendent justification rooted in the Word of God. Which prompts the urgent question of whether those who repudiate slavery today are better interpreters of what Scripture says about slavery than were its defenders a century and a half ago. Let me offer four suggestions in dealing with the biblical evidence.

First, recognize that slavery was so pervasive in the ancient world that it could not fail to find a prominent place in the biblical story. But this does not mean that God intended for time to stand still so as to perpetuate political arrangements and social institutions that were prevalent in the time of Abraham, Moses, Jesus, or Paul. Rather, it means that God was willing to work with humanity just as it was then rather than waiting for more ideal conditions to emerge.

Second, God is never defeated by our sinful circumstances but acts redemptively to overcome such limitations in ways that honor our freedom of choice. In the case of biblical slavery, he was forever insisting on the more humane treatment of slaves, a strategy that came to a climax in Paul's skillful appeal to Philemon on behalf of Onesimus. In this forward thrust of the slavery texts, we see God sowing the seeds of change in the rocky soil of human exploitation where their harvest would ripen slowly, even fitfully, in response to human growth long after the collection of Scripture was completed.

Third, always follow this redemptive movement of the text to its climax in Christ as the criterion by which the whole Bible is to be understood. Jesus could not fail to know that the majority of persons in the Roman Empire of his day were slaves; yet, his teachings on sacrificial love in human relationships undercut every rationale for slavery (Mt. 5:21–48). That is why the Apostle Paul insisted that life in Christ offered unity to slave and free alike (Gal. 3:28): they were members of one body (1 Cor. 12:13), they shared one Spirit (Eph. 4:4), they constituted one new humanity (Eph. 2:15). A new social order of voluntary equality had invaded the old order of enforced hierarchy and now coexisted within it to express, in advance as it were, the life of a new spiritual order already inaugurated but not yet consummated.

Fourth, set the sweep of God's saving history in the context of creation and consummation. First ask: what was God's original intention from the very beginning before human sin entered the picture? Then ask: what is God's ultimate intention for this world when time shall be no more? As regards slavery, the creation accounts make clear that we are all made in the image of God[2] and thus destined for "dominion" rather than servitude (Gen. 1:26–27). The consummation accounts promise that creation will one day be set free from every form of subjection and bondage so that it may "obtain the glorious liberty of the children of God" (Rom. 8:21 RSV). In other words, slavery belongs neither to the Alpha nor the Omega of God's purposes but is a tragic interlude in human affairs introduced by our determination to rule over others rather than being ruled by God. It has no place either in Eden or in Eternity, which is precisely why it should have no place "in Christ."

The Power of Popular Consensus

In the antebellum South, slavery had been viewed for centuries as an established way of life. It was as much a part of the social landscape as church and school and home. In particular, it was viewed as essential to the plantation system without which the economy would quickly collapse, resulting in the degradation of the culture. Lacking a dependable source of enforced labor to supply emerging world markets, there would not be the money needed to send young men to the better schools and to cultivate in young women a life of refinement. Therefore, those who challenged slavery in the South paid a high price for their protest. Any who freed their slaves or failed to punish runaway slaves were subjected to bitter criticism or even ostracism within their community.

Why was religion unable to serve as a corrective to this repressive cultural consensus? Primarily because Southern religion had become such an integral part of the prevailing culture, it was never able to get the critical distance needed to challenge the abuses of slavery. Pastors were so immediately answerable to their congregation that they lacked the leverage to fulfill a prophetic role. The church was so enmeshed in the power structure of the day that the voice of the people became the voice of God, making the pulpit little more than an echo of the pew.

Here we are confronted in its most blatant form with what might be called the tyranny of the majority. To those accustomed to view majority rule as a cardinal principle of democracy, it is important to remember that, up until the Civil War, slavery was approved in the South by an overwhelming majority that approached unanimity. In both overt and covert ways, virtually every denomination except for the Quakers lined up solidly behind slavery. The minority was not even free to form a loyal opposition and debate the issue. In our day, it is almost impossible to realize how hopeless it was to question the views of leading opinion-makers in the community regarding slavery, especially when the prosperity of the economy was at stake.

Needless to say, this cultural consensus contributed absolutely nothing to making slavery morally right. If slavery was indeed a sin, then we must recognize that it was a sin, not so much of individual ethical choice, as of complicity in a vast collectivity of oppression from which it was almost impossible to escape. The autonomous conscience, which we cherish so highly today, was no match for this monolithic Southern mindset. Even though only a small minority of Southerners were wealthy enough to own slaves, this influential aristocracy received such solidarity of support that it created a vast social system with the power to legitimize slavery and marginalize dissent.

There is one more dimension to this dilemma that highlights its bitter irony. The Bible is replete with calls to repentance and warnings of judgment, so how did the clergy fulfill their calling to preach against sin if slavery itself was exempt from this indictment? The answer is that they succeeded in making a moral crusade out of this hideous system by seeking to bring it up to biblical standards. We have already seen that the Scriptures urge a more humane treatment of slaves in comparison with the harsh practices of their day, and this ancient concern was translated into an antebellum appeal to end such abuses as breaking up families by selling off individual members, enforcing literacy laws making it a crime to teach slaves to read and write, and refusing to allow slaves to testify in civil and church trials. Some religious leaders sternly warned that God would not honor the Confederate cause unless the most flagrant abuses of slavery were corrected, and when the war was lost, the prevailing theology of defeat was rooted, not in punishment for the evils of slavery, but in the failure of white owners to do their biblical duty to their black dependents.

Salutary as these calls for reform may have been, the constant stress on making slow, minor improvements in the conditions of slaves distracted attention away from the central issue of the legitimacy of slavery itself, particularly in its nonbiblical form based squarely on African racism. The creation of an increasingly idealistic concept of scriptural slavery made the appeal for reform more theoretical than practical. No matter how strongly preachers fulminated against flagrant abuses, their congregations failed to discipline slave owners guilty of brutality. Finally, the gradualism urged by the clergy to soften the cruelty of slavery became nothing more than an earnest effort to treat the symptoms rather than to cure the disease!

The Rise of a Political Messiah

When the Southern church used its Bible to sanction rather than to condemn slavery, thereby enlisting God in support of the dominant cultural consensus, the

Confederate cause was captured by the ideology of racism. Once the South gave its soul to this artificial construct, it lost its capacity for self-criticism. Slavery won by silence, because dissent could not be tolerated. There was neither a free pulpit in the churches nor a free podium in the schools nor a free press in the communities. Soon the region was isolated by its cherished ideology, losing touch with the conscience of the world at a time when slavery was being abolished in Europe, and the emerging monetary economy was producing revolutionary changes in the role of workers everywhere.

In such a closed society, how could the terrible shackles of slavery ever be broken? Enter a strange, even enigmatic, figure named Abraham Lincoln. Abolition was not his burning cause. Indeed, he hardly bothered himself with the slavery question until it was thrust upon him by necessity. Nor was he quick to play the religion trump card as the South delighted in doing. Son of a poor Baptist farmer, he was early stamped with the severe Calvinism of his parents, but he could never bring himself to affiliate with the church, even though it would have been politically expedient to do so. Intellectually, he was the opposite of those Southerners who found God cheering them on no matter where they opened the Bible. Rather than jumping on a religious bandwagon to advance his cause, Lincoln "increasingly wrapped his political ideas around religious themes, appealing at the very end to a mysterious providence whose inscrutable and irresistible workings both baffled and comforted him."[3]

Strange as it may seem, it was this lonely, reluctant redeemer president, with his "wearying sense of 'metaphysical isolation' "[4] who proclaimed "release to the captives" and "set at liberty those who are oppressed" (Lk. 4:18 RSV). For this act of emancipation he paid with his life on Good Friday of 1865. As pastor Joel Bingham would put it a week later, his was "a bloody sacrifice, upon the altar of human freedom" that "wrought out the painful salvation of the Republic."[5] When Lincoln had visited the Confederate capital of Richmond on the day after it fell, he was surrounded in the streets by African Americans shouting, "Glory! Glory! Bless the Lord! The Great Messiah."[6] This spontaneous tribute filled Lincoln with awkward embarrassment, for he was at best a secular messiah. We are reminded of how Scripture hailed the Persian King Cyrus as the Lord's "anointed," or messiah, for his defeat of the Babylonians (Isa. 45:1 NRSV).

Like Cyrus, Lincoln was forced to use the "terrible swift sword" of war to accomplish his work of deliverance. And what a costly redemption it was! More than 620,000 soldiers lost their lives, more than all the casualties in our nation's other wars combined.[7] The South saw twenty-five percent of its white males of military age slaughtered in the carnage.[8] But the religious cost was equally great in terms of the loss of credibility. Historian Mark Noll remarks with biting irony of the biblical debates over slavery:

> The North—forced to fight on unfriendly terrain that it had helped to create—lost the [scriptural] war. The South certainly lost the shooting war. But constructive orthodox theology was the major loser when American believers allowed bullets instead of [a mature interpretative method] to determine what the Bible said about slavery. For the history of theology in America, the great tragedy of the Civil War is that the most persuasive theologians were the Rev. Drs. William Tecumseh Sherman and Ulysses S. Grant.[9]

Clearly this heartbreaking bloodbath would never have been necessary if the evangelical faith of the solid South had been mobilized to solve the slave question by the deepest teachings of its Scriptures on sacrificial love instead of by committing regional suicide without a foreign shot being fired. Does this mean, therefore, that we should relinquish religion and resort to political and military action to achieve our moral aims? Not at all, for the Christian faith can become a powerful force for constructive change when its teachings are insightfully understood and courageously implemented, as the role of the Black church in the civil rights movement illustrates. Antebellum Southern religion proved ineffective in solving the slave question, not because it was worthless and needed to be discarded, but because it was rigid and needed to change!

The good news here is that, even when the church's faith refuses to grow, God has other contingency plans at his disposal. His agenda is too important to entrust to any one representative of his cause. When religion neglects its messianic mission, he can use secular messiahs, such as Cyrus and Lincoln, to do his bidding. It is liberating to realize that clergy are not the only agents of moral progress. As in the great struggle against slavery, lawyers and politicians and journalists and, yes, even soldiers can also serve as the Lord's anointed. If it offends you to think of God using the rough-and-tumble side of life to accomplish his will, remember that, in the crusade against slavery, precious few volunteers stepped forward in the stained-glass ghetto of Southern sanctuaries. As Lincoln saw so clearly from his profound doctrine of divine providence, sometimes the will of God is done *because of* our goodness, while at other times it is done *in spite of* our evil, but, in either case, it shall be done!

Here, then, are three important lessons of slavery: First, it is dangerous to champion the Bible when you do not know how to interpret it aright. Second, societies that suppress dissent in support of an ideological consensus sow the seeds of their own destruction. Third, when God is not well served by those who represent his cause, he will use surprising substitutes to do his bidding. Let us learn well these lessons of the past and use them to face the challenges of the future.

NOTES

1. Mark A. Noll has helpfully clarified biblical and theological issues in the debate over slavery that precipitated the Civil War. See his "The Bible and Slavery," *Religion and the American Civil War*, eds. Randall M. Miller, Harry S. Stout, and Charles Reagan Wilson (New York: Oxford University Press, 1998), 43–73; *America's God: From Jonathan Edwards to Abraham Lincoln* (New York: Oxford University Press, 2002), 365–438; *The Civil War as a Theological Crisis* (Chapel Hill: University of North Carolina Press, 2006).

2. On the struggle of the South to affirm the image of God in a context of white supremacy see H. Shelton Smith, *In His Image, But . . .: Racism in Southern Religion, 1780–1910* (Durham, NC: Duke University Press, 1972).

3. Allen C. Guelzo, *Abraham Lincoln: Redeemer President* (Grand Rapids: William B. Eerdmans, 1999), 5.

4. Guelzo, *Abraham Lincoln*, 20, citing A. N. Wilson, *God's Funeral* (New York: W. W. Norton, 1999), 10.

5. For the sermon see Joel F. Bingham, *National Disappointment, A Discourse Occasional by the Assassination of President Lincoln* (Buffalo: Breed, Butler, 1865), 36. Pitts Theology Library (Candler School of Theology, Emory University), http://beck.library.emory.edu/lincoln/sermon.php?id=bingham.001&...

6. James M. McPherson, *Battle Cry of Freedom: The Civil War Era, The Oxford History of the United States*, vol. 6 (New York: Oxford University Press, 1988), 847.

7. McPherson, 854.

8. McPherson, 856.

9. Noll, "The Bible and Slavery," 66.

PART FOUR

—→·←—

WE SHARE OUR MUTUAL WOES

The Lord God has given me the tongue of a teacher,
that I may know how to sustain the weary with a word.

Isaiah 50:4 NRSV

When Christianity defined itself as a religion of growth in maturity, it deliberately embraced the necessity of dealing with failure. We are not able to spend a lifetime "pressing on the upward way" toward "higher ground" without experiencing many setbacks before reaching the summit. In the quest for physical development, how easy to neglect a balanced diet and postpone regular exercise. In seeking to gain wisdom, how quickly we forget the lessons of yesterday and fail to prepare for tomorrow. Even our most intimate relationships are sometimes undermined by hostility and alienation. Just so, progress on our spiritual journey is often fitful at best, characterized by two steps forward and one step backward. Beset by insecurities and temptations on every hand, it is not easy to grow, especially in goodness!

Jesus prepared his disciples for their share of defeats by linking their lives together in a shared commitment to his cause. Facing the ultimate threat of the cross that would scatter them to their homes (Jn. 16:32), he taught them to love one another as he loved them (Jn. 13:34). This bond could not be broken by his physical departure from earth. Instead, as his followers reached out to include others, they defined their new movement as a fellowship, a sharing of their life with Christ in ways that transcended differences of ethnicity, gender, and nationality (Gal. 3:28). Regardless of background, they had become members of one body (1 Cor. 12:27), citizens of one commonwealth (Phil. 3:20), and family of one household (Eph. 2:19). This sense of commonality, or *koinonia* as they called it, became a safety net undergirding any who might fall with the combined spiritual resources of the group.

The sermons clustered here address many of the pitfalls that lie along the path to maturity: natural disasters that threaten bodily harm, physical death that forces us to face eternity, spiritual myopia that blinds us to the true meaning of life, and frustration with the slow pace of needed change. The final message deals with the most tormenting problem of all: what do we do when, as one put it, God seems to be an ever-absent help in time of trouble? How I hope that you will find here a word to encourage and sustain your heart when it grows weary.

18

GOD AND THE TSUNAMI

—➤•◄—

When the waters saw you, O God, . . . they were afraid; the very deep trembled. . . . Your way was through the sea, your path through the mighty waters; yet your footprints were unseen.
Psalm 77:16, 19 NRSV

The most catastrophic natural disaster in recent memory was the giant earthquake that erupted under the Indian Ocean on December 26, 2004, caused by the movement of two tectonic plates four thousand fathoms under the surface of the sea. Registering 9.0 on the Richter scale, this two-hundred-megaton jolt thrust up giant waves that raced at nearly five hundred miles an hour to devastate three thousand miles of unprotected shoreline. Saturation media coverage makes it unnecessary to dwell here on the carnage that initially caused at least 225,000 deaths, 200,000 of them in Indonesia alone. Instead, we focus on the profound religious issues raised by the sheer arbitrariness of the disaster. Since tsunamis do not play politics, there are no enemy terrorists to blame. So does that make God the culprit?

Efforts to explain the divine role in such calamities left much to be desired. As might be expected, some were ready with theories of retribution: one popular author covered all the bases by insisting that God was punishing our enemies for persecuting Christians and punishing us for our moral laxity as a wake-up call to repent. To critics challenging the severity of his verdict, he retorted, "You ought to see what hell is like. It's going to be an eternal judgment of God on all people."[1]

Others used scriptural descriptions of upheavals in nature (Mt. 24:7–8; Lk 21:25–26) to view the tsunami as a sign of the last days when the rewards of heaven will more than compensate us for the severe trials that we must endure here on earth. However, to explain this tragedy in terms either of heaven or of hell leaves it a mystery that will not be solved until we reach eternity, thereby diverting our attention from responses that are urgently needed in the present.

If we as Christians refuse to face head-on the hard questions that arise whenever nature becomes our enemy, that very denial of the problem will create a dark closet of doubt within the house of faith. After all, we are endlessly threatened, not only by earthquakes, but by floods, tornadoes, landslides, and plagues. It is the megascourges that get media attention, but our heartbreaking dilemma is mirrored in the face of one tiny baby dying of leukemia. What do we say when nature seems not only capricious and cruel but downright callous about those whom it hurts the most? As Christians we make some very strong claims about the essential goodness of our world as a gift of God. But how can we sing "For the Beauty of the Earth" on beaches littered with rotting corpses? Let us honor the dead by grappling with the tough issues raised by those terrible realities that cost them their lives.

The Creator

The religious questions raised by the tsunami fall into a predictable pattern, which has surfaced many times in the past. First, "How could God allow such a terrible thing to happen?," and, second, "Where was God when it happened?" The assumption is that, if God is all-loving, he would not permit such a cataclysm to occur;

and if he is all-powerful, he would prevent any other force from causing it to occur. Since the Christian faith insists that God is intimately concerned with each individual life (Mt. 10:29–31), we cannot assume that he was indifferent or detached like the Deist god of The Enlightenment. If we have no answers to these questions, does this imply that God is vindictive rather than loving, or that he is weak rather than strong, or that he is absent rather than present with us? Clearly, the tsunami calls into question our most fundamental understanding of God.

We begin with the issue of power. Many simply assume that God, by definition, is in charge of everything that happens. We like to use the "omni" words, stressing that God is omnipotent, omniscient, and omnipresent. When we shift out of that philosophical framework, we often speak of God as sovereign, almighty, and majestic. Or as one theologian put it, "God is in control of the entire universe, and there is not even a single atom outside His sovereignty"[2] Descriptions of God's absolute power abound, which imply that he could instantly halt the most ferocious storm if he desired. Sometimes it seems as if Christians are in a contest to claim more for their God than other religions claim for theirs, which causes us to insist that our God can do anything he pleases.

Let me trouble you to think about whether this is the best way to understand the greatness of God. Obviously God cannot do anything that is inherently impossible or contradictory, such as make a rock so heavy that he cannot pick it up. Furthermore, God can only act consistent with his character. Thus, for example, God cannot sin or do anything that would be ungodly, which puts off-limits for him many things that humans do. According to the Bible, the holiness of God means that he is unique, radically different from us in what he thinks and does (Isa. 55:8–9). To say that God can act only for good does not mean that he is restrained by some power greater than himself, but rather that he chooses to limit his power by his perfection. In short, God is *not* free to *not* be God!

Now let us look more closely at the common platitude that God is all-loving. We all know that the word "love" has great latitude, which is well expressed by acknowledging that we love our God, our country, our family, as well as cold watermelon and our favorite flavor of ice cream. One kind of love can easily become so smothering possessive that the beloved is crushed by its embrace. Another kind can lead to a pampering of the beloved that results in their corruption. All of us know parents who coddle their children until, like bad fruit, they become "spoiled."

In the Bible, God is pictured as having a very distinctive kind of love that is different from our own, so much so that it required a new word to describe it. This *agapē* is what we might call "tough love," sacrificial rather than selfish or smothering in nature. By the time of the Apostle Paul, the followers of Jesus came to realize that it was redemptive love because it was causing them to grow toward maturity (Eph. 3:14–19; 4:13–15). The central truth of the New Testament is that the nature of God was most fully revealed by Christ's death on the cross, which represented a revolution in our understanding of just how vulnerable his love was willing to become on our behalf (Phil. 2:6–11).

When we combine these insights regarding God's power and love and apply them to his role as creator, we begin to understand why God did not decree that earth always remain a perfect planet that never changes, a place where there are no germs or snakes or hurricanes. God did not make a robot world for the same reason that he did not make robot people to inhabit it, namely, because such a world would leave no room for choices, for growth, for the achievement of maturity. Trapped in a world of total predictability, we would be forced to bow to the inevitability of the way things always have been and will be.

Theoretically, it might seem easier to live in a perfect world where nothing ever goes wrong, but such a world would deny us the most precious dimension of our humanity, namely, the freedom to decide what to believe and who to love and how to relate to the world about us. Think of the parents who do everything possible to create a perfect world for their children only to watch them grow up unable to cope with the harsh realities of human existence. There is no maturity without freedom and no freedom without risk. That is why God chose to use his power in accomplishing the hardest task of all: to love us in such a way that we will freely choose to love in mature fashion. So let us begin to think about the kind of world where responsible freedom is encouraged for our benefit.

The Creation

Only after we sharpen our understanding of the character of the Creator are we able to ponder what kind of creation is compatible with his nature. Just as we often adopt an absolutist idea of God that puts no limits on the way he uses his power and his love, even so we often entertain a simplistic idea of creation by assuming that God began with a nice clean slate, a perfect emptiness filled only with himself. It is always easier to start like that, in a vacuum with no clutter or carryover from the past. Many of our problems stem from our inability to start from scratch. We lament the legacy that others have left behind but assume that God was not encumbered with such restrictions.

The biblical account in Genesis 1, however, is not so simple. For no sooner does verse 1 declare that God created the earth than verse 2 immediately goes on to say that, before this began to happen, the earth was (1) devoid of form or content, having no shape or substance, no law or order. (2) Furthermore, there was a dark watery void underneath this chaos called "the deep." (3) Again, upon the face of the deep there was a brooding "darkness." And yet God faced down this bleak abyss. The wind of his breath blew across its shadowy face. He moved in to hatch something new like a bird sets on an egg. The creative God came up against the most uncreative, unpromising raw materials imaginable and determined to use them as building blocks for a livable planet earth.

Such a startling picture of chaos leaves us hungry to speculate about where this amorphous nothingness, this watery emptiness, this overarching blackness came from, but on such issues the creation account in Genesis is silent, as is its New Testament counterpart where the origin of "darkness" is not explained but simply posited (Jn. 1:5). The key point lies rather in the sharp contrast drawn by Genesis. The opening verses insist that creation must be understood in light of its antithesis: what our world would be like without the intervention of God. In other words, the creative activity of God did not mean making something out of nothing but it meant bringing order out of chaos, making a place where life could flourish with purpose.

One does not create a painting simply by gathering oils and brushes, or create a cathedral by assembling lumber and bricks. These are only raw materials waiting to be transformed. Just so, to say that our world was "created" means more than to say that it "exists," for the former implies design, coherence, and beauty such as God superimposed by gradually sorting out the confusion that confronted him.

A second startling insight in the biblical understanding of creation is that it is unfinished because the nothingness of the void was overcome but not forever banished. Always the possibility of reverting to corruption and disorder remained an option. In our incredible capacity to choose, we are free to lay waste to God's good creation by ravaging its forests, polluting its streams, and fouling its air. The prophet Jeremiah pictured a relapse of creation to its pre-created chaos (Jer. 4:23–26), but God asserted his determination to work within the constraints of our freedom to renew creation and bring it to completion (Jer. 4:27–28). That is why Jesus affirmed, not only that God was still engaged in his creative work, but that the Son joined him in that endeavor (Jn. 5:17). His miracles, for example, restored small fragments of creation to their original goodness (compare Gen. 1:31 with Mk. 7:37). Indeed, the work of creation will not be completed until there is "a new heaven and a new earth" as envisioned in the last book of the Bible (Rev. 21:1).

Pause to reflect for a moment on the meaning of evolution, which has become so controversial in contemporary religious life. To be sure, there are those who would use an extreme view of scientific or social Darwinism to discredit the Christian faith, but the growing evidence for a vast process of development over billions of years, if understood properly, may actually enhance our understanding of creation. For what it means is that there is an amazing drive toward order, purpose, and wholeness built into the very way that things are made. There was a time when our planet was little more than an uninhabitable mass of fiery magma endlessly pummeled by celestial meteors. Why should this utterly unpromising beginning lead eventually, not only to animal and human life, but to intelligence and community, even to goodness and beauty, rather than collapsing into a meaningless jumble?

There are few places to see the work of the creator God more clearly than in the millions upon millions of ways in which nature has decided, in the use of its own God-given freedom, to grow to the point of development it has now reached. And why should these choices that the evolutionists call "natural selection" result in such purposeful progress except that this was the intention of the Creator from the beginning? Clearly nature's quest for harmony and order is not yet complete, which is why the tectonic plates that have been grinding against one another for some three billion years may still overlap in ways that cause unintended disasters. But the progress made thus far in nature is simply breathtaking despite the fact that it is still a work in progress.

The Creature

What does it mean to live as unfinished creatures in an unfinished world? Despite enormous progress, the world is just as broken as we are; thus, there is much work yet to be done. Meanwhile, the existence of the void reminds us of how finite, vulnerable, and thus, necessarily interdependent we really are. Life is a hazardous venture at best, not only because we cannot predict what may happen next in nature, but also because we cannot predict what may happen next in the human heart. The only way to cope with the many contingencies that belong both to the freedom of nature and to the freedom of humanity is to be prepared for the worst but committed to work with God for the best in renewing the creation.

It may sound audacious to suggest that God has invited us to help him tame the chaos, to literally be co-creators with him in making a better world, but that is precisely why he has endowed us with what we call "creativity," which means exactly what it says, namely, the capacity to make things new and better! Why would God ask us to "subdue" the earth and "have dominion" over it (Gen. 1:28 NRSV) unless he had fitted us for that very task? Unfortunately, many Christians have a vague and weak doctrine of creation that leaves them indifferent to the plight of nature. What is needed is an attitudinal change according to which it becomes an overriding passion of us all to leave the world better than we found it. It is a scandal that some environmentalists who claim to have no god are more actively involved in the care of the earth than are some Christians who claim to worship its Creator!

To take seriously our role as partners with God in guiding creation to attain its full potential is to honor science and technology for the great strides made in understanding the physical world and what its most pressing needs might be. Since the 1960s, seismologists have begun to understand the workings of tectonic plates, and therefore, gained the ability to predict well in advance when upheavals may occur. Regarding the recent tsunami, several hours of warning time were available, but no alarm systems were in place despite the fact that they utilize a simple technology, which has been in existence for almost a century.

Third World countries often plead the excuse of poverty for their neglect when the problem is really one of priority. Most of them spend far more on weapons of destruction than on an early-warning system able to alert citizens to this danger. If we but have the will to do it, we can make this world a much safer place instead of squandering our ingenuity and resources on that which can only destroy life and fracture its habitat. That is precisely the kind of choice that God gave us: "I call heaven and earth to witness against you this day, that I have set before you life and death, blessing and curse; therefore *choose life*, that you and your descendents may live" (Deut. 30:19 RSV).

To be sure, this will not be a quick or easy task, and in our petulance, we whine at God for not having already solved our problem for us. But remember, God himself has been toiling on behalf of our world for a lot longer than we have. At the outset, he spread his labors over six days rather than commanding an instantaneous creation that would be complete from the outset. Instead of pulling the world out of a hat full-blown, God followed a gradual progression, an orderly sequence, a purposeful process that continues to evolve. We must infer from this approach that he "took his time" because the kind of creativity that honors freedom takes patience, even for God. If God never gives up in his efforts to create something worthwhile, if he is willing to work one step at a time, who are we to refuse to join him in that task?

The fact that the job is not finished, either for God or for us, does not mean that he has consigned us to live with a succession of tragedies as acts of judgment, punishment, or warning. Rather, he has joined us in the struggle and made himself vulnerable to their impact. In the magnificent eighth chapter of Romans, the Apostle Paul wrote of the emptiness, brokenness, and sense of futility that haunts the whole created order (Rom. 8:20). No one could have depicted the tragic dimension of life on a vaster canvas than did Paul in his personification of every part of creation joining together in a common chorus of cries. But he moved swiftly to interpret this writhing as the travail of an expectant mother about to bring forth her most cherished hope (Rom. 8:22b). The spasms that convulse life are but the labor pains by which the creation is struggling to "be set free . . . and obtain the glorious liberty of the children of God" (v. 21 RSV).

Paul's key word in this passage is "groaning," which he attributes not only to creation (Rom. 8:22) but to the Christian community as we share creation's ordeal (Rom. 8:23) and to the divine Comforter who intercedes on our behalf with "groanings too deep for words" (Rom. 8:26 AT). Herein lies our ultimate hope for the transformation of tragedy, not that we have discovered a neat theodicy that somehow explains the problem of suffering, but that we have experienced the creator God striving with us in all things until he once again makes them good (Rom. 8:28).

So, to answer directly the question, "Where was God when the tsunami struck?," he was on every mile of those battered beaches weeping with those who wept, groaning for the day when nature and all of its inhabitants will live together in harmony. As the daughter of Cooperative Baptist Fellowship missionaries working in Asia put it:

When wave upon wave of water hit shores
thousands of miles from where they began,
You were there.

When these waves crashed away
everything in their path,
You were there.

When the people You loved enough to die
for ran for their very lives,
You were there.

When houses fell and possessions
were swept away,
You were there.

You saw as these waves broke buildings, stole
lives, left terror and grief in their wake.

Did Your heart break? I don't have to ask.
I imagine Your tears would put the waters
of tsunamis to shame.

In the midst of death and destruction,
the God of the Universe was there.
You were there.[3]

NOTES

1. Henry Blackaby cited by *BP News*, January 24, 2005.

2. R. Albert Mohler, Jr., "God and the Tsunami: Theology in the Headlines," http://www.crosswalk.com/news/weblogs/mohler/?adate=1/3/2005.

3. "He was There: A Personal Reflection," *CBF Fellowship!*, February/March, 2005, 3. The identity of the author could not be given because of security concerns.

19

THE LAND BEYOND THE STARS

And all these, though well attested by their faith, did not receive what was promised, since God had foreseen something better for us, that apart from us they should not be made perfect.

Hebrews 11:39–40 RSV

Shortly before he died in his eighty-ninth year, Robert Frost was talking with his friend Victor Reichert about a recent trip to Russia when suddenly he interrupted himself to ask, "Victor, what do you think are the chances of life after death?" His friend answered with a question, "Robert, what do you think?" Frost bent his head and remained silent for a long time, then lifting his face he replied, "With so many ladders going up everywhere, there must be *something* for them to lean against."[1]

This conversation between a poet and a rabbi prompts us to wonder whatever became of that "invincible surmise" that Christians once called their "blessed hope"? Years ago, the theme of eternal life was a staple of most Protestant pulpits. Every revival series featured climactic sermons on heaven and hell. But now, that horizon seems to have receded or even disappeared from the religious landscape. To be sure, every recitation of The Apostles' Creed concludes with "I believe in the life everlasting," but it sounds like little more than a mild palliative designed to mitigate the terrors of death.

Are we really better off to suppress what Wordsworth called our "intimations of immortality?"[2]

Does this posture of detachment cause us to become more concerned for the world around us, less addicted to an escapist religion? Or does our indifference to the world beyond result in a shriveling of that dimension of transcendence that should overarch the earthly journey? Let us revisit this neglected agenda in the hope of raising one more ladder to the skies so that we may reflect on what it leans against.

The Future

In seeking a fresh approach to the function of eternity in the life of the believer, I have found guidance from a passage that has had little or no influence on our understanding of the world beyond. As the majestic roll call of faith recorded in Hebrews 11 comes to a climax, the author draws from the pilgrimage of the People of God in the Old Testament a number of conclusions that merit our closest attention:

> And all these, though well attested by their faith, did not receive what was promised, since God had foreseen something better for us, that apart from us they should not be made perfect (Heb. 11:39–40 RSV).

What provocative insights throng this single sentence! (1) God's promises are not always fulfilled as soon as we prove faithful. Indeed, their bestowal may be deferred longer than our earthly lifetime, even for centuries on end. (2) This delay is not a matter of divine indifference, as if God were either fickle or forgetful, but is based on his determination to provide "something better" however long that effort may take. (3) Perfection is not automatic or instantaneous even when we go to be with God after death. Rather, it is a dynamic process of development that may progress in stages according to God's providential plan. (4) Reaching the wholeness and maturity of perfection is not simply a matter either of individual achievement or of divine provision but is profoundly relational, something that happens in concert with all the People of God. In other words, each of us participates in the blessings that come to *all* of us. No matter how early or how late we may have joined the earthly race, every one of us benefits equally from the fulfillment that comes at the end of the journey.

It is just here that we discover the one insight most crucial to our quest for understanding. We know very well from Hebrews that the "something better" causing God to delay the fulfillment of his promises to the Old Testament worthies was none other than Jesus Christ: his better revelation (1:4), better hope (7:19), better covenant (7:22), better priesthood (8:6), better sacrifice (9:23), better possessions (10:34), better life (11:35). Therefore we would expect our text to say that "apart from *Christ* they should not be made perfect." But no, it says "apart from *us*," which means that we who have benefited from the finished work of Christ will be permitted to share our blessings with those who lived before Christ in time and so waited in hope to claim God's promises. Because redemption unfolds throughout history, none of us can capture its fullness within a single earthly lifetime, but eternity will offer the opportunity for each of us to benefit from all that God has ever done for his people from creation to consummation.

In a word, this text is telling us that God's blessings are *retroactive*. As long as we live in time, we can never share with others all of the "better things" that God is continually doing with our lives. All that we can do here on earth is to live "by faith," which means to live in the creative tension between desire and delay, promise and postponement, wanting and waiting. But when time shall be no more, when all the people of God shall at last be gathered in "that city which has foundations, whose builder and maker is God" (Heb. 11:10 RSV), then we shall be able to bless, and be blessed, by all who were ever part of the earthly pilgrimage of faith. Then we shall be able to spend as many forevers as our poor minds can imagine building that wholeness of maturity both in ourselves and in others which is God's agenda for his people throughout all ages.

The cultural event of 1996 in Birmingham, Alabama, was an exhibit at the Museum of Art on The First Emperor of China, Qin Shihuangdi (259–210 BC). After unifying China between 230 and 220 BC, Qin moved quickly to become absolute sovereign of a vast domain rivaling the conquests of Alexander the Great and Julius Caesar. But the one foe he could not defeat was death, despite a frantic quest for the elixir of immortality, which included drinking potions of mercury. And so Qin decreed the construction of a vast mausoleum covering twenty-two square miles. As many as 700,000 laborers were conscripted to work thirty-six years building an elaborate underground fortress containing 8,000 terra cotta warriors with 40,000 bronze weapons. When finished, this artificial mountain was sealed with all of the Emperor's childless concubines, as well as the artisans who could have led grave robbers to its vast treasures, and there it lay undisturbed until accidentally rediscovered in 1974 by farmers digging a well.[3]

Why did Qin surround himself in death with the

likeness of an army in battle array? Because he was convinced that in the afterlife he would have to defeat every foe in order to triumph once again. Eternity for him would be but an endless extension of the conquests of earth. Qin was a brutal tyrant who once had 460 scholars buried alive merely for questioning some of his views, and he would visit the same havoc on heaven if anyone there dared to oppose him. By contrast, the author of Hebrews saw heaven as a place of sharing the best gifts that have come to us from the Christ whose greatest victory was won on a shameful cross. Here we see how tightly the two worlds are tied together. If salvation in this life is seen as attained by violence and destruction, then the next life is seen as an opportunity to expand and intensify that chaos. But if salvation in this life is seen as an endless quest for growth in the wholeness of maturity, then the next life is seen as the fulfillment of that goal in the perfecting of the saints.

The Past

What does this breathtaking vision of heaven in Hebrews say to our earthbound souls? Throughout my working lifetime, I have always ended a job with the same haunting refrain: "If only I could start again—not where I was at the beginning, but where I was at the end!" In one sense, I never really learned how to do a job until the job was over. But, in a deeper sense, what this means is that, by the time I finally figure out how to live effectively, my life will be over! It is not just that I want to be forgiven for my immaturities and inex- perience, important as such pardon may be. Rather, what I want is a chance to share the best gifts of my maturity and experience with those who graciously tolerated my fumbling first efforts, but that option is forever denied me by the irreversibility of time. Or is that denial to be forever? To be sure, we cannot turn back earth's calendar, but is there another realm in which time itself will no longer be a threat to our deepest longings for maturity?

Arthur Gordon tells of a wintry afternoon in Manhattan when, frustrated and depressed, "chewing the bitter cud of hindsight," he sought solace from an elderly friend who was also an eminent psychiatrist. The counselor took him to his office and insisted that he listen to three tape recordings of patient interviews, then identify the two-word phrase that was their common denominator. After hearing these tales of woe, Gordon was clueless until his counselor pointed out "the two saddest words in any language": *if only*. He explained: "'*If only*,' they say to me, 'I had done it differently' . . . '*If only* I had been wiser.' The trouble with *if only* is that it doesn't change anything. It keeps the person facing the wrong way—backward instead of forward."

Gordon's problem was that he was living in the past tense. His older friend's advice: "Shift the focus . . . change the key words from *if only* to *next time* . . . push aside the roadblock of regret." As the conversation ended, the psychiatrist reached in his bookcase and pulled out a diary kept by a schoolteacher in his hometown. Her husband, Jonathan, was an amiable ne'er-do-well whose inadequacies as a provider left her to care for the family and pay most of the bills. The journal was full of angry entries on his many shortcomings, which ended when he died except for one addition written many years later that read: "Today I was made superintendent of schools, and I suppose I should be very proud. But if I knew that Jonathan was out there somewhere beyond the stars and if I knew how to manage it, I would go to him tonight."

The Old Man closed the book gently and returned it to the shelf with this comment: "What she's saying is, 'if only I had loved him while I could.' That's when those sad words are the saddest of all; when it's too late to retrieve anything."[4] With that the story ended but our questions just begin. Does death mean that there are no more "next times" ever again? When our earthly journey comes to an end, is it forever "too late to retrieve anything"? Or are our Jonathans whom we never quite learn to love in this life "somewhere out there beyond the stars," and will we manage to go to them when night has fallen for us all?

The Present

With the ladder of deferred fulfillment rising to the skies, why are we so reluctant to consider what it may lean against? Notice how the insights of our text speak directly to the reasons for our neglect of the life beyond. One reason for that indifference is that our traditional understanding of the future is based on a rather vague and uninviting conception of heaven. Suppose that we survive death with our identity intact. Then what do we do? Without fleshly bodies, we are no longer preoccupied with the earthly quest for food, shelter, and clothing.

About the only thing that preachers can suggest, particularly from passages in the Book of Revelation, is that we will go to church all the time, praising God before his throne. But when we try to imagine what it would be like to do that for an eternity, the nagging possibility of boredom begins to set in. After all, how many verses are there to the "Hallelujah" chorus, and what will we do when we have sung them all? We seem unable to imagine how heaven could be meaningful in a timeless eternity. Against such static notions of perfection, which tend to imply a life of endless repetition, Hebrews pictures a dynamic heaven in which we will spend an eternity learning to become mature by sharing the best gifts of life with all who join us there.

Another reason for our neglect of the life beyond is that we tend to view it only as an answer to the problem of death. The afterlife is seen as guaranteeing survival beyond the grave and thus is of interest primarily to the elderly nearing the end of their earthly sojourn. The problem with this approach is that it makes the life above of no real relevance to the life below. This difficulty arises when we relate the two worlds *sequentially*, as if earth comes first and then heaven comes after it, rather than relating them *simultaneously*, as if the eternal world above invades and inter-penetrates the temporal world below. Hebrews 11 suggests that we do not live one world at a time. Rather, we live a bipolar existence according to which both worlds are equally real and present at all times.

A final reason why this world is "too much with us" is that we absolutize present experience—the more momentary the better! We act as if destiny is decided by the latest football victory or presidential election or technological marvel, but our deeper sensibilities know better. The writer of Hebrews insisted that only those who live with the disarming awareness of a greater world find the courage to bear a countercultural witness. Only those with a temperament for eternity, whose eyes are fixed on "a land that is fairer than day,"[5] are willing to sacrifice themselves as did the martyrs recounted in our scripture passage (Heb. 11:32–38).

Those who believe that this earthly life ends with a period will finally capitulate to the terrible tyranny of the status quo. But those who believe that it ends with a comma, setting apart what is at best a subordinate clause in the long sentence that is our life, will use their earthly days as an apprenticeship in the kind of perfection that takes an eternity to complete.

As John Bunyan neared the completion of *Pilgrim's Progress*, he described the summons by which Mr. Valiant-for-truth was called to leave this world for another. Gathering his friends he said to them:

> I am going to my Father's; and though with great difficulty I am got hither, yet now I do not repent me of all the trouble I have been at to arrive where I am. My sword I give to him that shall succeed me in my pilgrimage, and my courage and skill to him that can get it. My marks and scars I carry with me, to be a witness for me that I have fought His battles who now will be my rewarder.

Then Bunyan added: "So he passed over, and all the trumpets sounded for him on the other side."[6] May all the trumpets sound again when that day is come for you.

NOTES

1. Andrew R. Marks, *The Rabbi and the Poet: Victor Reichert and Robert Frost*, (Alton, NH: Andover Green Book Publishers, 1994), 2–3.

2. William Wordsworth, "Ode: Intimations of Immortality from Recollections of Early Childhood," reprinted in *The New Oxford Book of English Verse*, 1250–1950, ed. Helen Gardner, (New York: Oxford University Press, 1972), 508–13.

3. For details see R. W. L. Guisso, Catherine Pagani, and David Miller, *The First Emperor of China* (Toronto: Birch Lane Press, 1989).

4. Arthur Gordon, *A Touch of Wonder* (New York: Jove Books, 1978), 68–72. John R. Claypool called this account to my attention and later incorporated it in his book, *The Hopeful Heart* (Harrisburg, PA: Morehouse Publishing, 2003), 68–71.

5. Sanford F. Bennett, "There's a Land That Is Fairer Than Day," stanza 1, *The Baptist Hymnal*, ed. Wesley L. Forbis (Nashville: Convention Press, 1991), #515.

6. John Bunyan, *The Pilgrim's Progress* (New York: Fleming H. Revell, 1903), 302.

20

THE CONQUEST OF DARKNESS

—➤•◄—

As he walked along, he saw a man blind from birth. His disciples asked him, "Rabbi, who sinned, this man or his parents, that he was born blind?" Jesus answered, "Neither this man nor his parents sinned; he was born blind so that God's works might be revealed in him. We must work the works of him who sent me while it is day; night is coming when no one can work. As long as I am in the world, I am the light of the world."

John 9:1–5 NRSV

How bad to be blind! To live without light is to grope instead of grasping, to stumble instead of striding. Fingers become a clumsy, fumbling tangle; feet shuffle and slide through a fog that will not lift. With the darkness comes a loss of initiative as the sightless settle into the predictable monotony of accustomed routine, dreading any alteration in the patterns that they have mastered by force of habit.

Blindness itself is bad enough to contemplate, but our scripture passage demands that we do more. By introducing us to "a man blind *from birth*" (Jn. 9:1 NRSV), it forces us to deal with one who was doubly smitten. Never had his eyelids opened on a shimmering sunrise, or a wayside flower, or a little child's face. He had never seen reality whole but was forced to piece together a few ragged fragments from the stray sounds and smells and shapes that came his way. I knew a minister who became blind at the height of his career, and yet, unlike this wretched victim, he was left with many vivid memories that provided a dependable frame of reference in his continuing struggle to apprehend the world about him.

To be blind from birth! That is the kind of senseless, hopeless tragedy that shakes our confidence in an ultimate benevolence. Huddled there in perpetual darkness, this nameless creature raises the grim possibility that, for some at least, life may finally have no meaning at all. Nor can we sidestep the searching questions in his blank stare. Jesus and his disciples, as they "walked along" (Jn. 9:1 NRSV), probably came upon him in the very courts of the Temple (Jn. 8:59), perhaps by the Gate Beautiful where the beggars sat (Acts 3:2), a dark stain on the dazzling splendor of the Holy Place.

The Disciples' Approach to Tragedy

As soon as the disciples caught sight of the blind man, they blurted out the stock question that religion had taught them to ask in the face of unexplained evil: "Rabbi, who sinned?" (Jn. 9:2 NRSV). We have always sought a simple cause-and-effect solution to the problem of suffering. Logic seems to demand that if God is both all-powerful and all-righteous, misfortune must be viewed as just punishment for those who thwart his will. Such was the earliest and most basic answer of the Old Testament: sin causes suffering.[1] Nor can it be denied that tragedy often springs directly from a disregard of divine law.

But here was a case that did not fit such a net formula, for the victim had been smitten from birth. The only way in which he could be blamed for that plight was to assume that he had sinned either during the prenatal stage as a fetus in the womb or during some preexistent state as a transmigrated soul. Rabbinic speculation was driven eventually to consider such bizarre possibilities but with inconclusive results.

The only other course that seemed open was to fall back on the Old Testament concept of God "punishing children for the iniquity of parents, to the third and the fourth generation" (Ex. 20:5 NRSV). Again, unambiguous instances of this process are at work, as when the venereal disease of an irresponsible parent may indeed cause blindness in the eyes of a newborn babe.

In what strikingly similar fashion do we debate the tragic issues of our times! Like the disciples of old, we begin by assuming that someone is to blame and, further, that to determine and assign guilt will somehow alleviate the problem. Perhaps it is symptomatic of our deep desire to be a judge that we so persistently ask, "Whose fault is it?" as if the answer will confer meaning on tragedy or at least make it more bearable. To be sure, in some cases it is both possible and important to make this kind of judgment. Although it does the victim little good, such a determination may help to protect the innocent and to warn others, lest they commit a similar folly in the future.

But what of those instances in which the ultimate causes are hopelessly obscured? Even then, as did the disciples, we continue to debate the same alternatives. Some still say, "He sinned"; that is, tragedy springs from one's indolence, ignorance, or irresponsibility. He has only himself to blame for whatever his predicament may be. But others still say, "His parents sinned"; that is, he inherited his problems, he was born and bred in hopelessness, he never really had a chance. Much of the diagnosis of our ills today is polarized by "conservatives" who characteristically place responsibility squarely on the individual, and by "liberals" who predictably stress the contributions of heritage and environment.

Illustrations of these tendencies abound wherever

tragedy rears its ugly head. Who is to blame for the slums that incubate riots of despair, the present tenants who were born into the ghetto with little chance of escape, or the generations of profiteers who bequeathed to them substandard housing? Why have racial minorities such as Native Americans and African Americans been ostracized from the mainstream of society: their own sloth or a hideous system of discrimination that will take centuries to overcome? On and on we might ask: Why the Appalachian indigent? Why the high school dropout? Why the chaos in young nations emerging from colonialism? And always the same debate between individual responsibility and inherited liability. How would Jesus deal with our great dilemma? "Rabbi," we ask with the disciples of old, "who sinned, this man or his parents, that he was born blind?" (Jn. 9:2 NRSV).

Jesus' Approach to Tragedy

As was so often the case, Jesus refused to embrace either horn of the dilemma posed by his disciples. Instead, he began by negating their whole approach: "Neither this man nor his parents sinned" (Jn. 9:3a NRSV). Both alternatives were wrong; indeed, that whole way of framing the issue was fallacious. Rather, "he was born blind so that God's works might be revealed in him" (Jn. 9:3b NRSV). With that word, light began to break for the first time through the darkness that had blinded both the man's sight and the disciples' insight.

What was the decisive difference in the stance that Jesus took toward tragedy? To his followers, suffering was an occasion for speculation. The blind man presented them with a problem to be solved. Thus, they asked the Rabbi to respond to their need for explanation, not to the victim's need for illumination. In other words, they wanted light for themselves on the enigma of evil, but were oblivious to the blind man's infinitely greater need for light by which to live. To utilize Martin Buber's philosophical categories, the man was for them an "it," an object of detached debate, an anonymous question mark cluttering their theological system. But for Jesus, the man was a "thou," a subject evoking compassion, a focus of concern with whom to become involved.[2]

Notice how this perspective of Jesus shifted not only the attitudes but the very assumptions with which the disciples approached tragedy. Their question sought to determine the causes of the problem, and so viewed evil in the light of the origins from which it had come; whereas, the answer of Jesus sought to deal with the *effects* of the problem, and so viewed evil in the light of the results to which it could lead. Starting at the same point, the two approaches diverged in opposite directions. The disciples wanted to understand tragedy by tracing it backward, while Jesus wanted to overcome tragedy by tracing it forward. This shift of concern from the past to the future was rooted in the conviction that his task was not to explain the antecedents of evil but to change its consequences by manifesting the works of God.

Have we not confirmed the wisdom of the Master's approach? All of our speculations about the origin of evil have brought us little nearer to an answer. However we may try to explain it, the darkness is simply there—a primeval reality contending with the light (Jn. 1:5)—and even the most profound theories do not make it go away. But when we are moved by compassion to light a candle, refusing to let perplexity paralyze involvement, do we not discover that the power of God can push back the frontiers of tragedy? After the philosopher and theologian have retired in confusion, some willing spirit goes to work and hammers out a solution on the anvil of struggle. *Tragedy is not redeemed by being explained but by being changed!*

This does not mean, however, that Jesus was a naïve idealist who believed that brutal suffering would always work out to one's advantage. On the contrary, his determination to make the works of God manifest even in tragedy was buttressed by two sober sayings, one an imperative and the other a premonition.

He began with the imperative: "We must work the works of him who sent me while it is day" (Jn. 9:4a NRSV). There can be no progress in the conquest of darkness without the necessity of courageous action. But this is not to be understood either as frenetic activism or as tedious drudgery. Such labors are not dependent on our improvisation or ingenuity but are "the works of him who sent me" (Jn. 9:4a NRSV). That is, God both initiates the divine activity and discloses its true nature in the ministry of Jesus (Jn. 5:17). The task to which the disciples were called is a gift in which God supplies both the power and the pattern. Furthermore, the sending of Jesus as the supreme work of God meant that the great "day" of salvation had dawned (Lk. 1:78). The grip of evil can be broken, not because our strength is sufficient, but because the light of the world has come (Jn. 9:5).

This summons to work was coupled with a warning: "night is coming when no one can work" (Jn. 9:4b NRSV). Here duty is linked to urgency so that the disciples will avail themselves of their unique opportunity before it is too late. Remembering the hard stones so recently lifted against his life (Jn. 8:59),

Jesus looked ahead to the darkness of the cross already looming on the horizon and urged his bickering followers to get busy before that sunset.

His words about day and night were not a despairing lament, because as the analogy drawn from nature suggests, God gives as much light as he does darkness. The wise gratefully make the best use of the daytime hours to accomplish their work before sunset. In the spiritual realm, the disciples were to make the best possible use of Jesus' power as the bringer of God's new day while the opportunity was available rather than waiting until they were engulfed in the darkness that sought to extinguish his light (Jn. 11:9–10; 12:35).

Again we have confirmed the realism of Jesus. Every time that we quench the light, whether by apathy or hostility, night comes once more, even as it did at Calvary (Mk. 15:33). The church flees to the affluent suburbs and darkness falls on the inner city. Vested interests exploit Appalachia and "night comes to the Cumberlands."[3] Missionary concern subsides, and emerging nations turn to secularism for their founding principles. Then, as now, light is a vulnerable commodity in a world that loves darkness. How swiftly may a nation, or an institution, or an individual be plunged into darkness when they suppose that they can take daylight for granted.

Our Approach to Tragedy

The dialogue involving Jesus and his disciples provides us with rich insights regarding a response to human tragedy, but what is its relevance for us today? After all, we lack the power of Jesus to make the blind see. Nor, does it help the sightless to remind them of a miraculous healing that took place two thousand years ago. But before we dismiss the story as a remarkable exception to reality as we must live it, notice from its sequel how the restoration of one man's sight immediately raised a momentous issue for everyone with whom he came in contact, forcing a choice that went to the very heart of their outlook on life.

In gaining the one thing he needed most, the blind man seemed to have lost everything else as a result. Gone was his vocation as a professional beggar since that role was based on his handicap (Jn. 9:8). His neighbors were confused (Jn. 9:9), his parents were intimidated (Jn. 9:22), and his religious leaders were exasperated (Jn. 9:34), all because the one who healed him was controversial (Jn. 9:16, 24, 29). Now that he could see for the first time, there was nowhere to go. He was not welcome at work or home or community. Furthermore, he had never seen Jesus and did not know where he was (Jn. 9:12). So Jesus took the initiative to find him and offer a second miracle (Jn. 9:35), this time not of physical sight but of spiritual insight (Jn. 9:38). Having learned how disillusioning it can be to see the world for what it really is, the man now learned how illuminating it can be to see Jesus for who he really is.

In commenting on this strange turn of affairs, Jesus pointed out that every person, not just one poor beggar, is faced with a choice between blindness and sight (Jn. 9:39). Those who are open to new light from God such as he was attempting to bring (Jn. 1:4, 9) would be given spiritual insight, but those who shut their eyes to "the light of the world" (Jn. 9:5 NRSV) would become spiritually blind. The key difference is whether or not we look at life through eyes of faith (Jn. 9:35–37). That is, are we truly receptive to God's new day launched by Jesus, daring to believe that the best is yet to be

(1 Jn. 3:2)? When we pray and worship, are we eager for divine surprises, or are we so bound by religious traditionalism that we are captive to the status quo? Do we read Scripture with the conviction of John Robinson who was reported to have bade our religious forebears farewell as they set sail from Holland to America in 1620 with the words, "the Lord has more truth and light yet to break forth out of his holy word"?[4]

If our first challenge is to avoid becoming spiritually blind, our second challenge is to help others do the same. When cherished friend John Claypool wrote a ministerial memoir for a series called Journeys in Faith, he entitled it *Opening Blind Eyes*.[5] By this he meant offering a ministry of awakening that would help others become aware of who they really are instead of chasing self-images rooted in fantasy. Today, we live in a culture so saturated with propaganda that it is difficult to discern the true nature of reality. Some become so enamored with a political ideology that they filter every perception through those lenses. Others rally around an inherited way of life rooted only in custom. Think, for example, of how many centuries we refused to recognize the crying needs of women and children when their abuse was plain to see. Some people deliberately shut their eyes to tragic circumstances, and it can be dangerous indeed to try to open them, as the history of the civil rights movement vividly illustrates.

This deep conflict between the sightless who are eager for light and the seeing who prefer to shut their eyes to harsh reality permits no easy euphoria on our part. Any confidence that physical or spiritual tragedy can be overcome is not guaranteed by a neat theodicy with all the answers. Rather, it is nourished by a commitment to take the light of Jesus wherever darkness abounds. Even that kind of costly compassion provides no absolute assurances, however, for the night can engulf his light today just as it has done many times in the past. But even that darkness may become luminous with a costly compassion that redeems its despair. Midnight is not final in the realm of the spirit any more than it is in the realm of nature. To be sure, "night comes," but the early Christians discovered that, just as surely, the dawn will soon follow (Rom. 13:11–14). The crux is not to debate why we have both darkness and light but to decide in which element we will do our life's work and then open our eyes to its fullness.

Lillian Smith was reminded of the plight of her region as she pondered the artistry of Lamar Dodd:

> I looked at those colors: the clay with sun on it, the clay with night deep inside it, the clay with the terror—the old red-purple clay on which I had slipped a thousand times; all the treachery of it was in that painting, the stickiness, the poverty, the bleakness and the ordeal. And yet it was singing at the top of its voice. Man, singing down his terror: standing off and looking at his ordeal, picking it up in his mind and heart and his hands, and making it smaller than himself; and sometimes, turning it into a thing so beautiful and true and precious that for a thousand years after he is dead, other men will care for it.[6]

That is what Jesus was trying to teach us to do, to take the dark clay of tragedy and transform it into a thing of beauty. He worked such a miracle on more than a canvas as his light flooded the dark recesses of a blighted man's eyes and heart. A beggar born blind was made to see (Jn. 9:25)! Likewise, there are many things of God that we have never seen since the day we were born. Such blindness makes us spiritual beggars when we might be rich. If we will but bring our darkness to his healing touch, then the works of God will be made manifest in our lives as they were in his and, through us, in the lives of those on whom we let our light so shine (Mt. 5:16).

NOTES

1. Genesis 18:25; Exodus 20:5–6; Numbers 16:20–35; 2 Samuel 24:15–18; Jeremiah 31:29–30; Ezekiel 14:12–20; 18:19–32.

2. Martin Buber, *I and Thou*, trans. Walter Kaufmann (New York: Charles Scribner's Sons, 1970).

3. The phrase is suggested by the title of Harry M. Caudill's study of Appalachia, *Night Comes to the Cumberlands* (Boston: Little, Brown Co., 1963).

4. The various accounts of this event are discussed by William Wallace Fenn, "John Robinson's Farewell Address," *Harvard Theological Review* 13 (1920): 236–51.

5. John R. Claypool, *Opening Blind Eyes*, Journeys in Faith, ed. Robert A. Raines (Nashville: Abingdon, 1983). See especially pp. 81–93.

6. Lillian Smith, *The Journey* (New York: W. W. Norton & Co., 1965), 138.

21

THE DREAM DEFERRED

—➤•◄—

"A little while, and you will no longer see me, and again a little while, and you will see me." Then some of his disciples said to one another, "What does he mean by saying to us, 'A little while, and you will no longer see me, and again a little while, and you will see me'; and 'Because I am going to the Father'?" They said, "What does he mean by this 'a little while'? We do not know what he is talking about."

John 16:16–18 NRSV

Out of his bitterness as a Black poet during twentieth-century segregation, Langston Hughes posed one of life's haunting questions:

> What happens to a dream deferred?
>   Does it dry up
>   like a raisin in the sun?
>   Or fester like a sore —
>   And then run?
>   Does it stink like rotten meat?
>   Or crust and sugar over —
>   like a syrupy sweet?
>
>   Maybe it just sags
>   like a heavy load.
>
>   Or does it explode? [1]

Here is a question that thoughtful persons are asking with new urgency: What does happen to a "dream deferred"?

Pathology

In the public sector, we are being rudely jolted by the politics of postponement. The "New Frontier" of

John F. Kennedy evaporated like a mirage on the horizon, while the "Great Society" of Lyndon Johnson got lost in the jungles of Vietnam. Richard Nixon endured the embarrassment of our national honor called Watergate, while Jimmy Carter found himself frustrated by a strange new fanaticism in Iran. The peace dividend gained by Ronald Reagan as the Cold War with Communism ended was soon replaced by a war on terror in Iraq that divided our nation even as it drew us deeper into the volatile politics of the Middle East. Closer to home, spiraling debt and endless scandals compromised the character of Congress in ways that disfigure the American dream.

Nor is the church exempt from this pathology of hope that has infected the body politic. Baffled by statistical attrition and widespread unconcern, some timid souls seem content to retreat into the bright memories of bygone days, while others experiment with radically new forms of "cyberchurch" beyond the boundaries of institutional religion. Many who remain loyal to traditional expressions of the faith continue to build more buildings, launch more programs, and hire more staff, yet never seem to reach the Promised Land of their brightest vision.

This mood of wistful nostalgia is also an intensely private malady of our times. Beneath the smooth surfaces of accustomed routine, many individuals are quietly suffering from a shortage of dreams. A little boy stood with his mother at a busy street corner just after a shower had transformed the oil slick from passing cars into a paisley patchwork of swirling colors. "Look, Mommy!" he cried, "There's a rainbow gone to smash." And so it is for many who seem caught in a fate that offers only the options of boredom, rage, or despair. "Ne'er morning wore to evening but some heart did break."[2]

Our question, then, is both crucial and complex: What shall we do with our frustrated hopes? Many suppose that we must capitulate to the present moment, either in the bland optimism that this is the best of all possible worlds, or in the forlorn realism of Albert Camus who would try to think clearly and not hope anymore. Some would move toward a cynicism that degenerates into indifference, while others would choose the opposite extreme of a coercion that attempts to bend tomorrow to their hearts' desire. Are these our only options? As Hughes put it in his poem, do dreams deferred either "dry up" or "fester," "sag" or "explode"?

Jesus Christ faced this question at the center of his ministry and to it gave life's deepest answer. In the darkest moment of defeat, when the future seemed helpless to rescue the present, he compressed his controlling conviction into a single word—in English, a single phrase—that recurs seven times in the four verses of John 16:16–19. If we, like the disciples, can but understand what he meant by "a little while" (Jn. 16:18 NRSV), we shall discover the clue to a Christian understanding of deferred dreams.

Promise

The very phrase, "a little while," is a Hebrew expression that turns us to the Old Testament for background. Do you remember how the story of God's people got started? They were such a tiny band of rebels, a splinter group recruited out of Egypt, a people of midgets in the midst of giants as they themselves confessed (Num. 13:32–33). Their leader, Moses, failed to carry them into the Promised Land. When, by force of circumstance, they finally forged themselves into a nation, it became a bottleneck of heartbreak across which marched the mighty armies of Egypt and Mesopotamia as constant reminders that Israel was equally vulnerable from opposite directions.

In the face of such restrictions, what was the Israelite response? Would you believe that the nation sought to counter reality with a dream? Here was to be not just another earthly monarchy but a unique theocracy. Its king was to be God's son. Conceived as a venture in hope, Israel dared to believe that it had a monopoly on the most precious commodity of all—the future. Its light would shine to all the nations. It would be the pivot of human destiny, the controlling clue to human history. Those audacious Israelites dreamed such unthinkable dreams!

And what happened? A series of cruel events remorselessly shattered their dream to bits. The nation was driven to its knees. The monarchy was stripped of its royal prerogatives. The leadership was taken into exile. There, in the furnace of affliction, bewitched by Babylon with its revived civilization, how easy it would have been to say, "Here is reality! Look at these dazzling cities, look at that ziggurat skyscraper. And what do we have? Just a bad dream left to dry up 'like a raisin in the sun.'" With their hopes in shambles, the sensible conclusion to have drawn was that Israel had been left clinging to the promises of God much like the Old South was left holding Confederate bonds!

But the remnant refused to embrace the practical lessons of history. Reeling under intense pressure to abandon their promises—and the God who gave them —they determined rather to defer the dream, to hold in reserve for the future those realities that the present could not provide. Divine guidance for this decision is recorded in Isaiah 26, a passage closely parallel to our larger context: "Like a woman with child, who writhes and cries out in her pangs . . . so were we because of you, O Lord; we were with child, we writhed . . ." (Isa. 26:17–18 NRSV). Then God answered the travail of their tragedy: "Come my people, enter your chambers, and shut your doors behind you; hide yourselves for *a little while* until the wrath is past" (Isa. 26:20 NRSV). Why? Because the Lord is coming to deliver his people (Isa. 26:21).

What is the incredible truth of this passage? Not that things are getting better. Far from it. Things will get worse "until the wrath is past." But enter your hiding place and learn there the secret of the "little while," of "waiting on the Lord." Tomorrow may be dark, but the day-after-tomorrow belongs to God! Out of that crisis, when the whole dream could have exploded, Israel rose to shout, "We will not give up our promises. If history demands it, we will defer the dream, believing against belief that the future belongs to God!" And in "a little while," before a generation had fully passed, they began to return to Jerusalem and rebuild their battered hopes. Fulfillment was slow in coming as they waited for their expectations to be fulfilled, but they never gave up on their dreams!

Paradox

This unshakable confidence in the future was supremely validated in the life of a solitary individual who fulfilled the deepest dreams of Israel in his brief ministry. Jesus of Nazareth came preaching as the custodian of his nation's highest hopes. Reaching back into the Old Testament, he began to pluck the promises that hung there like buds in the conviction that they

242

were about to burst into full bloom. His whole ministry was essentially an explosion of dreams among a dispirited people. He radiated a powerful new enthusiasm that galvanized his followers. Hope blazed in the hearts of his disciples as they sped about on an urgent mission to Israel. With what majestic instancy God seemed to be breaking into the world of ordinary human existence.

But then, the storm clouds began to gather. Killers of the dream were determined to defend their vested interests in the status quo. Because Jesus had challenged the tired traditionalism of his day as lacking substance or spirit, a coalition of foes was driven to plot his death (Mk. 3:6). Soon his forerunner felt the blade, as Herod struck down John the Baptist for dreaming revolutionary dreams out of turn. Word reached Jesus that the "fox" sought his life as well (Lk. 13:31).

The crossroads had come all too quickly. Jesus withdrew for a time of retirement to rethink his threatened mission. Should he go home to tiny Nazareth as his family implored (Mk. 3:21, 31)? Should he pander to the multitudes who seemed ready to abandon his cause as a forlorn hope (Jn. 6:66)? Should he unsheathe the sword, as Zealots were eager for him to do, and try to coerce the dream (Mt. 11:12)? In this bitter exile of rejection, Jesus claimed for himself the faith of Israel in its most tenacious form. Out of spiritual Babylon he came with an invincible hope: he would not renounce the dream.

Brave son of fact that he was, Jesus did not dodge reality. With a shattering candor he solemnly announced to his disciples that "the Son of Man *must* suffer many things, and be rejected . . . and be killed . . ." (Mk. 8:31 RSV). Again and again he reminded them that the dream was going to die (Mk. 9:31; 10:33; 12:8; 13:14; 14:24). As our pivotal passage has it three times (Jn. 16:16, 17, 19), echoing the same refrain earlier in the Fourth Gospel (7:33; 12:35; 13:33; 14:19), "a little while," and they would see him no more. Jesus knew that his dream was vulnerable, that the present could so easily assert its power over the future.

But would that be the end of the affair, a dream defeated by the guardians of the religious establishment? No, with equal conviction Jesus announced that he would "rise again" (Mk. 8:31), that they would see him once more (Jn. 16:16, 17, 19), that the dream would not be destroyed even by his death. If disaster was sure to come with savage swiftness, victory would certainly follow with equal haste "after three days" (Mk. 8:31b RSV). The Fourth Gospel sharpened the paradox of tragedy and triumph in its twofold use of our key expression (Jn. 16:16–19):

> "A little while—and you will *not* see me."
> and again:
> "A little while—and you *will* see me."

There is a profound tension here between the two "little whiles" that are inseparable. On the one hand, his immediate future was utterly uncertain and defenseless against tragedy. Soon he would know the desolating loneliness of a cross. Soon his parched lips would cry, "My God, my God, why . . .?" (Mk. 15:34 NRSV) But on the other hand, his eventual future was utterly certain, as triumphant as the promises and power of God. His truth, crushed to earth, would rise again.

With these paradoxical convictions held firmly in balance, Jesus went forth to fulfill Isaiah 26. He entered his chamber of Gethsemane and drank the bitter cup. He hid himself for a little while in the noonday darkness of Calvary until the wrath was past. The dream was deferred for three days while he went into exile from the land of the living. Then, in a little while, before anyone expected it, he was back in the midst of his disciples. And the dream, so tragically but briefly postponed, at last began to come true as he said it would.

The resurrection of Jesus was, for the disciples, like a sunrise of faith after a three day eclipse. In their encounter with the risen Lord, the first Christians experienced God's vindication of the "little while" through which they had lived with him. In the light of the power unleashed by that event, can we really fault them for supposing that history was nearing its end, that Christ's glory would soon fill the skies, that all the promises of God were on the verge of fulfillment?

Indeed, the early church understood itself fundamentally as God's vanguard in a world without hope (Eph. 2:12), a colony of heaven (Phil. 3:20) in whose life the secrets of the future were hid. Paul even pictured the whole universe standing on tiptoe, waiting "with eager longing for the revealing of the children of God" (Rom. 8:19 NRSV). Christ was, in them, "the hope of glory" (Col. 1:27 NRSV). The future had already invaded the present. The church was living where the ages overlapped (1 Cor. 10:11).

But, once again, a shadow fell across this shining hope. Those who should have been most receptive to the gospel proved most resistant. No sooner did Rome view Christianity apart from Judaism than persecution erupted, as Nero and Domitian tried to stamp out the dream. Harassed, scattered, even martyred, the church was forced into an agonizing reappraisal of its hopes. As God seemed to delay, scoffers began to mock, saying,

"Where is the promise of his coming?" (2 Pet. 3:4 NRSV).
Exiled to the isle of Patmos, the prophet John
struggled once more with this age-long dilemma of a
dream deferred. In Revelation 6 he depicted the
martyrs under the altar "who had been slaughtered for
the word of God and for the testimony they had given;
they cried with a loud voice, Sovereign Lord, holy and
true, how long . . .?" (Rev. 6:9–10 NRSV). Then they were
"told to rest a *little longer* . . .," not while things were
getting better but "until the number would be
complete both of their fellow servants and of their
brothers and sisters who were soon to be killed as they
themselves had been killed" (Rev. 6:11 NRSV). Once more
the paradox: for a little while affairs would go from bad
to worse, but "The one who testifies to these things says,
'Surely I am coming soon'" (22:20 NRSV).

This tension between the "little while" of tragedy
and the "little while" of triumph is characteristic of
every section of the New Testament. Luke took the
one-generation hope of Mark and stretched it like a
canopy over the entire era of church history. The
Pastoral Epistles recognized that the Church might
have to live for a long time in a slowly changing world,
but they did not thereby abandon the ardor of the
Apostle Paul. The scriptural conviction is that one can
be both a realist and an enthusiast. The vocations of
serving the present and showing forth the future are
not mutually exclusive.

Patience

Here, then, in the biblical meaning of God's "little
while," is the answer to our question, "What happens to
a dream deferred?" It is a double-edge answer. On the
one hand, the ordeal is only for the short space of

"three days." Heartbreak does not last forever. The cross may be savage, but at least it is swift. As William Cullen Bryant put it, "The fiercest agonies have shortest reign."[3] On the other hand, travail will give way to triumph sooner than we suppose. The darkness may be all about us, but in "a little while" comes the morn. A dream deferred is not a dream destroyed!

This truth is especially applicable to our nation in the new millennium. America was also a land founded on the future. The Declaration of Independence was essentially a declaration of dreams: one nation with equality, freedom, and opportunity for all. Many have tried to be keepers of those dreams, to express in each new generation what the destiny of this nation was intended to be from its beginning. Yet, how hard we have found the fulfillment of our highest hopes. More than once we have been detoured into exile in a search for our "Promised Land."

A single illustration will suffice that is developed more fully elsewhere.[4] During the first century of our national history, the dark shadow of human slavery fell across the dream. For thousands of years it had been a permanent ingredient of the social structure. Countless Southern ministers waxed eloquent in its defense, convinced that so ancient an institution must be rooted in God's eternity and would remain so forever. But slavery belonged to the status quo; it did not belong to the dream. Some well-intentioned folk thought that they could end it without exile, travail, or a cross. They tried with words, with threats, even with legislation; they tried, but their dream would not come true. Then came the fearful struggle that ravaged our land and drenched the dream with blood.

For many, the Civil War was proof that slavery could

not be conquered. The South seemed ready to sacrifice its finest flower for the cause, while the North bitterly complained that the emancipation of illiterate Negroes was scarcely worth the price of such costly conflict. But when everyone seemed to think that war had destroyed the dream, one man knew that it had only been deferred. Abraham Lincoln was not unrealistic about all of the tragedy and heartbreak that surrounded him. The national agony revolted him more than it did those partisans yapping at his heels. Yet he knew that, even if tomorrow grew darker, the day-after-tomorrow belonged to the promise. If only the nation could hold on for "a little while," the dream would finally come true.

Matters did get worse before they got better. An assassin never let Lincoln live to enter his "Promised Land." Then came the terrors of Reconstruction, the anguish of rebuilding, the ordeal of change. But after "a little while," when sanity returned and grief subsided, the shackles of slavery never snapped shut again. The dream that had been deferred so many times at last came to pass. Today, there is not one among us who would advocate a return to that dreadful system. An evil which had seemed as permanent as the centuries finally evaporated like a myth, all because a tiny handful of patriots refused to give up on a dream deferred.

Each of us as Christians is called to live in that creative tension between the "now" and the "not yet" of dreams deferred, to trade the frustrations of the present for the fulfillments of the future. Our words of witness may fall on apathetic ears or be lost in the screams of a frenzied mob. We may be tempted to leap into the fray and fight with the enemies' weapons rather than to wait for the vindication of God. We may be forced to endure the desolating loneliness of that "little while" when truth seems buried in a tomb and there is no one to roll away the stone. But the dreaded "three days" is also an emblem of hope. For truth dies like a seed being cast into the soil, soon to burst forth and bear much fruit (Jn. 12:24). Tragedy is but the prelude to triumph. The tomb in which some try to bury truth becomes the womb in which fresh wisdom is born that will outlive its pallbearers. Time is on the side of truth. It is the counterfeit word, like the counterfeit coin, whose days are numbered.

NOTES

1. Langston Hughes, *The Panther and the Lash: Poems of Our Times* (New York: Alfred A. Knopf, 1967), 14.

2. Alfred Lord Tennyson, "In Memoriam A. H. H.," pt. 6, lines 7–8, *The Poems and Plays of Alfred Lord Tennyson* (New York: Modern Library, 1938), 297.

3. William Cullen Bryant, "Mutation," line 4, *American Poetry and Prose*, 3rd ed., Norman Roerster, ed. (Boston: Houghton Mifflin Co., 1947) 1:354.

4. See chapter 17 on "Learning the Lessons of Slavery."

22

THE SOUND OF SILENCE

—➤•◄—

Then the word of the LORD came to him, saying, "What are you doing here, Elijah?" He answered, "I have been very zealous for the LORD, the God of hosts; for the Israelites have forsaken your covenant, thrown down your altars, and killed your prophets with the sword. I alone am left, and they are seeking my life, to take it away."

He said, "Go out and stand on the mountain before the LORD, for the LORD is about to pass by." Now there was a great wind, so strong that it was splitting mountains and breaking rocks in pieces before the LORD, but the LORD was not in the wind; and after the wind an earthquake, but the LORD was not in the earthquake; and after the earthquake a fire, but the LORD was not in the fire; and after the fire a sound of sheer silence.

1 Kings 19:9b–12 NRSV

Preachers are supposed to be professional purveyors of words with a ready response to human need. Because we speak on the authority of Holy Scripture, we are expected to have an answer for every question, a solution for every problem, an explanation for every dilemma. So insatiable is the craving for certainty that many of our fastest growing churches are built around a pulpit that never hesitates or equivocates on any issue but rather proclaims non-negotiable positions without a hint of doubt or perplexity. In the popular stereotype, a preacher without a word to declare is like a pitcher without a ball to throw, a musician without an instrument to play, a soldier without a weapon to fire.

I found myself caught up in that very predicament when the daughter of my best friend, John Claypool, was diagnosed with acute leukemia. Because John was our pastor, he and his family had no pastor, a role they asked me to fill during the eighteen months that Laura Lue struggled to survive. At first, John sought to share the anguish of his little family of flesh with our larger family of faith. As he put it at the outset of his first such attempt, "see me this morning as your burdened and broken brother, limping back into the family circle to tell you something of what I learned out there in the darkness."[1] But as the end approached, and he often stayed up all night trying in vain to placate her savage pain while listening to her cry "Why?," he began to say to me in poignant lament, "Bill, I have no word for what is happening to Laura Lue."

A few weeks later I joined him in that heart-rending confession. Standing to preach her funeral sermon, I began by saying:

> I am chagrined to confess that to this critical hour I bring no ready word. . . . alas, I am filled not with sound but with silence as I stand mute before the mystery of the event that we here celebrate with such sorrow. For all of my training in sacred rhetoric I possess no semantic sleight of hand by which to bend our question marks into exclamation points before this hour is over. The Apostle Paul confessed that because we know in part we also prophesy in part. Having offered you in the past from that fragment of prophecy which is mine to declare, I must today bear witness to that part which has not yet been given me.[2]

But in that experience of wordlessness prompted by Laura Lue's death, I discovered that God can use silence as well as sound to heal our broken hearts.

Our Silence

Let me be honest with you about the puzzles of the human predicament. I do not know why nature is so capricious and even malevolent. I do not know why a cosmic cruelty seems to stalk so many innocent children. I do not know why the human nervous system has a built-in capacity to experience such excruciating pain. I do not know why my daughter's body was so buoyantly healthy and the body of John's daughter was so fatally flawed. And so I am left with questions that hang like fish hooks in the mind, all of our neat analogies about caterpillars, cocoons, and butterflies notwithstanding. Perhaps others can offer a clear explanation for the seeming unfairness of life, but I am not persuaded that our compulsive talkativeness will ever resolve such baffling quandaries.

To be sure, our futile stammerings are often relieved by the gracious outpouring of support mobilized to combat despair. Friends throng to lavish their affection upon our open wounds. From unexpected quarters come expressions of support in calls, messages, flowers, food, and a thousand acts of simple kindness. But soon the merciful blur of busyness prompted by crisis is stilled. Friends go home, flowers fade, dishes are returned, thank-you notes are written. Then, we are left with our emptiness, with our silence, with that ineffable void of solitude when someone we love is claimed by death.

Does this mean that, when we have nothing to say, we are bereft of hope, destined to be struck dumb with no language but a cry? Far from it! In our companionship with silence we are surrounded by one of the most eloquent modes of expression ever known. To instance: silence may be sullen, even ominous, as when a crowd gathers outside a despot's chambers to convey its grievances. Silence may be sinister, as when a thief stalks his prey along a lonely pathway. Silence may be shallow, as when listening to a vacant mind chattering away with nothing useful to say. Silence may be comic, as when a humorist pauses before delivering the punch line. Silence may be ecstatic, as when two lovers at a loss for words have only symbolic acts by which to express their affection. Mozart was once asked to identify the most beautiful moment in music. "The pauses," he replied, those momentary interludes of silence when sound can work its magic in the chamber of the heart. Silence is at once a potent yet perplexing form of speech.

God's Silence

With all of its versatility, is silence ever a way to encounter God? For some theologians, such a question borders on blasphemy. Divine revelation, they insist, comes only by the spoken word. But is it so? Or can the God who often conveys himself to us through audible speech also come to us in the brooding silence? Is there a speechless profundity that says more than all the half-formed words that stick in our throats? Perhaps we could learn to cope with silence, with the utter absence of meaningful words, if we knew it to be the silence of God!

The very Bible that is often called "the Word of God" provides rich resources for understanding the limits even of sacred utterance. It speaks not only of the superficial silence into which the wicked and ignorant lapse but also of that profound silence that belongs only to God. Three passages depict this dimension in Father, Son, and Holy Spirit so as to give us, as it were, the basis for a trinitarian theology of silence.

(1) At a critical moment in the history of Israel, Elijah challenged the prophets of Baal to a contest in order to contend for the supremacy of Yahweh. No sooner was victory in his grasp, however, than he was sent running to the wilderness by a wrathful Jezebel where he despaired of life itself (1 Kings 19:10). There at Horeb, the mount of God, the prophet who had called down fire from heaven on Mt. Carmel learned something new about God: "And, behold, the Lord passed by, and a great and strong wind rent the mountains, and brake in pieces the rocks before the Lord; but the Lord was not in the wind: and after the wind an earthquake; but the Lord was not in the earthquake: and after the earthquake a fire; but the Lord was not in the fire: and after the fire a still small voice" (1 Kings 19:11–12 KJV). The Hebrew original is even more surprising: the "still small voice" is better translated by the New Revised Standard Version as "a sound of sheer silence." After all of the clamor subsided, Elijah had to negotiate an eerie stillness so still that it could be heard.

B. F. Westcott has commented on this spiritual pilgrimage which we are all invited to make from Mt. Carmel to Mt. Horeb, from the God of sound and fury to the God of sheer silence:

> "earth's children cling to earth" . . . longing for some visible system which shall "bring all heaven before their eyes," for some path to the divine presence along which they can walk by sight . . . who shrink from the ennobling responsibility of striving with untiring effort to hold communion with the unseen and the eternal . . . who are required to listen like Elijah on the lonely

mountain, when the thunder of the earthquake is stilled and the violence of the fire is spent, for the still small voice. [3]

(2) "Jesus came . . . preaching" is the way that the record of his ministry begins (Mk. 1:14 RSV). How much he had to say! Never did truth find more perfect expression than in his word-pictures, called parables. As the Gospel of John realized, he was the Word become flesh, the self-disclosure of God in the life of his Son (Jn. 1:14). But finally, when his life reached its climactic moment, there was no sound to be heard from his lips. An ancient prophet of the Exile had already provided an appropriate description of that wordless event: "He was oppressed, and he was afflicted, yet he did not open his mouth; like a lamb that is led to the slaughter, and like a sheep that before its shearers is silent, so he did not open his mouth" (Isa. 53:7 NRSV). Pilate marveled at that magisterial silence but could not fathom its depths (Jn. 19:9–10).

What does it mean, that awful silence of the cross when, as the spiritual puts it, he uttered not a "mumbling word"? Does it not mean that God was never more eloquent than in that moment when he had nothing to say? Does it not mean that even the silence of unimaginable suffering may be the silence of God? Does it not mean that there is a divine silence interpreted, not by word, but by love in which we can find strength to face even death?

(3) Finally, in that remarkable eighth chapter of Romans, Paul grappled with the groanings of the whole creation. And what was his deepest insight? "Likewise the Spirit helps us in our weakness; for we do not know how to pray as we ought, but that very Spirit intercedes

with sighs *too deep for words.* And God, who searches the heart, knows what is the mind of the Spirit, because the Spirit intercedes for the saints according to the will of God" (Rom. 8:26–27 NRSV). Incredible as it may seem, the apostle dared to suggest that there are times when even the Spirit of God chooses to say nothing, that there is a depth of anguish that leaves the heavenly family speechless in the face of the human predicament.

At the very least this passage makes clear that God understands and that he cares, but surely much more. Can the conclusion be avoided that God also experiences our silences and gathers them up into the great silence of his Spirit? Somehow the inexpressible groanings of Gethsemane belong to a cosmic struggle by which God is bringing a new creation into being at infinite cost to himself. Somehow God can be both above us in his sovereignty and within us in his suffering, for he is Lord both of sound and of silence.

Living with Silence

If divine reality can communicate with us in silence as well as in sound, then what may we say about the creative role of silence in rebuilding our battered hopes? The one who has taught an impulsive talker like me more about the ministry of silence than any other was Thomas Merton. Leaving behind a brilliant career in the world, he deliberately chose a vocation of solitude in a monastery near Louisville, Kentucky. Although he had much to say, his life was primarily a sacrament of the silence of God. Of those persons who share his secret he wrote:

> They do not speak. They do not pray aloud. . . .
> They are not busy with anything. They simply

enter into themselves, not in order to think in an analytical way, not in order to examine, organize, plan, but simply in order to be. They want to get themselves together in silence. They want to synthesize, to integrate themselves, to rediscover themselves in a unity of thought, will, understanding, and love that go beyond words, beyond analysis, even beyond conscious thought. They want to pray not with their lips but with their silent hearts and, beyond that, with the very ground of their being. [4]

And what happens when, in silence, we reach "the very ground of our being," when we enter the interior of the silent self and begin to pray, Speak, Lord, for thy servant listeneth, rather than Listen, Lord, for thy servant speaketh? (1 Sam. 3:8–10)? Then we begin to discover that God is in the depths of our solitude, that he "is able to do far more abundantly than all that we ask or think" (Eph. 3:20 RSV), that his grace is not limited to the words we are able to use. The Psalmist put it simply: "Be *still*, and *know* that I am God!" (Ps. 46:10 NRSV). Beyond all of our explanations of God waits God himself. Beyond all of our best verbalization, even in prayer, lies a seldom explored level of human passivity that permits the divine activity. As Isaiah put it: "In returning and rest you shall be saved; in *quietness* and in trust shall be your strength" (Isa. 30:15 NRSV).

Now we begin to glimpse the kind of silence that is sacred. Pico Iyer described it well when he commented that

silence is the tribute we pay to holiness; we slip off words when we enter a sacred space, just as we slip off shoes. A "moment of silence" is the highest honor we can pay someone; it is the point

257

at which the mind stops and something else takes over (words run out when feelings rush in). . . . Silence, then, could be said to be the ultimate province of trust: it is the place where we trust ourselves to be alone; where we trust others to understand the things we do not say; where we trust a higher harmony to assert itself. [5]

If silence is more than the absence of noise, if indeed it is "that enchanted place where space is cleared and time is stayed and the horizon itself expands,"[6] then is that kind of spiritual stillness not a denial of hope but precisely an affirmation of its immense potential? Wrote Thomas Merton: "The purest faith has to be tested by silence in which we listen for the unexpected, in which we are open to what we do not yet know, and in which we slowly and gradually prepare for the day when we will reach out to a new level of being with God. True hope is tested by silence in which we have to wait on the Lord in the obedience of unquestioning faith."[7] Paul put it simply: "Now hope that is seen is not hope. For who hopes for what is seen?" (Rom. 8:24 NRSV). We may reword the same principle, "Now hope that is *heard* is not hope. For who hopes for what is heard?" That is, anything that can be adequately put into words is, in some sense, already present and known; whereas, our hope is for a new order that we have not even begun to name!

Some of the most significant changes affecting our existence take place in silence. The gravitation that keeps us earthbound comes unawares and is neither seen nor heard. The tides churn in upon our shores in obedience to silent forces. Tiny sprouts grow to become huge oaks without a whisper. Massive clouds move about without the slightest swish of sound. So it is with broken hearts. Not with many words but in fellowship with the divine silence do we discover the strength to cope with our brokenness.

> How silently, how silently
> The wondrous gift is giv'n!
> So God imparts to human hearts
> The blessings of his heav'n.[8]

Although the suggestive symbolism of the last book in the Bible has often furnished comfort in time of distress, one text from Revelation is seldom claimed when words fail us: "When the Lamb opened the seventh seal, there was silence in heaven for about half an hour" (Rev. 8:1 NRSV). This remarkably dramatic passage depicts the final disclosure of human destiny, the opening of the book of life with the names of those who will live forever. Before such a momentous issue is resolved, however, the heavenly hosts are hushed in awe and dread. One expositor has commented: "Heaven, hitherto resonant with voices, now holds its peace: neither Elder nor Angel offers a word of explanation; there is neither chorus of praise nor cry of adoration . . . no thunders issue from the Throne. This silence does not spell a cessation of the Divine workings, but a temporary suspension of revelation."[9]

I shall never forget that Saturday afternoon when I sat with my wife in the Claypool's family room at the foot of the stairs while the parents gathered around Laura Lue for a final farewell. When the end came at sunset, an indescribable silence settled about the house. Earlier in the day, and so often before, I had heard from the upstairs those muffled sobs of pain and the heavy footfalls of parents racing to the bedside. But now the sounds of suffering were stilled. And I knew that I would never again hear a little girl's laughter coming down those stairs or the dancing steps of a young lady ready for her first date. And so I tested the silence that day to see if it could be endured.

The silence lasted "for about half an hour" as the family said their goodbyes. When they came down, there was really nothing that I could say to them. Except that the seemingly endless half hour of silence is in heaven, too. I learned that afternoon that even the most heartbreaking silences could be endured. For the silence belongs to God.

NOTES

1. John Claypool, *Tracks of a Fellow Struggler: How to Handle Grief* (Waco: Word Books, 1974), 26.

2. William E. Hull, "The Sound of Silence," (sermon, Crescent Hill Baptist Church, Louisville, KY, January 13, 1970), 3. The present sermon is an adaptation for more general use of the earlier sermon with this same title.

3. Brooke Foss Westcott, *Christus Consummator* (London: Macmillan, 1887), 45.

4. Thomas Merton, "Creative Silence," *The Baptist Student*, February, 1969, 19.

5. Pico Iyer, "The Eloquent Sounds of Silence," *Time*, January 25, 1993, 74.

6. Iyer, "The Eloquent Sounds of Silence," 74.

7. Merton, "Creative Silence," 21.

8. Phillips Brooks, "O Little Town of Bethlehem," stanza 3, *The Baptist Hymnal*, ed. Wesley L. Forbis (Nashville: Convention Press, 1991), #86.

9. Henry Barclay Swete, *The Apocalypse of St. John* (Grand Rapids: Wm. B. Eerdmans, 1951 reprint of the Third Edition of 1909), 106.

PART FIVE

---→▸•◂←---

MENDING THE BROKEN CENTER

Things fall apart; the centre cannot hold;
Mere anarchy is loosed upon the world, . . .
The best lack all conviction, while the worst
Are full of passionate intensity.

William Butler Yeats, "The Second Coming"

We live in a time of fragmentation when the cohesiveness of our culture is threatened by competing factions. Though long a nation of immigrants, we once enjoyed a common language and religious heritage, but now the newcomers to our shores bring with them a Babel of tongues and increasingly diverse faith traditions. Our politics have become more partisan, our dialogue more polemical, as special interest groups press their single issue agendas in uncompromising fashion. As one observer put it, the glue is gone that held us together. The U. S. motto, *e pluribus unum,* calls us to become "one out of many," but at present the *pluribus* seems to have overwhelmed the *unum.*

Does the Christian faith have anything constructive to contribute to the quest for cohesiveness in these contentious times? Do those reconciling realities that are able to overcome our enmity with God and neighbor have the potency to mitigate the rancor that divides our world into warring camps? The Apostle Paul was convinced that God has acted to "reconcile to himself all things, whether on earth or in heaven" (Col. 1:20 NRSV); that in Christ "all things cohere," or "find their unity" (Col. 1:17 AT); and that the church is to make all of this known to "rulers and authorities" no matter

261

how exalted they seem to be (Eph. 3:10 NRSV). These audacious claims are an ancient way of saying that the gospel is not only personal and social but cosmic in scope, hence its message of redeeming love is to be addressed to all of our hostilities no matter how widespread and entrenched they may be (Eph. 2:11–22).

The sermons in this section address a wide range of animosities that fester in our world, especially since the terrorist attacks of September 11, 2001. I begin closer to home with the kind of pluralism that can quickly harden into polarization, then look at how these same kinds of antagonisms vex the entire global village. Unfortunately, even tragically, religion is playing a major role in many of our conflicts by providing theological justification for outright hatred, thus I end with a look at how faith could become so toxic. That is a somber note on which to conclude a book of sermons, but we live in troubled times. Still, there is hope if only we can find it and provide a secure home in which it may flourish.

23

LET THEM GROW TOGETHER
—→►•◄←—

He told another story. "God's kingdom is like a farmer who planted good seed in his field. That night, while his hired men were asleep, his enemy sowed thistles all through the wheat and slipped away before dawn. When the first green shoots appeared and the grain began to form, the thistles showed up, too.

The farmhands came to the farmer and said, 'Master, that was clean seed you planted, wasn't it? Where did these thistles come from?'

He answered, 'Some enemy did this.'

The farmhands asked, 'Should we weed out the thistles?' He said, 'No, if you weed the thistles, you'll pull up the wheat, too. Let them grow together until harvest time. Then I'll instruct the harvesters to pull up the thistles and tie them in bundles for the fire, then gather the wheat and put it in the barn.'"

Matthew 13:24–30 MSG

What we call the Parable of the Wheat and the Tares (Mt. 13:24–30) is a little story that Jesus told, based on first century Palestinian farm life, about what to do with some weeds that threatened to ruin a crop. He did not tell such tales to entertain his hearers but as a way to communicate with them in a context of bristling controversy. Indeed, the seven parables clustered in Matthew 13 were in response to the mounting conflicts recorded in Matthew 11–12.

To skeptics with closed minds that made it hard for them to give his message a hearing, Jesus reached for fresh images, clear comparisons, even curious riddles in an effort to prompt them to think in different categories. This account, for example, is full of surprises, many of them deliberately enigmatic despite the fact that they are rooted in ordinary experience. So beware: if this sermon is true to the strategy of Jesus, it will seek to slip up on your blind side, breech your defenses, and provoke you to ponder some challenging perspectives that you might prefer to ignore. We begin, as did Jesus, with a strange story that is not easily understood or forgotten.

The Story

The plot seems simple enough: a farmer sowed his field with seed to prepare for another crop of grain (Mt. 13:24). But no sooner had this work been completed than an adversary slipped in under cover of darkness to sow bad seed among the good (Mt. 13:25). No clue is given as to why a neighboring farmer would do such a dastardly deed, except to identify him as an "enemy," for the ultimate sources of such animosity are hidden deep within the human heart. We are left with the sober realization that even our best efforts can be under-mined by spite, jealousy, and ambition when least expected. There is a mystery to human meanness that defies any explanation.

In order to grasp the cunning of this dark deed, we need to identify the kind of bad seed that was scattered on top of the good. It was not "tares," as traditionally translated, which is a kind of vetch. Rather, the Greek word here (*zizania*) referred to bearded darnel, which we sometimes call cockle, thistle, or cheat. The problem is that it cannot be distinguished from wheat in the blade but only in the ear after it has ripened enough to make a head which becomes poisonous from hosting a fungus. If harvested and ground together with the wheat, the flour is ruined, and therefore, the whole crop is lost. Because the Hebrew name for darnel was derived from a word meaning "to commit adultery" or "to play the harlot," it was thought of as degenerate or illegitimate wheat.[1]

With this clarification we are able to grasp the dilemma that confronted the farmer once his crop was discovered to be corrupted. The field hands wanted to pull up the wretched weeds immediately so as to keep the field clean and thereby protect their labors (Mt. 13:28). But the owner realized that, by now, the buried roots of the wheat and the weeds had become so entangled with each other that to yank out one would uproot the other as well. Concerned not for appearances but for a maximum yield from all their efforts, he wisely decided, "Let both of them grow together until the harvest" (Mt. 13:30 NRSV). Then everything could be reaped and the separation take place in such a way that the weeds would be bundled up and burned as fuel while the wheat would be gathered into the barn. To be sure, this approach required more time and patience on the part of everyone, but the results would be well worth the wait.

The Setting

Why would Jesus tell such an earthy story and liken it to the grandest theme of his gospel, "the kingdom of heaven" (Mt. 13:24)? For one thing, his parable warned against the dangers of a premature separation between good and evil that the Judaism of his day was attempting on every hand. The Pharisees practiced a rigid code of conduct that built a wall of exclusion between them and those less observant of religious law. The Essenes relocated to a desolate wilderness so that they would not be defiled by what they considered a corrupt priesthood in Jerusalem. The Zealots were agitating for a decisive break with Rome even if it meant all-out war with a fight to the finish. Because of this separatist mentality, many expected that a primary role of the Messiah would be to gather a purified remnant of the righteous, but here was Jesus consorting with publicans and sinners, harlots and centurions— letting bad weeds infest good wheat!

Closer to home, John the Baptist had prepared for the ministry of Jesus by picturing the coming Messiah with a winnowing fork in his hand that would separate the wheat from the chaff so that the latter could be burned "with unquenchable fire" (Mt. 3:12 NRSV). Arrested for these fiery denunciations and facing imminent execution, John sent his disciples to Jesus with the wistful query, "Are you the one who is to come, or are we to wait for another?" (Mt. 11:3 NRSV). This was but a polite way of asking, Why are you letting me rot in prison without lifting a finger against Herod who may kill me any day? And the answer of Jesus implied in this parable is, "I know you have enemies. I have them too. But, in the mercy of God, it is not yet time for the unquenchable fire to fall. Judgment tarries, but God is patient. Time is on his side, if not on ours. He is willing to wait for a better day."

Closest to home, a terrible weed was growing within the innermost disciple band. Judas seemed to have Zealot sympathies, which would have put him at the opposite extreme from a Roman collaborator like Levi. Surely the core of followers needed to be purged of its poisons if the movement was to have any integrity. But if Judas were suddenly uprooted and cast out, who might leave with him because their "roots" were entangled with his? James and John were called "Sons of Thunder" (Mk. 3:17 NRSV), which suggested an impatient itch to take militant action, and a Simon other than Peter was called the Zealot (Lk. 6:15). Rather than satisfying those who may have wanted Judas expelled, or angering others who may have shared his misguided dreams, our parable explains why Jesus stuck with him to the very end. After love's last appeal was rejected in the upper room (Mt. 26:20–25), Judas finally excluded himself from the twelve by an act of betrayal in which none of the others joined him.

The Significance

In light of these challenges to his ministry from without and within, what new insights did Jesus seek to plant in the minds and hearts of his hearers by telling this little story? Let us look at four of them:

First, inclusivism is a hard sell, and its foes abound on every hand. Jesus sought to sow the seeds of the kingdom on a field as wide as the world (Mt. 13:38), to universalize the grace of God by making it available to every person regardless of race, gender, ideology, or nationality. But the custodians of the status quo felt so threatened by outsiders that they restricted their legacy to only one small group, arbitrarily limited by ancestry, willing to embrace a common culture. And so Jesus warned, "My kind of kingdom makes enemies. If you follow me, expect opposition (Mt. 11:12). Realize that a lot of weeds come with the turf. There is no way for me to broadcast the good seed of unconditional inclusivism without provoking those who scatter the bad seed of narrow exclusivism." To this day, most people prefer sameness to otherness. They find more security in homogeneity than in heterogeneity. Especially in times of tension, they would rather circle the wagons and huddle up with their own kind than to risk openness to those who are different.

Second, in this kingdom under siege, often driven underground like seed planted in soil, it is difficult to tell friend from foe, for weeds may come disguised as wheat. The devil never likes to be noticed, but works in the darkness as an imitator of God, sowing seed that grow into counterfeit disciples. Because authenticity cannot be determined until their fruits are known (Mt. 7:16–20), it is always dangerous to attempt premature separation, which is precisely why it is so difficult to be a zealous reformer. As Robert Farrar Capon put it provocatively:

> . . . the enemy turns out not to need anything more than negative power. He has to act only minimally on his own to wreck havoc in the world; mostly, he depends on the forces of goodness, *insofar as he can sucker them into taking up arms against the confusion he has introduced,* to do his work. . . . he simply sprinkles around a generous helping of darkness and waits for the children of light to do the job for him. Goodness itself, if it is sufficiently committed to plausible, right-handed, strong-arm methods, will in the very name of goodness do all and more than all the evil ever had in mind.[2]

Third, the presence of so much ambiguity, even in our most idealistic impulses, calls for the practice of patience to give people and ideas a chance to prove themselves. As the Jewish teacher Gamaliel wisely counseled when religious hotheads wanted to stamp out early Christianity, ". . . let them alone; because if this . . . undertaking is of human origin, it will fail; but if it is of God, you will not be able to overthrow them"

(Acts 5:38–39 NRSV). Paul reduced this reasoning to an axiom: "Pass no premature judgment" (1 Cor. 4:5, NEB). As we might put it, Live and let live! Wait and see! Since anything new can seem suspicious, at least give it the benefit of the doubt. Our story takes this practice of patience one step further by suggesting that we learn to tolerate differences even when they seem to be the work of an enemy. In such cases, we may need to buy time and put up with what is bad for the sake of a greater good. Our options do not always involve a clear-cut choice between black and white; sometimes, like wheat and bearded darnel, both sides seem to be a tattletale grey.

Fourth, none of this means that Jesus encouraged an easy relativism that was indifferent to moral reality. Both the story and even more the interpretation (Mt. 13:36–43) come to a climax at harvest time when there will be an absolute separation between the wheat and the weeds with the former destined for the barn and the latter for the fire. This is but a vivid way of saying, "Do not judge" (Mt. 7:1 NRSV) but let God do the judging (Rom. 12:19) for, as the Parable of the Sheep and the Goats makes clear (Mt. 25:31–46), the One who knows the secrets of every heart renders verdicts that are very different from our own. Meanwhile, as we await that final reckoning, we are to "let *both* of them grow *together* until the harvest" (Mt. 12:30 NRSV). Only then will the fruit of every life be fully known; meanwhile, the kingdom of heaven must make its way on earth as an embattled reality contending with alien kingdoms for the human heart.

The Summons

These insights may be given the widest possible

application because, as the interpretation of our story explains, "the field is the world" (Mt. 13:38 NRSV). I have selected three areas in which the truths of this strange story are especially relevant today:

(1) *The individual.* When we experience a transforming encounter with Christ and are ushered by him through the door to the kingdom of heaven, it is easy to be gripped by a certitude that approaches perfectionism. Having found ultimate answers to the riddle of existence, we yearn to remake all of life in conformity to our new-found convictions. But once we try to implement those impulses, two problems arise. In regard to ourselves, certainty easily gives rise to over-confidence, and over-confidence to pride, and pride to arrogance as if our way is the only way. In regard to others, this sense of superiority then leads to intolerance of those who resist our claims, and we end up viewing them as the "enemy." In demonizing anyone who gets in the way of our holy crusade, the poisonous weeds of polarization begin to grow from the good seed of the gospel that was sown in our hearts.

One of the greatest threats to human survival today is a creeping fundamentalism in the culture of every major world religion that would absolutize its understanding of good and evil to the point of justifying violence in the name of the sacred. Whether it be the ultra-Orthodox Jew who gunned down Prime Minister Yitzhak Rabin in Israel, or the Protestant and Catholic Christians who mercilessly murdered one another in Northern Ireland, or the Shiite and Sunni Muslims who daily terrorize each other in Iraq, they are all united with the field hands of old in saying, "Let's pull up and destroy the bad weeds we don't like in order to protect the good wheat that we have." And it all sounds so sensible, even godly, until we realize how many weeds of bigotry, prejudice, and hatred are sown by such misguided zealotry. There are enough weeds even in the best of us, as Paul confessed in Romans 7, that we dare not reach for the winnowing fork lest it pierce our own hearts.

Aleksandr Solzhenitsyn experienced evil of unimaginable horror in Stalin's Gulag and devoted his life to exposing its atrocities; yet he came to see that the issues were not so simple:

> . . . it was only when I lay there on rotting prison straw that I sensed within myself the first stirrings of good. Gradually it was disclosed to me that the line separating good and evil passes not through states, nor between classes, nor between political parties either—but right through every human heart—and through all human hearts. This line shifts. Inside us, it oscillates with the years. And even within hearts overwhelmed by evil, one small bridgehead of good is retained. And even in the best of all hearts, there remains . . . an unuprooted small corner of evil.[3]

(2) *The nation.* Each presidential campaign permits the mass media to engage in a year-long orgy of divisiveness on the theory that everybody loves a good fight. Political gurus urge their candidates to disparage opponents so relentlessly that whoever is elected will be discredited before taking office. When the results are in, the states are then divided into red or blue and every voter made to feel like a winner or a loser. Pundits peer into the future and predict a massive realignment of America into conservative and liberal camps that will continue to oppose each other ever more bitterly over

a whole range of irreconcilable issues. Some even celebrate this disuniting of America that leaves us with plenty of *pluribus* but not much *unum.*

Is it wise to divide up our country into a party of wheat and a party of weeds? Every day I deal with those who have nothing but utter contempt for "the other side." The issue here is not which political candidate you prefer but the simple fact that only one of them can be elected to lead us all. Grateful that we are offered a free choice, the question remains whether such acrimonious campaigning prepares us to unite in support of the candidate who prevails. To the victor belongs the spoils, we say, but does it make our nation stronger for those who voted for the winning candidate to disenfranchise those who voted for the losing candidate? The wisdom of our story is, "let them grow together" (Mt. 13:30 MSG)—even if each side thinks that it is the wheat, and the other side is the weeds! The two-party system has served our nation well throughout its history. The majority party in office needs the critical scrutiny and informed dissent of the minority party to protect it from the intoxication with power that is the Achilles heel of every politician.

(3) *The Church.* You doubtless know that every major denomination in America has been engaged in outright civil war over the past generation, none more so than Southern Baptists. At the root of the conflict is an unwillingness to tolerate some of the sharp differences that characterize contemporary life. Thus we have the culture wars with their pitched battles over such issues as abortion, homosexuality, and social welfare. Or the theological wars over biblical inerrancy, evolution, and the role of women. Or the ideological wars that pit conservative hardhats against liberal eggheads, rural

traditionalists against urban innovators, and older preservationists against younger progressives. When this volatile mix of issues is seized upon by religious absolutists, the predictable result is polarization. Nowhere is there a greater tendency to divide all of life into wheat and weeds than in a church with an authoritarian mindset. Remember the medieval Crusades, the religious wars that wracked Europe after the Reformation, and the splintering of Protestantism into a thousand denominations once it reached our shores.

To be sure, there are plenty of weeds in every church, superficial members who join only for the business contacts, or for the free babysitting, or for the use of facilities to hold their weddings and funerals. But where better for such "counterfeit Christians" to be? To uproot them only denies them the opportunity to hear and see a witness that might one day change their lives. The comment of Helmut Thielicke points to a better way:

> Must we not rather love, in order that in this very venture of love we may learn to realize that wheat is sown even in the most weed-ridden lives and that God is waiting and yearning for it to grow? Dostoevski once spoke this profound and unspeakably helpful word: "To love a person means to see him as God intended him to be." [4]

Do these applications, and the story on which they are built, imply that we are to be moral pacifists who fail to oppose evil until the weeds overwhelm us? No, "let *both* of them grow *together*" (Mt. 13:30 NRSV) is the imperative of our text. We are not to give up sowing good seed and let bad seed take the field. If we cannot eradicate evil in our kind of world, neither are we to let it choke out the good. Rather, we are to be busy growing an ever stronger faith that can more than hold its own even in a weed-choked field. Further, growing "together" rather than in isolation points us to a life of dialogue in creative coexistence with those who differ, however difficult that may prove to be.

After all, people are more than plants and, in the give and take of honest sharing, change can occur. Luther Burbank once remarked that "every weed is a potential flower."[5] All it needs is the right kind of crossbreeding and cultivation. Jesus offered the human weeds of his day the chance to plant their lives in the company of those who had joined him to scatter the good seed of the gospel. That is why it should be easy to get in the church but hard to get out: easy to be accepted because we are welcoming of all who respond to Christ's inclusive call; hard to be rejected because we are patient with those who allow weeds to grow in their lives. Instead of trying to decide what will happen to the weeds that never seem to change, let us trust that God will know best what to do with them in his own good time.

NOTES

1. For details see A. B. Bruce, *The Parabolic Teaching of Christ*, second edition (London: Hodder and Stoughton, 1887), 45–47.

2. Robert Farrar Capon, *The Parables of the Kingdom* (Grand Rapids: Zondervan, 1985), 102. Italics in the original.

3. Aleksandr I. Solzhenitsyn, *The Gulag Archipelago, 1918–1956: An Experiment in Literary Investigation*, III–IV, trans. Thomas P. Whitney (New York: Harper & Row, 1974), 2:615.

4. Helmut Thielicke, *The Waiting Father: Sermons on the Parables of Jesus* (New York: Harper & Brothers, 1959), 81.

5. Cited by Charles B. Templeton, *Life Looks Up* (New York: Harper & Brothers, 1955), 161.

24

THE MYSTERY OF MISSIONS

---+>•◄+---

These twelve Jesus sent out with the following instructions: "Go nowhere among the Gentiles, and enter no town of the Samaritans, but go rather to the lost sheep of the house of Israel."

Matthew 10:5–6 NRSV

There is a mystery at the center of the Christian mission that originated in the ministry of its founder. Ultimately, this global enterprise cannot be supported with confidence, even though the Apostle Paul and a host of successors were passionate missionaries, unless it is consistent with the intentions of the Master. The problem arises from the fact that Jesus never left his native land.[1] Nor did he win a growing constituency as his work progressed. In fact, he ended his efforts with only a handful of followers who fled the cross leaving him as a lonely remnant of one. Granted that Jesus was a great teacher, a powerful healer, a courageous martyr, but was he in any sense a missionary to the wider world?

The mystery deepens when we ask whether he failed at missions because he never even tried. To be sure, at the very end of his earthly sojourn, the risen Christ issued the Great Commission (Mt. 28:19–20), which was preceded by predictions that his disciples would be "dragged before governors and kings . . . as a testimony to them and the Gentiles" (Mt. 10:18 NRSV), and that the gospel would be preached "throughout the world, as a testimony to all the nations" (Mt. 24:14 NRSV). But in this same gospel he charged the Twelve, "Go nowhere among the Gentiles, and enter no town of the

Samaritans, but go rather to the lost sheep of the house of Israel" (Mt. 10:5–6 NRSV). Later, Jesus told a Syro-Phoenician woman that he himself "was sent only to the lost sheep of the house of Israel" (Mt. 15:24 NRSV). Is this why he refused to adopt Jewish missionary practices but instead scathingly denounced the scribes and Pharisees for traversing "sea and land to make a single convert" (Mt. 23:15 NRSV)?

The issue is especially acute in the Gospel of Matthew where these seemingly pro-missionary and anti-missionary passages stand side by side in equal strength. There can be no appeal to the need for harmonizing different gospels since both tendencies are emphasized in the same gospel. But that, in itself, is a prime clue in our search for a solution, for the First Evangelist was able to harmonize both sets of texts in his own thinking. Somehow, he came to understand the lesson we must learn: that to go only to the lost sheep of the house of Israel is consistent with the command to go and make disciples of all nations. Once we grasp that paradox, we solve the mystery of missions. But more: only as we obey the former injunction are we prepared to fulfill the latter. Therefore, let us ponder the reasons why Jesus insisted that the way to the whole world started in tiny Israel, that the route to universality began with particularity.

The Need of the Disciples
The first suggestion is that this sequence of priorities was exactly what his fledgling disciples needed. In the face of their inherited prejudices, which were flagrant enough for all to see, Jesus did not talk in grandiose terms about "winning the world." For "the world" is finally an abstraction referring to an amorphous

aggregation of social groups; whereas, Jesus wanted to establish the reign of God in the only real world of the spirit that existed, which was in the hearts of living persons. Thus, he did not try to get his teaching adopted by the Sanhedrin or legislated by the Romans. Rather, "he took the slower, and in the long run perhaps the more effective, way of living the principles out before individual men and women, and then accepting these men and women as apprentices to that way of living."[2]

Within the circumscribed territory that Jesus used as a manageable laboratory for training in ministry, he demonstrated for his hotheaded disciples a revolutionary new spirit designed to teach them compassion at close-range. Strangely enough, this education began with a strategy of silence. Jewish thought at that time was filled with belittling references to the Gentiles. In the messianic age to come, their fortunes would be reversed, and at best, they would become subservient to their Jewish masters while, at worst, they would perish together in hell. There is no hint in the Gospels that Jesus ever resorted to such invective. Any trace of revenge or retribution against the Gentiles was missing from his message.[3] Despite the centrality of circumcision as the key practice in the Jewish hereditary religion, Jesus never once advocated this rite that arbitrarily excluded all Gentiles by virtue of birth (Jn. 7:22). Instead of familiar references to the ancestral God of Abraham and David, he spoke of a universal Father "in heaven" (Mt. 5:45; 6:9). An entirely new climate free of provincialism, contempt, and vengeance was created by Jesus' refusal to make derogatory statements about the Gentiles, despite the fact that he was constantly badgered to do so (Mk. 12:13–17).

Into this creative vacuum, cleansed of its venom,

Jesus set the boundless grace of God. Judaism was a religion with barriers that Jesus pointedly ignored. His sweeping assertion, "I have come to call not the righteous but sinners" (Mk. 2:17 NRSV) demonstrated the true missionary spirit, not by how he moved *outward*, but by how he moved inward. "Neither to the sick who were segregated on cultic and ritual grounds, nor to the prostitutes and sinners who were boycotted on moral grounds, nor to the tax-collectors who were excluded on religious and nationalist grounds, did he refuse contact, help, and fellowship."[4]

Inevitably this new boldness that breached barriers erected within Judaism was tested beyond that society not only in relation to "half-breed" Samaritans but to outright Gentiles as well. We need to remember that, as a result of worldwide Roman conquest, foreigners were present everywhere in first-century Palestine, especially in Northeast Galilee, the Decapolis, and Syro-Phoenicia—all areas where Jesus worked. When he did encounter a Roman centurion (Mt. 8:5–10) or a royal court official (Jn. 4:46–54), a Samaritan (Jn. 4:1–42), or a Canaanite woman (Mt. 15:21–28), these outsiders were readily offered the same blessings of God that he was seeking to share with his own people. What this means is that almost every facet of the central issue of universality was fully present within the particularity of Israel; thus, Jesus did not need to go beyond this limited arena to apprentice his disciples in what was involved in becoming transcultural missionaries.

This example teaches us the powerful truth that we are not likely to develop universal compassion for the "Gentiles" unless and until we first develop particular compassion for our own "house of Israel." We frequently hear appeals to enlarge the scope of our outreach, all of which is well and good, but the danger is that we may succeed so well at loving the world in general that we never get around to loving anybody in particular. For example, we may glamorize foreign missionaries in their colorful dress and romanticize their overseas work in exotic cultures, all the while neglecting or ignoring the missionary imperatives that stare us in the face here at home. The only antidote for this expansive tendency, which, in the name of missions, pushes the real world beyond our reach, is to balance the need to *broaden* our vision with the need to *narrow* it to a workable focus.

At first glance, an emphasis on localism might seem to be "provincial." Some scholars have accused Jesus of a limitation in the understanding of his mission and assumed that he never intended to found a worldwide movement because of "parochialism" in the passages that we are examining. The whole point, however, is not an either/or by which Jesus opted for Israel to the exclusion of the Gentiles. Rather, he built the larger mission squarely on the smaller mission so as to ground it in sober realism.

I am convinced that nothing would do more to clarify our understanding of, and deepen our commitment to, international missions than for us actually to engage in that very kind of mission work right here at home. As with first-century Palestine, so with twenty-first century Birmingham: the "foreigners" are already here; the barriers are already up. At least in microcosm, we can find every problem that our overseas missionaries are up against without driving one-hundred miles from home. If we fail to become missionaries here in our American "Israel," then all our efforts around the world will rest on a theoretical foundation at best.

The Need of the Church

The second suggestion is that Jesus turned initially to his own people, not only because the disciples needed this ministry, but because "the lost sheep of the house of Israel" needed it as well. We begin to understand his concern by recognizing that this very description would sound shockingly contradictory to Jewish ears. For the phrase "house of Israel" (Mt. 10:6; 15:24) referred to the chosen people, the children of promise, the Old Testament people of God. This means that those whom we today would call "the *saved*," Jesus called "the lost"! The issue here was not so much individual salvation as it was a conviction that Jewish religion had "lost" its true sense of mission. Because the shepherds of God's flock had led the sheep astray, Jesus first sought to call those in the Old Israel back into the fold of service so that they might then join with his followers as the New Israel in ministering to a wider Gentile world.

Ironically, Jesus felt constrained to lodge this indictment in the Golden Age of Jewish missionary activity. Never before had zeal been more intense or success more gratifying. But the entire enterprise combined spiritual conversion with ethnic custom. Salvation was equivalent to naturalization; that is, becoming a believer was tantamount to becoming a Jew. Moreover, those unwilling to accept the rituals of ethnic affiliation, especially circumcision, were increasingly rejected as Israel's enemies. Palestine was beginning to fester with political passions that interpreted Judaism's highest mission as ridding the land of Roman tyranny by violent means, whether human or divine. The mood of many was influenced by a zealotism more interested in *killing* Romans than in *winning* them. The sheep had strayed so far without a shepherd (Mt. 9:36) that they were itching to wage a Holy War, to solve the "Gentile problem" with a sword, and to embrace Jesus only if he would consent to lead such a bloody crusade.

It was this fatal fusion of missionary service with national sovereignty that caused Jesus to denounce Pharisaic proselyting as hypocrisy (Mt. 23:15). But even though he categorically rejected every suggestion of warrior kingship as a legitimate expression of his ministry, he refused to give up on the misguided multitudes who flocked to him for help. Rather than making them his enemies because of their wayward-ness, and thereby repeating the mistake of his opponents, "he had compassion for them" (Mt. 9:36 NRSV) and so urged his disciples to call them back into the true fold that he had begun to reconstitute with a remnant of twelve (Mt. 9:35–10:7).

Reluctant as we may be to admit it, the primary group needing to be won to world missions may be found within our Baptist churches and denomination. The really great scandal in world missions is not how few of the lost have been won, but rather how few of the saved are doing anything about it! Actually, mission results among Southern Baptists have been remarkable considering that less than twelve percent of the denomination's membership are enrolled in any form of missionary education,[5] while only about five percent of church-related workers are engaged in a foreign mission vocation.[6] Although it is tragic to contemplate the multitudes without Christ, at least we can leave the fate of those who have never heard the gospel in the hands of an all-wise and merciful God. But as much cannot be said for those who have heard and done nothing about it. It was to those who had "heard" but "drifted" that the devastating question was asked, "how can we escape if we neglect so great a salvation?" (Heb. 2:3 NRSV).

Therefore, our mission always involves two fronts rather than one, not only calling the lost to salvation but also calling the saved to service. These two tasks are not competitive, as if the particularists are pitted against the universalists. Nor are they consecutive, as if one first wins the sheep and then the goats will follow. Rather, the two tasks are concentric, inreach to God's people providing a foundational core for outreach to the wider world.[7] As we win more of the church to its missionary imperative, we will win more of the world to Christ.

The Need of the Savior

My final suggestion is that the launching of a world mission was delayed until after Jesus universalized the faith of Israel by his death on the cross. A clue to this insight is provided by the fact that all positive references to missions during the ministry of Jesus are in the future tense (Mt. 10:18; 24:14). This is especially true of Matthew 8:11–12, which pictures Gentiles streaming into the Kingdom from every direction, but only in a future era yet to come. The Great Commission was not mandated until after Jesus' earthly life was over, because only then had the resurrection vindicated his struggle to purge religion of the provincialisms that contributed to his rejection.

As the Gospel of John repeatedly emphasizes, the "hour" to turn to the Gentiles did not arrive until after the cross was squarely faced (Jn. 12:20–27). For only at Calvary was salvation defined exclusively in terms of radical obedience and selfless love, which are no respecters of race or religion. During his earthly ministry, Jesus never explicitly annulled that elaborate system of legalism that was the main barrier to a universal mission, but even his Jewish followers came to realize that the law, in its separatist sense, was abrogated by his death on the cross (Gal. 3:13; Eph. 2:15; Col. 2:14). Jesus cherished no facile optimism that centuries of restrictive tradition would disappear in a day, but he did dare to believe that the breaking of his body and the shedding of his blood would finally expose the limitations of such a system. Once God confirmed this conviction by raising him from the dead and investing him with cosmic authority (Mt. 28:18), then, and only then, was he ready to announce that a way had been opened for all to accept this good news.

It is here that we plumb the depths of the mystery of missions. For we learn that Jesus laid the foundation for the greatest mission effort in human history even though he was not a missionary in the traditional sense. He did not win either the house of Israel or the Gentiles; instead, he died alone on a cross, forsaken by friend and foe alike. But there was a strange potency to that seeming tragedy, for by his death the grace of God was liberated for the Gentiles. In a profound sense this means that we are not ready to go into all the world until we have first been crucified with Christ (Gal. 2:20), not ready to bear much fruit among the Gentiles until we have first died to pride and prejudice and to the provincialisms that they foster (Jn. 12:20–25). It is relatively easy to launch a worldwide mission—Hitler did as much for Nazi Germany with an all-consuming passion. But Hitler was not willing to nail his mission to a cross, and so it perished as will ours unless, like Jesus, we first offer it to God in the Gethsemane of obedience at any cost (Mt. 26:36–46).

Finally, then, the mystery of missions is solved by the

paradox that, if our commitment is first purged by the crucifixion, it will then be empowered by the resurrection. The earthly Jesus clearly saw world missions as a future hope; not in some remote future, rather in the near future. In other words, for him missions belonged to a promised era of fulfillment that was coming soon, and he would have a crucial part in bringing it to pass. Nor will we get serious about missions until we truly believe that God wants a new day for our world, that such a transformation is possible, and that we can be agents of the needed change. After all, missions is the most audacious effort to remake the world ever attempted! It takes incredible power to produce worldwide change, but such power is available in the risen Christ if only we will claim it for our cause.

NOTES

1. This conclusion has been reached on the basis of careful geographic study by Albrecht Alt, *Where Jesus Worked: Towns and Villages of Galilee Studies with the Help of Local History* (London: Epworth, 1961).

2. T. W. Manson, *Only to the House of Israel? Jesus and the Non-Jews*, Facet Books: Biblical Series, 9 (Philadelphia: Fortress, 1964), 18.

3. Joachim Jeremias, *Jesus' Promise to the Nations*, Studies in Biblical Theology, 24 (London: SCM, 1958), 41–46.

4. Ferdinand Hahn, *Mission in the New Testament*, Studies in Biblical Theology, 47 (London: SCM, 1965), 30.

5. In 1992, before serious splintering began within the denomination, there were 614,366 enrolled in Baptist Brotherhoods, 1,190,908 in Woman's Missionary Unions, for a total of 1,805,274 enlisted in some form of missionary education out of 15,365,486 SBC members (11.75%). See *Southern Baptist Handbook*, 1993 (Nashville: Convention Press, 1993), 7.

6. In 1995, there were 4,054 foreign missionaries under appointment, while in the same year there were well over 60,000 paid staff positions in SBC churches.

7. Cyril Blackman, *The Biblical Basis of the Church's Missionary Enterprise*, Essays on Mission, No. 3 (London: London Missionary Society, 1961), 18.

25

THE STRUGGLE FOR A GLOBAL FAITH

—➤•◄—

For neither circumcision nor uncircumcision is anything;
but a new creation is everything!

Galatians 6:15 NRSV

There are many reasons why you may have never heard or read a sermon such as this. One is that we tend to take an idealistic view of the New Testament church as an idyllic fellowship free of conflict, a model of harmony because of the love that the first Christians had for one another. In actuality, however, an explosive conflict raged at the heart of apostolic Christianity, particularly during the ministry of Paul. That painful struggle not only defined the essential nature of our faith, but it permanently determined the relationship between Christianity and Judaism.

Again, most of our preaching seeks to meet the spiritual needs of the individual rather than addressing those larger realities on which our religion rests. We have defined the "plan of salvation" in such personal terms that our pulpit agenda seldom deals with a pivotal decision that shaped the course of Christian history. Today, we pay a heavy price for our failure to probe the biggest single problem that vexed the first century church even though it is directly relevant to the tensions that have surfaced in almost every modern denomination.

One of the main reasons why we are timid about digging into this problem is because the conflict was originally framed around the issue of circumcision. To us, that practice is viewed as an elective surgical procedure without any religious significance. Circumcision is seldom mentioned in a church setting, not only because of the inherent delicacy of the subject matter to our modern tastes, but because it does not seem to speak to our spiritual needs in any meaningful fashion. Indeed, many church members declared their faith as children long before they had any idea what circumcision is!

But before you dismiss the subject out of hand, remember that circumcision was the most explosive issue in Paul's pivotal letter to the Galatians (2:3–9; 2:11–13; 5:1–12; 6:12–15) and that it recurred as a key theme in several of his later epistles as well (1 Cor. 7:17–19; Rom. 2:25–29; 3:30; 4:9–12; Phil. 3:2–3; Col. 2:11; 3:11; Eph. 2:11–13; Titus 1:10). Moreover, it was the central controversy prompting the Jerusalem Conference of Acts 15, which became, in many ways, the watershed event of the apostolic era. Are we wise to ignore so important an issue just because, at first glance, it seems to be irrelevant in our day?

The Problem

The New Testament period was a time of escalating tensions between Judaism and its enemies. Palestine had been culturally conquered by the Greeks and militarily conquered by the Romans. As a result, the Jewish population felt threatened with assimilation into the foreign culture of the Mediterranean world that would cause Judaism as a distinctive way of life to disappear. Just as many religious leaders in America today are alarmed by what they view as the increasing power of a secular culture, the Jewish leadership of that day practiced the politics of polarization, which eventually erupted in a fight to the finish against the mighty Roman Empire. Indeed, the apostolic era came to an abrupt end with the Jewish war of AD 66–73, which resulted in the fall of Jerusalem and the loss of a homeland in Palestine until the modern nation of Israel was established in 1948.

Since, in their ancient struggle for survival, the Jews had no flag around which to rally, they made circumcision the symbol of their embattled identity. Far from being an optional hygienic technique, circumcision became the boundary marker that separated Jews from the rest of the world (Eph. 2:11). Its decisive importance in first century Judaism is seen clearly in Jubilees 15:26 from that era:

> And anyone who is born whose own flesh is not circumcised on the eighth day is not from the sons of the covenant which the Lord made for Abraham since (he is) from the children of destruction. And there is therefore no sign upon him so that he might belong to the Lord because (he is destined) to be destroyed and annihilated from the earth and to be uprooted from the earth because he has broken the covenant of the Lord our God.[1]

Aware of the sacred significance that the Jews were attaching to circumcision, their Greek and Roman masters pressured them intensely to renounce what they viewed as a repugnant practice (1 Macc. 1:14–15 OT Apocrypha). An operation to remove its mark surgically became common among the urban upper class and was viewed by the historian Josephus as forsaking Jewish customs to adopt a Greek way of life (*Jewish Antiquities*, XII, 241). Those who refused to repudiate circumcision were ostracized from the gymnasium, the public bath, and the athletic contests, all of which involved only males who participated in the nude. In some instances, the defiant practice of circumcision could lead to punitive taxation, loss of citizenship, or even death, as when Antiochus IV Epiphanes slaughtered those families who circumcised their children and hung the infants from their mother's necks (1 Macc. 1:60–61; 2 Macc. 6:10 OT Apocrypha). By the time that Paul began his missionary work around 50 AD, circumcision had become the battle cry of patriotic Jews determined to avoid extinction as God's chosen people in a pagan culture.

Paul had been born and raised as an observant Jew, "circumcised on the eighth day" (Phil. 3:5 NRSV). As we know from Romans 9–11, his heart's deepest desire was to win his fellow countrymen (Rom. 10:1). Therefore, he was willing for Timothy to be circumcised to facilitate his acceptance by Jews in their synagogues (Acts 16:3), but Paul adamantly refused to require it of Titus, a Greek who would work primarily with Gentiles (Gal. 2:3). He knew that most non-Jews would never accept his message on condition of circumcision, because it would entangle them in a cultural and political controversy with which they wanted no part. This does not mean that Paul simply abandoned a practice clearly taught in his Hebrew Bible. Rather, he had learned from the martyr Stephen that the Abrahamic covenant of circumcision (Acts 7:8) failed to circumcise the heart and ears of the people, causing them to resist the Holy Spirit and reject God's messengers (Acts 7:51–53). Far from ignoring or repudiating circumcision, Paul internalized its meaning so that his Christianity would become a religion of the spirit, rather than of the flesh (Col. 2:11–13).

THE STRUGGLE FOR A GLOBAL FAITH

The Solution

Paul's insistence on eliminating circumcision from his gospel to the Gentiles was bound to result in open conflict with Jews (Gal. 2:4–5). Put as simply as possible, it raised the issue of what practices in Judaism one had to embrace in order to become a Christian. The first effort to address this problem resulted in what might be called a "two-spheres" solution according to which there would be dual strategies, a mission to circumcised Jews led by Peter and a mission to uncircumcised Gentiles led by Paul (Gal. 2:7–9). Again and again, Paul tried to honor this compromise in evenhanded fashion (1 Cor. 7:18–19). After all, his driving passion was to win as many as possible regardless of whether they were Jew or Gentile (1 Cor. 9:19–22). For a brief time this strategy seemed to succeed as Christianity flourished, not only in Paul's Gentile churches, but in the Jerusalem church led by James where "many thousands . . . among the Jews," who were "all zealous for the law," had become believers (Acts 21:20 NRSV). The solution seemed so fair and simple: Gentiles did not have to become Jews in order to become Christians, nor did Jews have to become Gentiles in order to become Christians. It was to be a win/win solution for those on both sides of the issue.

Soon this strategy began to fail, precisely because of its success, as a growing number of Jewish Christians and Gentile Christians began to mingle in great cosmopolitan centers, such as Antioch. The reason for its failure was that a small but fanatical group within the church called Judaizers refused to accept the "two-spheres" accommodation but instead insisted that *every* Christian obey the ancestral customs of the Jews as set forth in the Hebrew Bible. These Judaizers organized themselves into "the circumcision party" and pressured Peter to stop eating with Gentile Christians in Antioch because they were not circumcised and did not observe kosher food requirements. In yielding to their pressure, Peter incurred the wrath of Paul who "opposed him to his face, because he stood condemned" (Gal. 2:11–12). By insisting on their understanding of the *purity* of the church, which involved a literalistic observance of such Old Testament practices as circumcision, the Judaizers were disrupting the *unity* of the church at the crucial point of table fellowship, which included the Lord's Supper.

As political and cultural tensions rapidly escalated in Palestine, the Judaizers increased their agitation by insisting that circumcision was essential to salvation (Acts 15:1). When this led to "no small dissension and debate" (Acts 15:2), it was decided to convene a summit in the Holy City, which we call the Jerusalem Conference. There a party of Pharisaic believers determined to prevail on the issue of circumcision by demanding that all Christians be "ordered to keep the law of Moses" (Acts 15:5 NRSV). As the debate unfolded, both Peter and James sided with Paul, emphasizing that salvation was only "through the grace of the Lord Jesus," and therefore, Jewish requirements should not be imposed upon "those Gentiles who are turning to God" (Acts 15:19 NRSV). A diplomatically worded Apostolic Decree was drawn up urging each side to be respectful of the religious scruples of the other side as shaped by custom and culture, but not to allow these human differences to impede anyone from accepting Christ (Acts 15:22–29).

With all of the key leaders in agreement, it might seem that the matter had finally been settled, but such was not the case. The next time that Paul returned to Jerusalem, he found a powder keg of political extremism ready to explode. This inflammatory atmosphere resulted in him almost being lynched in the shadow of the Sanctuary as the result of a rumor that he might have carried a Gentile, Trophimus the Ephesian, into the Temple (Acts 21:27–32). Paul's life was spared by the intervention of Roman soldiers, but the rest of his ministry was spent as a prisoner processing judicial appeals to ever higher levels of the Roman government. No wonder he became so frustrated over the circumcision issue that, in exasperation, he invited those who were insisting on the circumcision of Gentiles apply the knife to themselves and be castrated (Gal. 5:12)! Paul washed his hands of the issue by insisting that circumcision simply did not matter to the Christian faith despite the claims of his detractors (Gal. 5:6; 6:15). To his heartbreak, the issue was finally settled, not by apostolic summitry, but by Roman armies that brutally crushed a suicidal uprising of Jews fomented by the kind of religious absolutism that had tried to wreck Paul's ministry.

The Relevance

The first thing we learn from this titanic struggle is that Christianity is not an otherworldly escapist religion but one that addresses persons in their own distinctive setting and seeks to become indigenous in that culture as far as possible. Because of its rootedness in the real world of time and place, earthly pressures on the faith can become enormous. Particularly potent is the combination of patriotism and piety that seeks to make the church an agent of some group's political agenda. Religious people take seriously their earthly citizenship as well as their ethnic identity, and they desire to be loyal to their inherited traditions. In Jewish Christianity this led to the emergence of a "circumcision party;"

whereas, in our country it has resulted in a strong tradition of exclusivism with its frequently violent expressions of hostility to anything foreign. Sad to say, religion has often been in the forefront of strident efforts to sanctify sameness and demonize differences. In light of the strength of religious isolationism, especially in the South, it is not surprising that organized expressions of this impulse have often included a "churchly" component, especially in the Klu Klux Klan with its Bible-thumping tirades against Catholics, Jews, and Blacks; its ritualistic use of white robes of purity; and its obscene use of fiery crosses as symbols of terror.

Second, in light of our enormous cultural diversity, it is not only legitimate but often necessary to have multiple strategies for evangelization. In the New Testament, this required one approach to Jews and another to Gentiles; whereas, today it may require different approaches to the first world and the third world, or to the older generation and the younger generation, or to liberals and conservatives, or to eggheads and hardhats. In the twenty-first century as in the first century, we still have bitter "culture wars" that divide our nation into opposing camps with the antagonisms between them accentuated by the mass media. The remarkable thing is that, no matter how diverse we become, the spirit of Christ has a universal appeal to all groups regardless of their nationality, gender, political persuasion, or ideological preference. When we start with interpretations of the Bible shaped by our religious traditions, we almost always end up with differing positions, such as on the issue of circumcision in the first century or on the role of women in the twenty-first century. But when we start instead with the life and teachings of Jesus, we find that his open arms are able to embrace us all.

Third, when we seek to resolve the tension between the particularity of our religious customs and the universality of our risen Lord, doctrinaire extremists can wreck havoc and subvert the worldwide outreach of the Christian faith regardless of the solutions we devise. Everybody in the early church saw the irreconcilable split coming as Paul made his final appeal in the Holy City (Acts 21:11–12); yet, they seemed powerless to halt the momentum of his enemies' reckless hysteria until it had wrought division and destruction on every hand. In troubled times of fear, an inflexible fundamentalism often triumphs for a season and inflicts terrible wounds on the faith. In the ancient conflict over circumcision, everyone was not right. The Book of Acts embraced a wide spectrum of opinion that included Stephen on the far left, Paul on the near left, Barnabas in the center, Peter on the near right, and James on the far right. But this tolerance did not extend to the Judaizers who, by their legalistic mindset, were splitting the church and hindering its world mission. We may assume that the Judaizers were trying to be sincere, devout Christians but, judged by the verdict of history, they were deeply misguided in their non-negotiable demands!

Fourth, even when an irreconcilable impasse is reached, that does not mean that we throw up our hands in despair. Rather, as Paul reassured the apprehensive Christians of Caesarea, our only choice is not between the two sides in whatever culture war is raging. We need not be stymied if various Christian groups reach a point where they cannot reconcile their differences. Our faith stands or falls, not on our ability to solve all of the problems presented by our diverse backgrounds, but on the credibility of Christ himself to redeem those of every background. Only God is the providential Lord of history who can use even our disagreements to accomplish his will (Acts 21:14).

Let me return to the question with which we began: Why address such a hard and heavy subject? The first reason is that this is precisely the struggle that brought Christianity to the Gentiles, and that, my friends, is who we are! If the Judaizers had won, if customs such as circumcision had been made prerequisite to salvation, then Christianity would have become little more than a small reforming sect within Judaism. Why is it that we may readily embrace the Christian faith even if we have no Jewish background? It is because Paul fought to the death for our right to do so and that is a struggle that we should never forget!

Another reason is that our churches are engaged in global missions stretching around the world. Why should Christians invest so much time and effort and money to help those in such different cultures? What do we as Americans have to offer Asians or Latinos? Why not just stay home and help our own kind? The answer is that we have something utterly crucial to offer every person in the world if we will do so, not as Americans, but as Christians. Ours is a global rather than a national or ethnic faith, and we discover that best when we go outside our culture to work with those who do not share our inherited customs but who want the respect and acceptance and love seen uniquely in Jesus Christ our Lord.

A final reason for the urgency of this message is that today almost all American denominations are divided by a variety of cultural cleavages that provide prime examples of polarization at work. Christians still need to convene contemporary "Jerusalem Conferences" to discuss and decide how to respond to these significant differences. In place of a long-held consensus about the meaning of their tradition, most denominations are in open turmoil over deep divisions.

In deciding how to be on mission in a fragmented world, does this history lesson from Holy Scripture provide any insight for our guidance? As I see it, the deepest truth of its message is unmistakable. When faced with conflict, do not commit your Christianity to one side in the latest culture wars but to the spirit of Christ who is lord of all cultures. Go with those who are trying to reach all peoples across every barrier. Avoid the polarizers who often win in the short term and embrace the reconcilers who are often vindicated only by the longer march of history. When the curtain fell on the earliest chapter of church history in Acts, the Judaizers seemed to be firmly in control in Jerusalem, while Paul was under house arrest in Rome. But today the Judaizers are in the dustbin of history, while Paul, as well as Peter and James, are honored for their courageous stand in advocating a universal faith. Such a faith does not come without a struggle, which may prove costly, but it is worth whatever price must be paid because, without it, Christianity would not have become an "equal opportunity" religion open to Jews and Gentiles alike.

NOTE

1. James H. Charlesworth, ed., *The Old Testament Pseudepigrapha* (Garden City, NY: Doubleday, 1985), 2:87.

26

RELIGION IN AN AGE OF TERROR

———➤•◄———

*He also said to the crowds, "When you see a cloud rising in the west,
you immediately say, 'It is going to rain'; and so it happens. And when
you see the south wind blowing, you say, 'There will be scorching heat';
and it happens. You hypocrites! You know how to interpret the
appearance of earth and sky, but why do you not know how to interpret
the present time?*

Luke 12:54–56 NRSV

In recent years we have witnessed a remarkable reach
for freedom in our world. The Berlin Wall came
tumbling down and with it the collapse of Soviet
Communism. Nelson Mandela was released from
prison, breaking the iron grip of apartheid in South
Africa. With a couple of symbolic handshakes, first by
Begin and Sadat, then by Rabin and Arafat, it seemed
that intractable hostilities between Israelis and
Palestinians might finally abate. As the half century
Cold War began to thaw, America relished the prospect
of a peace dividend that would usher in a new era of
unrivaled prosperity.

But before these millennial expectations could be
fulfilled, an ominous new threat arose that
foreshadowed a cultural clash of global proportions.[1]
Each of its three defining moments launched a decade:
First was the 1979–80 hostage crisis in Iran, which our
diplomatic and military might proved impotent to
solve. Then came the 1990–91 Gulf War, which despite
the success of Operation Desert Storm, left Saddam
Hussein as entrenched as ever in Iraq. The third was
defined by the terrorist attack of 2001 upon our citadels

of commerce and government, which we seemed helpless to anticipate or prevent. In all three instances, a fanatic wing of Islam in the Middle East has been able to hold hostage our long deferred dream of universal peace. Despite overwhelming military victories in Afghanistan and Iraq, those countries continue to sink into the chaos of civil wars fomented to a large extent by rival religious parties.

My purpose is not to second guess our national leaders by proposing a political solution to the current crisis. Nor do I claim any special competence in the military or diplomatic aspects of the confrontation. Rather, my aim is to "interpret the present time" (Lk. 12:56 NRSV), to discover the claims of God that this momentous crisis lays upon our lives. I shall seek to do that by probing the religion embraced by the overwhelming majority of the populace in the Middle East. Unfortunately, the Islamic movement has long been a mystery to Americans, especially as regards its long history. Since this is the dimension most neglected in media analyses, let us begin with a swift sketch of how the past has profoundly shaped the problems that we now confront in the present.

The Islamic Crisis in Historical Perspective
The founding of Islam is dated to the life of its supreme prophet Mohammed (born c. 570 AD) who, in the month of Ramadan, 610, experienced a "Night of Power" when he began to hear the voice of the Angel Gabriel revealing to him the Koran—God's eternal and infallible word. In 622, Mohammed made a fateful migration from Mecca to Medina, thus marking the start of the Muslim calendar. In the next ten years, before his sudden death in 632, he virtually completed

his mission of unifying the diverse tribes of the vast Arabian peninsula under a theocracy governed by the one and only God, Allah. During the following century his movement spread like a devouring fire to the East and the West. Turned back in Europe at Tours, 135 miles southwest of Paris, by Charles Martel in 732, Islam's expansive force was spent only after it had planted itself firmly in Africa and Asia to become the last great empire of the ancient world.

The magnitude of medieval Islam has seldom received its rightful place in world history. George Sarton, the Harvard historian of science, has written that, in the tenth century, "The main task of mankind was accomplished by Moslems.[2] The greatest philosopher . . . mathematicians . . . geographer and encyclopedist" were all Moslem. From Islam came the rediscovery of Aristotle and the first scientific astronomy and medicine since the Greeks. By the time Columbus discovered America, this desert faith was not only the largest religion in the world but, in some respects, its most universal. For as the medieval empire decolonized itself, vast stretches of the world's great sunbelt were left "permanently caught in the light but unbreakable net of a common Islamic culture."[3]

The centuries following this Golden Age were unkind to Islam, leaving it intellectually stagnant, politically impotent, and economically exhausted by the opening of the twentieth century. Perhaps its low point came in 1924 when the Caliphate, or dynastic rulership, was abolished by Turkish leader Kemal Ataturk in connection with the dismantling of the Ottoman Empire. This move was part of a herculean effort to modernize the fossilized civilization of Islam, an effort that has deeply divided it ever since. When enormous wealth suddenly became available with the discovery of vast oil reserves, an aristocratic elite set out to transplant Western technology to the Arabian peninsula. But with that westernization came a set of cultural values repugnant to the traditional Islamic faith, which grew from 300 million adherents in the mid-twentieth century to 1.3 billion today.

This background prepares us to grapple with our first key insight: the crisis in the Middle East, at its deeper level, is the manifestation of a head on collision between the modernizing power of Western consumerism and the tenacious conservatism of Islamic culture. The problem is that, since the Middle Ages, this region has been dominated by the West. We travel as tourists to glimpse the monuments of the Crusades, but those who live there face these galling reminders of their subservience on a daily basis. In their eyes, every time the United States intervenes with massive military force, it is but the latest in a series of "crusades" against their way of life. Moreover, they interpret this intervention as support for the oil sheiks who have invested untold billions of petrodollars in the West, even as the Middle East, for all of its vast resources, is trapped in economic squalor.

Once the problem is defined in this fashion, many Americans are left wondering why the Middle East should get so upset over the imposition of something as wonderful as "Western civilization." Does not this legacy bring with it all of the benefits of the scientific revolution? The great Islamic scholar Bernard Lewis answers plainly: "For vast numbers of Middle Easterners, Western style economic methods brought poverty, Western style political institutions brought tyranny, even Western style warfare brought defeat."[4]

But that still does not bring us to the heart of the problem, which is: How could admittedly profound cultural differences cause these two civilizations to engage in such violent conflict? In particular, how could the Islamic concept of *Jihad*, meaning "struggle" or "exertion," which Mohammed interpreted as the individual's lifelong struggle to resist temptation, be used to justify random acts of mass terror?

Before we fly into a rage of religious judgmentalism in answering such questions, let us remember a few sobering facts. The Jewish and Christian scriptures of the Old Testament contain numerous references to "holy wars" that include the idea of *herem*, a Hebrew word meaning "anathema" or "separated," according to which the enemies of Israel were to be utterly destroyed without mercy (Deut. 7:1–2; 20:16–18), including men, women, children, infants, and animals (1 Sam. 15:3). Even those Israelite towns that compromised the faith were to be torched "as a whole burnt offering to the Lord" that would become "a perpetual ruin, never to be rebuilt" (Deut. 13:16 NRSV). This kind of extreme militancy has surfaced repeatedly in both Jewish and Christian history, notably in the medieval Crusades (1096–1396), which provided papal armies with abundant opportunities to ravage and plunder Muslim lands.

In the light of this historical background, our challenge is much larger than capturing a few extremists and destroying their terrorist network. It is the challenge of overcoming the bitter confrontation between Western modernism and Islamic traditionalism that has festered for centuries. Therefore, let us see if we can discover a way beyond the impasse that so deeply divides these two approaches to life.

Islamic Traditionalism and Western Modernism

The reactionary mentality long prevalent among Islamists throws into bold relief the dangers inherent in all forms of religious fanaticism. Here is a militant religious movement offering authoritarian opinions based on a literalistic interpretation of one ancient book to which zealous followers give unquestioning obedience. Quite simply, it is old-fashioned religious fundamentalism raised to the level of national and international policy. The problem is not that Muslims have no right to their convictions, or that they are not entitled to base them on the Koran, or that they are wrong to urge them on others. The problem, rather, is that their views are both determined and delivered with finality, that there is no room for alternative viewpoints, that self-criticism has been overwhelmed by certainty. In a word, the basic problem is that of religious absolutism, treating understandings that are human and therefore contingent as God's decrees which are divine and therefore categorical.

The tragic consequences of this mindset unfolding in the Middle East should warn us against some of the same symptoms that have emerged in American life. The "noise level" is rising in many pulpits as popular preachers bellow and scream with a stridency that says unmistakably, "Don't talk back, I have declared the last word, take it or leave it!" A new zealotism welcomes this bombast as a way of verbalizing gut feelings of anger and frustration over the course of human events. One veteran participant in the life of his denomination remarked after attending a highly publicized showcase of such preaching, "Anybody who brought his mind to this meeting wouldn't know what to do with it." Whenever we allow others to do our thinking for us just because they rant and rave while waving a Bible in the air, we are starting down the same dangerous road that Islamic fundamentalists are now walking.

A particular problem with the religious totalitarianism in Islamist militancy is that it is fused to the political ideal of a theocratic government. Throughout its history, Islam has steadfastly advocated the union, rather than the separation, of church and state. That is why ayatollahs can issue edicts touching on every aspect of private and public life, from decisions of national diplomacy down to minute details of manners and morals. Again, the issue is not whether God's will embraces the totality of life, or whether clerics may hold an opinion as to what God's will might be on any particular point. The issue, rather, is whether expertise in the Koran, or in any other scripture, confers an omnicompetence in areas not directly related to religion. Do religious leaders have a monopoly on the full range of human wisdom, or does God guide laypersons into secular callings where they may become far more expert in the affairs of statecraft than scriptural specialists ever could?

To be sure, it would simplify things if we could put all of the problems of life into one basket and hand them over to a prophet for solution. But God does not offer any such shortcuts to building a better world. If politicians could find all the answers by becoming experts in Scripture and theology, they would line up to enroll in the nearest seminary. But our most sensitive and spiritually committed public officials have learned, on the contrary, that true faith, far from conferring easy answers to complex problems, may actually intensify the difficulty of finding a just but workable solution. Issues of governance need to be discussed on the basis of input from a wide range of viewpoints, with differing conclusions likely from equally sincere and dedicated Christians.

To reject Islamic fundamentalism, however, does not mean that we are to embrace the westernized modernism that is championed as its alternative. For even in the West we are beginning to realize that this way of life is not an unmixed blessing. The scientific method has brought a vast increase in knowledge but with it a positivism that questions the reality of anything transcendent. Technology has brought a cornucopia of prosperity but with it an insatiable materialism shot through with competitive selfishness. Psychology has brought an introspective individualism but with it a narcissistic infatuation that shreds the fabric of community and leaves an aching loneliness in its place. Too often, the controlling ideology of modernism has brought with it a superficiality of spirit, a relativism of values, a reductionism of purpose calculated to erode the foundations of Western civilization.

In this anguished moment of human history, therefore, we must transcend the temptation to embrace either extreme that has polarized our two cultures almost to the breaking point. Instead, we need to search for a way to unite the passion for material progress in the West with the passion for spiritual stability in Islam. The deepest lesson of the present confrontation is that both antagonists stand judged, Islam for its effort to turn back the clock and so have no future, the West for its effort to abandon its spiritual foundations and so have no past. Finally, it is theologically illegitimate to choose between the Western drive to have dominion over the secular and the Islamic drive to have dominion over the sacred.

After all, God is both our creator and our redeemer who calls us to honor both the physical and the spiritual, to love both the earthly and the heavenly, which is exactly why "the Word became flesh and lived among us" (Jn. 1:14 NRSV).

Moving Beyond the Present Crisis

If these are some of the issues involved, how shall we as Christians respond? There are at least two stages involved. The first is to support our duly constituted public officials in providing necessary deterrence to the threat of terrorism wherever it exists. The second is to learn how to wage peace just as aggressively as we have waged war. Indeed, a long range strategy for making peace should be integral to our short range strategy for making war. In formulating plans for a religious response, I have three suggestions to offer regarding our responsibilities as global Christians, plus a concluding remark regarding our role as American citizens.

First, let us as Christians lead the way in rejecting the use of violence to fight "holy wars" in the name of God. In all three Abrahamic faiths—Judaism, Christianity, and Islam—a small but noisy minority of funda-mentalists use a simplistic and literalistic understanding of Scriptural inerrancy to sanction the kind of slaughter that long ago accompanied the Israelite conquest of Palestine. Measured by the ministry of Jesus, and by the example of his first followers, the use of violence to fight "holy wars" has no place in the will of God for his people. We as Christians cannot invite Judaism and Islam to join us in that understanding unless we first put our own house in order.

Second, let us strengthen rather than weaken the wall of separation between church and state. In Baptist history this relationship was needed because we were a despised minority persecuted by the magistrates on behalf of an established church. But in the present crisis it is needed so that Christianity will be clearly perceived by all, not as an American religion or even a Western religion, but as a global religion not beholden to any country or culture. Both Judaism and Islam find it difficult to adopt this stance because of theocratic assumptions in their traditions, which means that it is all the more important for American Christianity to provide an unambiguous example of how this may be done.

Third, let us concentrate on the commonalities Christianity shares with Judaism and Islam rather than on our differences. To be sure, there is a time and place to emphasize the distinctives of our faith, but now we need to explore the extent to which we can present a united front against extremist partisans in all three movements who would sanction lawless violence as a legitimate response to one's enemies. The central point to be considered in such trilateral conversations is surely the monotheism that is central in all of the Abrahamic religions. For if there really is only one God, as all three faiths emphatically affirm, then this universal deity must be the God of us all, friend and foe alike.

The consensus of the commentators is that the twenty-first century did not begin at 12:01 a.m. on January 1, 2000 in Times Square, but at 8:45 a.m. on September 11, 2001 in the World Trade Center. In this new era when things will never be the same again, we now live in an interconnected, interdependent world threatened by powerful forces that transcend the national borders behind which we once felt secure. One of the most destructive of those forces is an intractable intolerance posing as religious fervor that enjoys more popular support than it deserves because of a seething resentment by the masses against Western imperialism. If the twentieth century taught us anything, it is that once ideological hatred is deified, its fury knows no bounds.

To rid the world of that hydra-headed monster, America will need not only its military might but a new mindset. Before September 11, all that we could talk about was how to cut taxes, reduce government spending, and prop up an economy that was in danger of falling below the double digit yields to which we had become accustomed. If 9/11 taught us anything, it is that the richest nation in the world cannot spend all of its time and energy becoming even richer and let the rest of the world go to hell in a handbasket. If we try that approach long enough, the embittered, whom we ignore, will bring their hell to our shores in a suicidal frenzy of wanton destruction.

So we are tutored by tragedy in the lessons of *noblesse oblige,* that privilege imposes obligations. The time has come to set aside our consuming greed for extravagance and relearn the disciplines of compassion for those homeless and starving millions living on the outer edge of human subsistence. It will not be easy to show the rest of the world that we care for others as much as we care for ourselves. Indeed, it may prove easier to win the war against terrorism than to win the peace against that desperation which makes it possible. But we do not have to look far to find models of the selfless global commitment so needed in our present crisis. They are called missionaries. For centuries they have served as agents of a universal faith intent on uniting the entire human race in a fellowship of life and love.

While we need Christian missionaries as never before to help overcome the cleavages caused by our religious animosities, we also need missionaries of the American way of life at its best: travelers, entrepreneurs, teachers, social workers, agriculturalists, engineers, and a host of others willing to go and give, willing to listen and learn, willing to save and share that a broken world might be rebuilt on the basis of mutual tolerance and respect. The task will not be easy nor will it be brief. While there is little hope of changing the entrenched attitudes of those long infested with the virus of violence, we can lay the foundations of a new world order in which the moderating forces of justice and compassion in all of our religions will have a chance to prevail. My hope is that we as a nation will not gain the whole world only to lose our soul. Rather, I pray that we give our soul to the whole world and thereby gain the chance to live in peace with all humanity.

NOTES

1. The thesis that geopolitics is entering a new phase in which conflict will be primarily cultural rather than national was advanced by Samuel P. Huntington, "The Clash of Civilizations," *Foreign Affairs* 72, no. 3 (1993): 22–49; subsequently expanded into a book, *The Clash of Civilizations and the Remaking of World Order* (New York: Simon & Schuster, 1996). On the discussion generated see *The Clash of Civilizations? The Debate. A Foreign Affairs Reader* (New York: Foreign Affairs, 1993).

2. Quoted in *Time*, April 16, 1965, 73.

3. Peter Brown, "Understanding Islam," *The New York Review of Books*, February 22, 1979, 30.

4. Bernard Lewis, "Western Civilization: A View From the East," *The Jefferson Lecture for 1990*, cited in the Chronicle of Higher Education, May 9, 1990, A4.

27

WILL WE BE "LEFT BEHIND"?

—→⊷•⊰←—

For the Lord himself, with a cry of command, with the archangel's call and with the sound of God's trumpet, will descend from heaven, and the dead in Christ will rise first. Then we who are alive, who are left, will be caught up in the clouds together with them to meet the Lord in the air; and so we will be with the Lord forever.

1 Thessalonians 4:16–17 NRSV

There was a time when most Christians learned their theology at church, which had many advantages. We could be assured that the pastor was familiar with the distinctive doctrines of our faith. If we didn't understand what was being taught, Sunday School teachers were readily available to answer questions. In case we disagreed with some emphasis, fellow church members were always willing to sharpen the issues through friendly dialogue.

But now the role of the congregation in shaping our convictions has an aggressive competitor in the secular marketplace. The most prominent example is the wildly popular publishing phenomenon called *Left Behind*. Originally conceived as a single novel by that title published in 1995, it had grown by 2006 into a fifteen-volume series with sales of more than sixty-five million copies.

The creation of this theological juggernaut was the result of a remarkable partnership. The idea was hatched by an independent Baptist minister from California named Tim LaHaye, who was known in earlier years for writing and speaking with his wife, Beverly, on Christian family life. In 1991, he became concerned about the decline of "pretribulational rapture Bible prophecy" and determined to reverse the trend by fictionalizing his views to make them accessible to the general public. He enlisted the veteran ghostwriter of sports memoirs, Jerry Jenkins, to assist him by writing every word of the *Left Behind* series while LaHaye ensured its "prophetic accuracy."

My purpose is not to attack or defend the series but to explain its main contentions and evaluate their adequacy as Christian doctrine. To do this, I shall base my critique primarily on LaHaye's nonfiction book *Revelation Unveiled,* which he published to serve as a scriptural companion to the *Left Behind* series.[1]

The Scenario

To understand what LaHaye means by being "left behind," we must define four key words, all of which are loaded with theological meaning. The first is "rapture," which we usually take to mean a state of emotional exhilaration or ecstatic delight. The biblical usage, however, has a quite different force. In 1 Thessalonians 4:17, Paul speaks of being "caught up" together with the dead in Christ to meet the Lord in the air. The Greek verb meant "to seize" something forcibly in order to carry it away, and so could be rendered "snatched up" in order to emphasize both the suddenness and power with which God would act. When this verse was put into Latin, the translators correctly used a comparable verb, *rapio,* which meant "to lay hold" of something both forcibly and quickly. The noun form *raptus* is the origin of such English words as "rapt" and "rapture." LaHaye uses the term rapture to mean the instantaneous conveyance of Christians to heaven from their abode on earth.

The second essential term, "pretribulation," obviously has two parts. The root of the word, "tribulation," refers to a period immediately preceding the end-times, which Jesus described as the most utterly corrupt era in human history (Mk. 13:19). Based on LaHaye's interpretation of Daniel 9:24–27, he calculates that this upheaval will last for seven years, from the appearance of the antichrist to the final battle between good and evil called Armageddon. The addition of "pre" indicates that the rapture will take place *before* the tribulation; whereas, a "posttribulation" view would indicate that the rapture will take place *after* the tribulation.

The third term is "premillennial," another compound with the same prefix. The root "millennial" comes from the Latin word for "thousand" and refers to the triumphant reign of Christ on earth for a thousand years mentioned in Revelation 20:3. Those who are "premillennialists" hold that the rapture and the tribulation will take place *before* the thousand-year kingdom is established; whereas, those who are "postmillennialists" hold that the rapture and tribulation will take place *after* the thousand-year reign of Christ is ended.

The final term "dispensationalism" refers to a system of interpreting prophecy, which incorporates the three positions just described. In short, dispensationalists are those who believe in a premillennial pretribulational rapture. The term itself refers to the belief that God deals with humanity in seven successive "dispensations" or epochs of history. In its entirety, dispensationalism is both a full-blown biblical theology and a philosophy of history, but of greatest interest to us is its two most distinctive contentions: (1) that prophecy does not apply to the Church Age, which is a "great parenthesis" in God's dealings with his people; and (2) that there are two prophetic tracks, one applying to the Gentiles and the other to the Jews, the latter involving the return of Israel to the Holy Land and the rebuilding of the Temple in Jerusalem.

Now, we are ready to understand what LaHaye means by being "left behind." He is referring to non-believers who remain on earth when all true Christians, whether living or dead, are suddenly translated into heaven. Their departure will unleash a worldwide upsurge of evil for seven years presided over by its ultimate embodiment, the antichrist. The first half of this period will see the rise of a one-world apostate church and a craze for one-world government, all of which will lead to sheer chaos in the second half of the period. Despite this hell on earth, a remnant of 144,000 Jews will be converted, to whom Christ will come in his glorious appearing to reign over a millennium of peace, at the end of which the final judgment will usher in eternity.

In case this end-time scenario seems a bit strange or even bizarre to you, LaHaye freely admits that his position has long been a minority view with only a negligible number of major theologians embracing it throughout the long history of the church. In the modern English-speaking world, the two most influential exponents of dispensationalism have been John Nelson Darby (1800–1882), a leader of the strict Plymouth Brethren sect in England who set forth his system in thirty-two published volumes, and Cyrus I. Scofield (1843–1921), an independent Bible teacher whose Scofield Reference Bible summarized

Darbyite dispensationalism in a series of notes printed beneath the Scriptural text.

The Evidence

Having identified the theological framework of the *Left Behind* series, let us now evaluate its adequacy in light of Scripture. Here, the crux of the matter is the methodology by which to interpret the relevant texts. As LaHaye recognizes, Christians of equal commitment to Scripture differ sharply on this issue because they explain the same texts in quite different ways. Here let me mention only three of the methodological issues that create this difficulty.

First, the centerpiece of LaHaye's system is the worldwide secret rapture that suddenly and surprisingly snatches up every believer from the earth. But notice how ambiguous is the biblical evidence for this position. In LaHaye's prime passage, 1 Thessalonians 4:17, the shouted command, the archangel's call, and the trumpet's sound described in verse 16 suggest that this will be a very public rather than a private event; thus most commentators conclude that it refers to the final advent rather than to the rapture. The second most cited passage, John 14:3, speaks of Christ coming to take his troubled disciples unto himself, but the larger context implies that this postresurrection "coming" will be to earth rather than to heaven (Jn. 14:18, 23). Finally, LaHaye appeals to Revelation 4:1–2 where John is invited through heaven's open door to glimpse God's plans for the future, but this is standard language for being granted a prophetic vision while remaining on earth (2 Cor. 12:1–4).

When we look carefully at LaHaye's best evidence, we find solid indications of God's determination not to neglect or abandon his troubled children here on earth. But these texts do not say anything about God plucking the whole church out of the world and leaving everybody else behind. LaHaye claims that there are 318 scriptural references to some phase of the second coming of Christ and lists twenty-six "rapture passages" among them, but his whole effort to split the final advent into two parts separated by seven years is just not supported by these texts. The first principle of sound interpretation is to begin with what the Bible says most clearly, most consistently, and most constantly. The notion of a pretribulationist secret rapture fails this test.

Second, if LaHaye does not get his scenario from the explicit teachings of the relevant biblical texts, then where does he get it? The answer is that it comes from the way in which he combines many Scripture passages that were originally unrelated to each other. Beginning with the seventy weeks of Daniel 9:24–27, he tries to fit virtually the entire sweep of biblical history from the Babylonian exile to the millennium into its cryptic timetable of heptads (seven sevens, then sixty-two sevens, then one final seven). The problem is that the Bible itself nowhere makes these connections. The New Testament frequently builds on the Old Testament, but it never utilizes Daniel 9 as the framework for a doctrine of the future in the way that LaHaye does. In other words, his system is like a necklace, each separate part a pearl taken straight out of Scripture, but the string holding these pearls together is taken straight out of Scofield!

In terms of methodology, we come to a second principle of interpretation. What God has joined together in Scripture, let us not put asunder. Conversely, what God has left separate in Scripture, let us beware of joining together lest the relationship thereby established reflects our own ideas rather than the plain teachings of Scripture. Fidelity to Scripture is determined, not only by the number of separate verses that we can cite in support of a particular theory, but also by the extent to which their use in an overall design corresponds to the way in which they were actually related to each other within Scripture.

A third issue arises from LaHaye's strong insistence on interpreting the Bible literally, as if only this approach "passes the test of 'making common sense' out of the Scripture."[2] The problem here is that the Bible itself does not teach, or even imply, that all of its descriptions should be understood literally. Take, for example, the key prophecy of Joel 2:28–32 which predicted that the coming of the Spirit in the last days would be so world-shaking that "the sun shall be turned to darkness, and the moon to blood" (Joel 2:31 NRSV). But when this passage was fulfilled at Pentecost (Acts 2:20), it was, at the literal level, a perfectly ordinary day, so ordinary that bystanders supposed that the Spirit-filled disciples were merely drunk (Acts 2:15)! Why, we must ask, does it make "common sense" to interpret a passage "literally" if it was intended to be interpreted symbolically?

This brings us to our last principle of interpretation: the type of literature which God chose to use in revealing his truth should be taken into account when explaining its content. If God wished to convey factual information, as in an historical narrative, then a literal interpretation would be entirely appropriate. But if God chose to speak through parable, poetry, and proverb, we should not subject this figurative language to a "literal" interpretation. This is especially true of highly symbolic writings such as Daniel and Revelation, which lie at the heart of LaHaye's enterprise.

The Issues

Why have I devoted this sermon to LaHaye's understanding of Biblical prophecy? Not only because of its enormous impact in the media marketplace, but because it raises fundamental issues lying at the heart of our hope for the future. Since, as they say, a picture is worth a thousand words, let us turn from LaHaye's use of the Bible to the ways in which his partner, Jerry Jenkins, has dressed this theology in fictional garb. Any thoughtful reader of the books would have to ask at least three questions prompted by his portrayal of the Christian faith.

First, does God really love the world, as John 3:16 affirms, or does he abhor it? The "signature scene" in Jenkin's fictionalized account is of a crowded 747 plane red-eyeing it from O'Hare to Heathrow when suddenly dozens of passengers including every child on board plus three crew members instantly disappear without taking any of their clothing and personal effects with them. The only thing that saves the plane is that the Captain and First Officer are "left behind." When they return to Chicago and finally manage to land, chaos abounds. The highways are littered with wrecks from disappeared drivers, mothers are screaming for their missing babies, a woman in childbirth watches her womb deflate as the obstetrician can find no trace of the fetus and must content himself with delivering the placenta! When the pilot, Rayford Steele, finally gets home, all that is left of his sleeping wife is an empty nightgown and her wedding ring between the sheets.

Surrounded by scenes of devastation caused by the

rapture, we are forced to wonder: Does Christ come for his own at the cost of such worldwide carnage? Does God want to strip the world of all its good folks so that the bad folks will stew in their own juices? Did Jesus try to separate his disciples from publicans and sinners or to bring them together at unheard of levels of intimacy (Mk. 2:13–17)? Is the strategy of the Gospel a deliberate effort to create so much earthly chaos that Christianity will be seen as a way to escape from its clutches? Are we drawn to God primarily by love or by fear?

Which leads straight to a second question: What awakens true faith in Christ? Another main character, Buck Williams, is a cynical young journalist always on the prowl for a fast-breaking story. On that fateful overseas flight, for example, instead of helping frantic mothers try to find their children, he quickly plugged in his laptop and began tapping out a scoop for his editor in New York. But when, a few days later, the now-converted pilot shows him a videotape on dispensational prophecy, Buck begins to view the events he is covering, particularly at the United Nations, in light of its predictions. Once he decides that history is, indeed, beginning to unfold in accordance with LaHaye's understanding of the tribulation, light dawns, he sinks to the floor in amazement, and soon joins a tiny remnant of those who share his clue to the meaning of world events.

Again we ponder: Is the struggle of faith a search for the right understanding of political events, especially involving the nation of Israel, or is it a search for personal and cosmic renewal from a risen Lord? Is faith confirmed when historical events unfold in a predetermined pattern, or when the Holy Spirit leads us through whatever the future may happen to bring?

Indeed, are we saved by an understanding of anything regarding the tribulation, or are we saved by a cross-bearing relationship with Jesus Christ (Gal. 2:20)?

During his earthly ministry, Jesus refused all requests for signs (Mk. 8:11–12), for times and places that could be observed (Lk. 17:20–21), insisting that even he did not know the day or the hour when the end would come (Mk. 13:32). Like him, we would do well to leave matters of calculation in the hands of God, for so often we have been mistaken in reading the "signs of the times" (Lk. 12:54–56). Just in my lifetime, I have heard the antichrist identified as a certain Pope, or as Adolf Hitler, or as Josif Stalin, none of which could be correct because, on LaHaye's timetable, the antichrist will appear for only seven years before the millennium begins!

Our final question is built on answers to the first two. If the gospel means that God loves not just the church but the world as well, and if faith means learning to love God back in return, then what is to be the attitude of his people toward their enemies in the world around them? *Left Behind* seems to offer two answers. First, flee from them by means of that miraculous evacuation called the rapture. Second, fight them in the greatest war ever waged called Armageddon. But did Jesus advocate this kind of instant escapism and unrestrained violence as a way of bringing history to its intended end? In his own apocalyptic discourse, he warned that wickedness would be multiplied and the love of many would grow cold (Mt. 24:12), to which we should respond, not by escaping, but by enduring to the end (Mt. 24:13). That endurance was not to be passive, however, but involved a preaching of the gospel of the kingdom to the ends of the earth (Mt. 24:14). Only then would the end come, not because our enemies have been destroyed by wars and rumors of wars (Mt. 24:6), but because we have given everyone an opportunity to believe.

In the midst of his ministry, Jesus took three of his leading disciples up a high mountain where they witnessed him communing with Moses and Elijah (Mk. 9:4). Neither of these Old Testament worthies had undergone a normal death and burial but, in a sense, had been "raptured" to heaven by God. Seizing the moment, Peter blurted out his wish to make this mountaintop experience more permanent (Mk. 9:5), but God interrupted with a command to keep listening to Jesus as he pointed them toward Jerusalem and the challenges that awaited them there (Mk. 8:31). All of us would, I am sure, welcome a shortcut to glory, but I would rather be left behind to share his saving gospel of suffering love with friend and foe alike until time shall be no more.

NOTES

1. Tim LaHaye, *Revelation Unveiled*, a revised and updated edition of *Revelation Illustrated and Made Plain* (Grand Rapids: Zondervan, 1999).

2. LaHaye, *Revelation Unveiled*, 106.

ACKNOWLEDGEMENTS

The most unusual thing about this book may well be the way in which it originated. One day a casual friend in our congregation, Dave Carder, invited me to lunch to discuss a proposal that took me completely by surprise. He related how he had been securing written copies of the sermons delivered once each month as part of my duties as the teaching minister in our church, duplicating them for distribution to a wide circle of acquaintances scattered around the world. Dave was so impressed with the feedback received from these efforts that he urged me to put a selection of sermons in book form as a way of extending and perpetuating my ministry as it neared its end.

Even though I had never contemplated harvesting the fruits of my pulpit work in this fashion, the entreaty of Dave Carder soon became irresistible, especially when it received the enthusiastic endorsement of our senior minister, Jim Moebes. At that time, in my other vocation as Research Professor at Samford University, I was finishing a book for pastors on Strategic Preaching, and it occurred to me that a collection of sermons might serve not only the spiritual needs of lay readers but also provide pastors with case studies of the kind of proclamation advocated in that book. With my consent, the Hull Legacy Project was soon established, a Steering Committee recruited, and generous funding secured to get the enterprise launched, the first-fruits of which you now hold in your hands.

At the time of this compilation, I had served as Theologian in Residence at Mountain Brook Baptist

Church, Birmingham, Alabama, for fifteen years. My regular monthly messages, plus additional presentations during Holy Week and Advent, meant that I had more than two hundred options from which to choose. The tithe of that total included here reflects my effort to be as comprehensive as possible in addressing a wide range of human needs. I was influenced by the response of the congregation to each sermon when delivered, by the frequency with which reprints and tapes were requested, and by my desire to utilize sermons that had not been published elsewhere. The Steering Committee contributed most helpfully to the selection process by identifying specific audiences beyond our church that it hopes the book will also serve.

When time came to secure a publisher, President Thomas E. Corts was most insistent that Samford University Press undertake the assignment. Having worked closely with him for many years as Provost, and having enjoyed office support and library resources for many more years as Research Professor, I found his request to be irresistible, particularly when his successor as president, Andrew Westmoreland, gave the project a high priority from the outset of his administration. Thus was an even closer partnership forged between the two institutions through which I have fulfilled my ministry for so long, Mountain Brook Baptist Church and Samford University. Their dual sponsorship of this book in the Hull Legacy Series well expresses my own deep desire to overcome the growing estrangement between faith and learning by offering the best resources of each for the enrichment of the other.

At Samford University Press I have enjoyed the expert guidance and skilled professionalism of Jack

Brymer as project coordinator, Sandy O'Brien as editorial supervisor, and Scott Camp as graphics designer. My office associate, Joellen Henson, has been of invaluable help in the preparation of a usable manuscript while responding to many other competing claims on her time. Sermons are especially difficult to revise for publication because they are often fashioned without time for the careful attention to documentation characteristic of more scholarly work. Joellen cheerfully tracked down obscure references, forgotten authors, and the sources of quotations so that others might also draw from the wells where I have drunk. I am privileged to have benefited immensely from every member of a team that cooperated beautifully to make this a better book.

As the dedication indicates, our immediate family includes several ministers, some of them with many years of rich pulpit experience on which I have freely drawn. All have been a great source of insight and encouragement as I toiled over this task. But preachers know that their most discerning hearer is the spouse who lives with them through the travail of sermon-making that others never see; who is there when the message is conceived, gestated, birthed, and sometimes incubated until it is strong enough to make its public debut from the pulpit. That is why my deepest thanks go to my wife, Wylodine, the only one who has heard them all; who knows which ones were born prematurely by forceps delivery; but who, after fifty-five years of listening, keeps coming back for more!

ABBREVIATIONS

———➤·◄———

The following abbreviations indicate the translation used when quoting from Scripture:

AT The author's translation by William E. Hull from the original languages of the Old Testament and New Testament.

JB *The Jerusalem Bible*, 1966, Darton, Longman, & Todd, Ltd. and Doubleday and Company, Inc. Used by permission. All rights reserved.

JBP *The New Testament in Modern English*, 1958, J. B. Phillips. Used by permission. All rights reserved

KJV *The King James Version.*

LB *The Living Bible*, 1976, Tyndale House Publishers.

MSG Scripture taken from *The Message*, 1993, 1994, 1995, 1996, 2000, 2001, 2002. Used by permission of NavPress Publishing Group.

NEB *The New English Bible*, 1970, Delegates of the Oxford University Press.

NIV *The New International Version*, 1978, New York International Bible Society. Used by permission. All rights reserved.

NRSV *New Revised Standard Version Bible*, 1989, Division of Christian Education of the National Council of the Churches of Christ in the United States of America. Used by permission. All rights reserved.

RSV *Revised Standard Version of the Bible*, 1952, [2nd edition, 1971] by the Division of Christian Education of the National Council of the Churches of Christ in the United States of America. Used by permission. All rights reserved.